SHAKESPEAREAN
SUBVERSIONS

SHAKESPEAREAN SUBVERSIONS

The trickster and the play-text

Richard Hillman

London and New York

First published 1992
by Routledge
11 New Fetter Lane, London EC4P 4EE

Simultaneously published in the USA and Canada
by Routledge
a division of Routledge, Chapman and Hall Inc.
29 West 35th Street, New York, NY 10001

Typeset in 10 on 12 point Baskerville by
Witwell Ltd, Southport

Printed and bound in Great Britain by
TJ Press (Padstow) Ltd, Padstow, Cornwall

British Library Cataloguing in Publication Data

Hillman, Richard
Shakespearean subversions: the trickster and the play-text.
I. Title II. Shakespeare, William, 1564–1616
822.33

Library of Congress Cataloging in Publication Data

Hillman, Richard
Shakespearean subversions: the trickster and the play-text/
Richard Hillman.
p.   cm.
Includes bibliographical references and index.
1. Shakespeare, William, 1564–1616—Criticism and interpretation.
2. Shakespeare, William, 1564–1616—Knowledge—Folklore.
3. Literature and anthropology—England.   4. Literature and
folklore—England.   5. Trickster in literature.   I. Title.
PR3004.H56   1992
822.3′3–dc20   91-33889

ISBN 0-415-07020-1

To Kristin, the two Malcolms,
the two Jessies – all the 'found' family

CONTENTS

ACKNOWLEDGEMENTS

Those sections of chapters 7 and 8 dealing with *Antony and Cleopatra* and *The Tempest* are adapted from articles published in *Shakespeare Quarterly* and *The University of Toronto Quarterly*, respectively. The discussion of *Hamlet* in chapter 7 draws on work that first appeared in *Essays in Literature*. All of this material is used here by permission.

A Sabbatical Leave and a Faculty of Arts Minor Research Grant from York University enabled me to concentrate my efforts on this project during 1987–8. Then and thereafter, the warm and generous people of Lunenburg County, Nova Scotia, provided the sustaining assurance that there were other things.

TEXTUAL NOTE

Shakespeare's works are cited from *The Riverside Shakespeare*, textual editor G. Blakemore Evans (Boston: Houghton Mifflin, 1974). For the sake of clarity, I have not followed that edition's practice of placing departures from the copy-text in square brackets. Abbreviations used in references follow Modern Language Association convention.

1

INTRODUCTION: TOWARDS A DEFINITION OF SUBVERSION AS A DRAMATIC FUNCTION

I take the tentative 'towards' in my title very seriously. The category of dramatic effects that concerns me needs a broad rubric – so much so that it risks forfeiting its right to one at all – and 'subversion', however unavoidably the term imposes itself, is merely an accommodating approximation. Its indispensability lies in its capacity to delineate a specifically dialectical process – as 'transgression', say, need not[1] – without assuming a context or implying a consequence. A disadvantage, perhaps, is the term's widespread but controversial adoption by recent criticism of Renaissance drama, especially the materialist schools classified as New Historicism and Cultural Materialism. In fact, disagreement over the significance and role of subversion serves, for a number of critics, to focus broad theoretical and methodological divergences. The central question, simply put, is whether elements in the plays that appear to challenge dominant political forms – including social and cultural practices – actually do so in any meaningful way, or whether, as Stephen Greenblatt puts it in an enormously influential essay setting out the New Historicist position in what might be called its 'pure' form, 'moral values – justice, order, civility – are secured paradoxically through the apparent generation of their subversive contraries' (Greenblatt 1985: 40).[2]

Even in these terms, one can have one's subversion and deny it too. Thus Jonathan Dollimore, applying the cultural model of Foucault, proposes that a 'reverse discourse . . . eventually challenges the very power structures responsible for its "creation" ' (Dollimore 1986a: 180). Indeed, from this position it is a disconcertingly small step to recuperating repression itself: 'rather than seeing containment as that which preempts and defeats transgression we need to see both as potentially produc-

1

tive processes' (Dollimore 1986b: 71). More useful for my purposes is the deconstructionist formulation of Jonathan Goldberg, following Derrida: 'dominant discourses allow their own subversion precisely because hegemonic control is an impossible dream, a self-defeating fantasy' (Goldberg 1987: 244). The latter idea, in so far as it implies the infinite renewing and proliferation of meanings, sets no limits to the creative potential of subversive processes. However, I prefer to bypass the theoretical issue, which is less urgent for me than for critics whose focus is the connections between literary and other 'texts' (cultural, historical, political). My approach allows the play-text not complete freedom from its contexts, but a reasonable measure of fictive autonomy. From this angle, the 'claim' to subversiveness of any given dramatic element depends upon its part in the play: subversion is as subversion ultimately does (or does not).

As this implies, I nevertheless find the subversion–containment dynamic useful in some instances. Indeed, I detect versions of it in several texts neglected from this point of view; I also apply it, more fully than seems to have been done, to the arena of sexual politics. But I do not confine subversiveness to collective processes, nor do I confine the collective to the political, however broadly defined. The epistomological bases of this study remain psychological and anthropological. Moreover, in the interest of remaining open to variations within and between texts, I resist erecting conceptual monoliths: my title promises not 'subversion', but 'subversions', and I find little critical use in such materialist reifications as 'power' and 'authority'. Most fundamentally, I take issue with the dismissal of *all* 'subversive voices' in the plays as inauthentic because 'produced by the affirmations of order' (Greenblatt 1985: 38). On the contrary, in my reading, subversiveness tends to construct the forces of 'order', whose 'affirmations' are thus cast in the role of negations: 'containment' becomes 'counter-subversion'.

I am proposing that, from a wide variety of subversive practices in Shakespearean drama – including certain (but not all) kinds of clowning and some (but not all) political rebellion, as well as confrontations with love, conscience, or death – a principle of subversiveness can be distilled that, in cutting across context and consequence, cuts deeper than particular 'subversive voices'. Because this principle signifies in elusive and contradictory ways, I have taken the risk of expounding it metaphorically by attaching it to the mythological figure of the trickster. In his case definition – by definition – can only go so far. The trickster's essence is his shape-changing, and he can only be known indirectly, through his entanglements. That will be the project of later chapters. This one, however, will equally testify, by its very method, to the necessity for indirection.

I

At one extreme of Elizabethan attitudes to genre stand the famous complaints of Sir Philip Sidney, in the course of defending poesie, against 'mingling Kinges and Clownes' (*Defence of Poesie,* 39). I should like to begin at the other extreme, with the struggle between personages called Comedy and Envy (the advocate of tragedy) for control of the generic identity of *Mucedorus* – that free-wheeling dramatic derivative of Sidneian romance whose naïveté, extreme popularity, and indeed anonymity make it the natural spokesman for subliterary stage practices. That the palm in this crude contest ultimately goes to Comedy is of little significance, for the text's gesture towards formal concerns is conspicuously beside the point. In their frenetic absurdity, these allegorical caricatures explode their pretence of enacting artistic policy, authorial control. On the contrary, they impress us as cast up on the metadramatic shore by the turbulence of the very action they claim to be generating – a mélange of fantastic improbabilities that is little beholden to them.

Yet it is worth noting that this irrelevant struggle over genre is conducted in terms of subversion – a point reinforced by the displacement of the classically impeccable concept of tragedy into Envy, whose spiritual patron is, of course, Satan. Comedy, like Eve in the garden ('Time fits us well; the day and place is ours' (Induction 7)), is confronted by the 'ugly fiend' (75), the 'envious disdainer of men's joys,/Whose name is fraught with bloody stratagems' (41–2). The result is a paradigm of subversion as not only challenging but intimately involved with the process of creation. This paradigm is self-consciously extended into the political sphere in the 1610 version of *Mucedorus* played before King James. Despite his failure within the text, Envy there threatens to enlist Comedy itself in a theatrical act of political subversion that will provoke 'a puissant magistrate. . . . To your great danger, or at least restraint' (Epilogue, 45–51). That threat

3

is laughed off but left unresolved. Thus the risk of losing control over genre is linked with the challenge of keeping theatre politically innocuous, just when the independent energy of the dramatic material itself has proved the futility of such control. The message, it would seem, goes beyond repudiating trouble-making playwrights as envy-driven to affirming subversion as an element of textual production.

Criticism of Shakespeare's tragedies has long outgrown the impulse to excuse (and therefore the impression of not excusing) the presence of fools and clowns with reference to that specious chimera, 'comic relief'.[3] Still, the assumption survives that such figures embody outlooks and modes of action more naturally at home in comedy, where the folly of their 'betters' does not have 'serious' consequences. That is, their much-admired contribution to tragedy comes from discordant rather than harmonious counterpoint. The 'clash' may be less acute than it seems in medieval religious art, according to Willard Farnham, but it is still 'great enough to make us highly sensitive to it' (Farnham 1971: 14). The 'grotesque' and the 'elevated' may form a 'bond of substance' but not a 'union in spirit' (20). Genre is not explicitly the issue in Richard L. Levin's analysis of clown subplots across the spectrum of Renaissance drama (R. L. Levin 1971: 109–47), yet the legacy of such formalist thinking is evident in his insistence on a distinction between 'foil' and 'parody'. And even when Robert Weimann persuasively refutes this distinction in arguing for 'complementary perspectives' (Weimann 1978: 237) that generate a much wider range of structural effects with 'no hermetic barriers' (239), he falls back upon the concept of 'polarity as a structural principle' (245). The 'careful placement' of the Shakespearean clown produces more than commentary upon the main action; rather, he 'enters into a highly complex relationship with it that is indispensable to the larger meaning' (244–5). Yet the basis remains a 'dialectic' reflecting the 'age-old contradiction between ritual and *mimesis*' (245), focused by the transitional position of Shakespeare's theatre between 'popular' and 'literary' modes (241).

The modern ear has progressively broadened its sense of harmony to include closer intervals, and perhaps it is time, as deconstructionist critics have argued,[4] to extend our proliferating perceptions of Shakespeare's generic self-referentiality towards a concept of generic fluidity. As is clear from the redundancy of

Comedy and Tragedy in *Mucedorus*, as well as from Theseus' baffled critical logic in the face of the 'tragic mirth' of Pyramus and Thisby ('That is hot ice and wondrous strange snow' (*MND*, V.i.57–9)), such an approach means recuperating attitudes lurking not far behind neoclassical lip-service. Already, a recognition of formal instability, if not insouciance, has been virtually forced on criticism in the cases at least of *Troilus and Cressida* and of the last plays, for which the catch-all category of 'romance' has superseded not only the First Folio classifications but the term its editors might have used, 'tragicomedy'. It will always be important that *Romeo and Juliet* is a star-crossed romantic comedy, *Pyramus and Thisby* a tragedy assimilated by comic forces; that the ending of *Measure for Measure* imposes comic closure with abnormal rigour; that *Othello* adapts comic patterns; and, more fundamentally, that the last plays bring comedy out of – and through – tragedy. It will continue to be useful to trace comic and tragic elements within the framework of the chronicle history. But we need also to be able to see how 'mingling Kinges and Clownes' may mean more than simply having both in the same play or even playing off one 'complementary perspective' against the other. As the work of William Willeford on the figure of the fool suggests, there may be a theatrical grammar that employs a single term for the dynamic interdependence of king and clown, conceived not as tension but as process, an undermining that perpetually renews precisely because it never resolves. And when king and clown are approached, not as characters, or even character-types, but as textual functions, it becomes clear that one possible name for such a part of dramatic speech is subversion.

I raise questions of genre and generic decorum at the outset precisely because they are not central to this book. They furnish neither its *raison d'être* nor its basis of organization. The preoccupation with genre since Bradley, though doubtless initiated by a desire to treat Shakespeare as a serious, because classically oriented, literary artist, has been amply validated by the uncovering of his complex uses of generic interplay. I shall often have occasion to use the language and the techniques of such criticism; and inevitably, especially since I am taking up plays in roughly their order of composition, I shall often be grouping together works in one genre or another. Moreover, I hope that my approach will shed its own light on generic issues.

But it will do so from a different angle – from a position outside the set of assumptions that has made it difficult, for instance, to see what Puck and Richard III and Cloten not only have, but do, in common.

II

Despite my attraction to the trickster as an emblem of subversion, the character-type of the trickster as defined and applied by literary historians is tangential to my direction. In the first place, by no means all of the characters that interest me fit obviously or easily into the pattern. In fact, relatively few even of Shakespeare's fools and clowns would necessarily qualify on their own merits, despite their well-established trickster-roots.[5] But then such roots do not necessarily make for analytical utility. As long as criticism settles for shadowy matters of literary ancestry and folk tradition, the trickster can shelter comfortably under the broad umbrella of the 'festive'. To get down to cases is to confront his elusiveness. Thus Leo Salingar, after exhaustively establishing the general influence on Renaissance comedy of the classical version of the trickster, comes to the conclusion that 'in Shakespeare at least the relationship is not one of direct descent' because 'his clowns are commentators, not intriguers' (Salingar 1974: 172). 'Intrigue' makes a convenient identifying sign; on this basis, at least, tricksters obviously abound in Renaissance drama,[6] even as their connection with festivity becomes more tenuous. But this criterion equally excludes the very figure I intend to take up first and centrally, Shakespeare's notorious 'shrew'. On the other hand, her husband–opponent's status for me is problematic, while Salingar would seem to admit him readily to the trickster-ranks – on the basis, oddly, that he serves the moral purpose of defending the institution of marriage. I take it that the archetypal trickster is above all – or beneath all – amorally subversive. So is Katherina, who functions analogously to other trouble-making characters – some clowns, some not – in actually constructing her theatrical presence by means of disruptive opposition. Petruchio's 'intrigue', by contrast, is a measure of his counter-subversiveness. In short, engaging in trickery as scheming does not automatically make a trickster in my sense. Thus I find that my concept hardly overlaps at all with the forms of 'practice' traced by Bertrand Evans in the tragedies, although I do share one aspect of his approach: it is as much types of action as types of characters that matter to me. And this is where the topic threatens to lose its shape by increasing its scope.

All deception is more or less subversive, after all, and deception is the basic stuff of drama. Even if one tries to exclude self-deception – and in Shakespeare one will inevitably be drawn back to it by some route – it is difficult to think of a play in any genre in any period in which some character is *not* deceived about something that matters. The multiple meanings of 'play' and 'plot' point strongly in this direction. Nor, for that matter, need significant deception depend on a deceiver as such. Salingar illustrates the blurring of dramatic trickery at the left- and right-hand margins of human mistaking and supernatural intervention, respectively, when he develops his study of the trickster in classical comedy as part of a chapter on ' "Errors" and Deceit', then follows with a section on 'Fortune as Trickster' (Salingar 1974: 76–174).

To pursue human mistaking for a moment, the basis of this form of deception is the truism that appearances can be deceiving, and on the Shakespearean stage they frequently possess an unassisted subversive power akin to that of manipulative agents. Thus in *The Comedy of Errors*, as the title suggests, the 'errors' themselves are implicitly given the power of creating the 'comedy' and so virtually acquire the status of dramatist. Yet even in that self-consciously mechanical farce, it is impossible to ignore the complicity of self-deception, and this element tends to become insistent, if not dominant, as characters become more fully developed psychologically. They are increasingly felt to distort appearances rather than to be misled by them, though where the balance lies in the case of, say, Hamlet or Othello is notoriously intertwined with larger and difficult issues of interpretation. The tendency reaches a grotesque extreme in the spontaneously misconstruing jealousy of Leontes. This study will be much concerned, especially in regard to the later tragedies and romances, with the question of self-subversion – what may be thought of as the trickster within. This is, of course, to take up, from yet another angle, Shakespeare's perennial, all-encompassing, subject – the role of the irrational.[7]

In sharp contrast to texts that incorporate subversive processes into primary dramatic 'reality' stands *A Midsummer Night's Dream*, which displays in Puck the most obvious trickster-figure

of all, the disembodied embodiment of self-delighting mischievous energy: 'those things do best please me / That befall
prepost'rously' (III.ii.120–1).[8] The fairies – through whom the
playwright takes his trickery out of the hands of human characters, yet still assigns it to an internal cause – in effect give such
energy 'a local habitation and a name': it suits their structural, as
well as their supernatural, status that they are at once visible to
the audience and invisible to their victims. This anomalous
position corresponds, in effect, to that of various internal
manipulators – from Aaron to Don John to Duke Vincentio to
Iago – up to the point where they become visible to their fellow
characters in their 'true' shapes. Before such *éclaircissement*,
these figures similarly operate by secretly creating, or taking
advantage of, appearances which have the potential for deception. Yet even from the first they are nominally human, and, as
will become apparent, the degree of humanity with which they
are credited has important implications for their relation to the
subversive principle. The late romances again introduce non-
human manipulation, in the form of fortune and the gods, while
The Tempest problematically combines the supernatural with a
controlling human figure who comes closer than might at first be
supposed to some of the trickster-like figures of other plays – yet
keeps a highly significant distance.

III

Having broadened my subject beyond trickster-characters, however defined, I should like to return to the archetypal trickster as
conceptual anchor – in effect, as a rationale for including some
forms of trickery and not others. There has been plenty of
anthropological documentation, beginning with anthropology
itself, of trickster stories from many parts of the world. From the
early days of psychology, this material has attracted analysis in
terms of psychic processes. Predictably, the Jungian school has
shown the greatest interest in the idea, detecting behind the
particular features of various tricksters a significant universal
archetype. One need not accept either Jung's premises or his
broader conclusions in order to value, as do virtually all students
of the subject, his perception that the trickster's activities constitute, for those who tell his story, not a mere source of
entertainment, but a nexus of therapeutic self-exploration.

Jung's slant, of course, is specifically psychological: 'The figure works because secretly it participates in the observer's psyche and appears as its reflection, though it is not recognized as such' (1953-79b: 270). This can indeed be a useful way of thinking about the trickster in a dramatic context, where characters tend to function symbolically, in some measure, as aspects of each other. As it happens, Jung's identification of this figure with the 'shadow', the archetype that for him embodies the primitive and instinctual side of the psyche, corresponds with Shakespeare's use of that term on several occasions – most notably in Puck's Epilogue: 'If we shadows have offended . . .' (*MND*, V.i.423ff.). Yet in fact the explicitly Jungian studies of which I am aware not only neglect the trickster as such but make limited use of the idea of the 'shadow' as subversive.

This is so despite the suggestive formulations of James P. Driscoll (1983) and Alex Aronson (1972). According to Driscoll, 'The self-deceived know nothing about their suppressed shadow; it emerges unexpectedly in confused, yet sometimes ruling, motives' (Driscoll 1983: 23-4). Such subversive villains as Richard III, Iago, and Edmund actually 'identify with their shadows' (24). Aronson considers that 'Shakespeare's villains frequently are embodiments of the tragic hero's unconscious' (Aronson 1972: 109). Still, the tendency of both critics is to reduce characters to case studies, imposing a restrictive naturalism, paradoxically, on the very dynamic they have defined in symbolic terms. Nor does this approach allow for Puck, who self-evidently cannot have a psychology. Similarly self-limiting, if more free-wheeling, is James Kirsch's application of Jungian principles to *Hamlet, King Lear*, and *Macbeth*. Disappointingly diffuse in construing the Ghost and the Witches, Kirsch is more stimulating in his brief remarks linking the Fool's role as 'spokesman for Lear's unconscious' with the subversion of the *persona* by the 'shadow' (J. Kirsch 1966: 218). Yet because for him, too, the psychological implications of the 'shadow' take precedence over the principle of subversion itself, the Gravedigger in *Hamlet* and the Porter in *Macbeth* cannot be accommodated. Finally, H. R. Coursen's more critically sophisticated Jungian approach by way of the 'compensatory psyche' is promising, in so far as it stresses that the shadow-side, if unacknowledged, will have its subversive revenge. My analysis of the late tragedies will largely share his premise that 'tragic man rejects the compensatory energy of the psyche' (Coursen 1986: 63). However, when Coursen goes on to identify the excluded part of the self with the feminine principle, as some feminist critics of Shakespeare would also do, the trickster as subversive dynamic is bypassed once again. Such precedents suggest that to pursue the archetype in narrowly psychological terms would involve imposing artificial limits on the scope and significance of trickery in the plays.

We can refreshingly open the issue up again, while keeping our focus on formal tricksters, by turning to the recent anthropological work of Robert D. Pelton, who uses his mainly West African data as the basis for what is, to my knowledge, the most comprehensive and probing consideration of the trickster-figure to date. In the light of his primary evidence, as well as material documented from other cultures, Pelton reviews the ideas of virtually all previous writers on the subject in an attempt to get a more satisfactory fix on a phenomenon whose very elusiveness and multivalence comprise its *raison d'être*. He draws on, but goes beyond, the psychological insights of both Freud and Jung; he rejects Lévi-Strauss's understanding of the trickster as a mere 'structuralist cog' in a 'vast intellectual machine of mediations' (Pelton 1980: 236). More to the point, for Pelton, are the views of Mary Douglas and Mircea Eliade, who have focused on the cultural value of sacred paradox. According to Pelton's analysis, it is as a symbol of such paradox that the trickster functions, endlessly producing meaning and order by endlessly challenging them:

> the delight that the trickster both creates and is finally springs from an intuition of the force driving the ironic dialectic of the imagination, which enables man himself to become a sacred world and human yearning to become the earthly synonym for that same force – this no-thingness that is the very antithesis of nothing. In touching nothing and finding joy the trickster reveals that this most supple energy of all is by its very adaptability the ultimate holiness made the moving power of ordinary human life.
>
> (Pelton 1980: 283)

This formulation emerges, needless to say, from a highly spiritualized and mythologized universe. Its wide-ranging significance, however, is suggested by a remarkable intersection with Foucault's depiction of transgression in a contemporary context

10

as 'profanation in a world which no longer recognizes any positive meaning in the sacred':

> In that zone which our culture affords for our gestures and speech, transgression prescribes not only the sole manner of discovering the sacred in its unmediated substance, but also a way of recomposing its empty form, its absence, through which it becomes all the more scintillating.
>
> (Foucault 1977: 30)

Several of Pelton's specific points are strikingly suggestive for a critic examining subversion in Shakespeare. When he makes an analogy, for instance, between the trickster as paradoxical sacred symbol and the symbol of the Christian cross (Pelton 1980: 283), he effectively forges a link between the fool as trickster-figure and the fool as emblem of Christian simplicity. It is this latter tradition that supports literary incarnations of truth-telling folly throughout the Renaissance – a phenomenon that has been valuably studied by such scholars as Walter Kaiser.[9] Similarly provocative is Pelton's reminder that the force embodied in the trickster can, as in the example of Loki, take a form that appears, at least, purely destructive (284). Obviously, this holds promise as an epistemological framework for Shakespeare's Machiavels.

These characters' affiliation with the trickster, which has been sporadically recognized, suggestively supplements their more direct debt to the Vice-tradition, besides deepening our understanding of that tradition itself. The pioneering work of Bernard Spivack has helped a generation of scholars to think in terms of non-mimetic character-types and the patterns of psychomachia. At the same time, despite his stress throughout on the subversive energy that such figures have in common, Spivack's exclusive focus on villainy may have fostered an unduly moralistic understanding of the dramatic ramifications of the tradition. Subsequent studies – notably by Weimann (1978), Farnham (1971), and Wiles (1987)[10] – have supplied a plentiful corrective. To grasp the archetype beneath the Vice-stereotype, to recognize subversiveness itself as the lowest common denominator, is to expand the field of relations among characters in a way that leaves behind not only generic but moral distinctions. We transgress nothing when we cross the artificial boundary drawn by T. McAlindon, in dealing with playful villains, between 'play which works in the service of truth and harmony, and play which deludes in

11

order to divide and destroy' (McAlindon 1986: 46). The Vice joins the Fool as what Kaiser terms 'an expression of all the mischievous and rebellious desires in man which society attempts to control or frustrate' (Kaiser 1963: 8). Yet this is also to reveal as having its own productive implications for criticism the question begged by the differentiation of the evil trickster: what gives the trickster's standard amorality an immoral cast – what makes a Loki, rather than, say, an Odysseus? In a mythological or anthropological context, the question may be pointless; but in terms of the give and take of fictive forces that comprises a Shakespearean dramatic structure, to approach a certain sort of villain as a figure of displacement, of creative energies gone awry, has exciting possibilities.

Again, however, this is a study of subversive practices, not merely of tricksters, and it uses the formulations of psychology and anthropology as a means to broader critical ends. For my purposes, the practical contribution of Pelton's work is that it establishes, in more comprehensive terms than other writers on the subject, the trickster as defined by his subversive activities and those activities as defining existential questions in terms of productive contradiction. Farther down this anthropological road lies the large and complex issue of rituals of inversion or transgression and their functions in systems of religious belief and social organization. Arnold van Gennep's delineation of initiatory patterns – a strong influence on criticism of Shakespearean comedy, in particular[11] – includes the now-familiar concept of 'liminality', a threshold state also discussed by Victor Turner in terms of 'communitas' and 'anti-structure'.[12] The eminently liminal figure of the trickster may be related to this state, and Turner explicitly makes the connection in dealing with the element of play in tribal rites (Turner 1977: 40).

Here, however, a caveat is in order; for in the context of ritual, the trickster's subversion comes ready furnished with a teleological context – a set of answers to his intrinsically unanswerable questions. Creation may be 'the play of the gods' (Turner 1977: 41), but sometimes they appear, at least, to 'kill us for their sport' (Lr, IV.i.37). The bias in Turner's formulation is built into the term 'play', as opposed to 'trick', and is reflected in most 'festive' criticism. It involves stripping trickery of risk, fear, and uncertainty – of its very destabilizing function – in service to an image of positive wholeness: 'Eros sports with Thanatos, not as a grisly Danse Macabre, but to symbolise a complete human reality' (Turner 1977: 41). Does Thanatos never play the trickster with Eros? Is not the 'grisly Danse Macabre' (note the emotionally loaded adjective) itself part of the 'human reality'? According to Claude Blum's analysis of that potently enigmatic late-medieval (and Shakespearean) coupling of the Fool and Death, the symbolic capacity of the Fool to bring life out of Death not only depends on Death's power but feeds into the Fool's radical subversiveness:

> La possibilité donnée au fou de dire la vérité et de transformer la mort en vie sera lourde de conséquences pour la suite de la représentation de la folie. La folie va s'affirmer comme subversion possible de tout discours; elle va s'affirmer comme un danger pour toute vérité installée dans une Loi, et pour la pensée chrétienne elle-même. Dans certaines de ses manifestations, elle finira par ne plus être que le signe de l'instabilité de tous les langages et de toutes les constructions humaines.
>
> (Blum 1983: 265–6)

Willeford has usefully considered the association of the Fool and Death (Willeford 1969: 88–93) in terms of the Fool's 'magical affinity with chaos' (101) – the key, as he sees it, to the figure's transformative potential. In what is certainly the most valuable analysis to date of clowning as a cultural phenomenon, Willeford proposes that fools 'wrest life from the "destructive element" while ridiculing the ancient dream that victory over it is possible' (101). Positing such a dynamic enables Willeford to go beyond the work of Enid Welsford and Robert Hillis Goldsmith in explicating the operations of folly in Shakespeare: his treatment of Lear and the Fool (208–25) is especially illuminating, whether or not one agrees (as I do not) that Lear is finally redeemed by a right relation to folly. In any case, however, folly is only one category of subversive practice, and by definition its subversiveness is limited. The fool is stigmatized, set apart, readily identifiable, more or less dependent, whereas the trickster is uninhibited, magically *hic et ubique*, the perpetual shape-changer. Willeford does not see in the trickster, whom he touches on merely as 'a special mythological form of the fool' (132), a more comprehensive emblem of the underlying principle of the production of meaning through its disruption.

13

We come closer to isolating this principle when we turn, as Willeford himself briefly does, to Eliade's observations on the broad psycho-cultural significance of chaos and boundaries. Eliade is consistently concerned with rituals of inversion as involving a symbolic re-creation of the universe 'preceded by a symbolic retrogression to Chaos' (Eliade 1965: xiii). In making the similar point that 'ritual recognizes the potency of disorder', Douglas effectively brings out the implications of 'Chaos' in this context:

> Granted that disorder spoils pattern; it also provides the materials of pattern. . . . This is why, though we seek to create order, we do not simply condemn disorder. We recognise that it is destructive to existing patterns; also that it has potentiality. It symbolises both danger and power.
>
> (Douglas 1966: 94)

Such disorder is the potent and ambiguous 'nothing' that the trickster touches.[13] As Brian V. Street puts it, 'the presence of the creative element in trickster tales is due to the integral relation of creativity and destruction' (Street 1972: 97). The figure's capacity to function as both 'deity and buffoon, creator and destroyer' makes manifest 'the presence of a potential saviour in every rule-breaker' (103). I wish to echo, however, the insistence by both Douglas and Street on potentiality: the trickster's creativity is indeed part of his significance, but he is essentially 'undifferentiated' (Street 1972: 102), and in many of his particular adventures he is merely destructive. This is where the subversive principle, as I conceive it, conflicts with the reassuring teleological orientation of more traditional 'festive' criticism, such as C. L. Barber's (1959), according to which 'ritual' disorder already contains its own undoing. My view presupposes that whether the potential is realized, whether the trickster finds 'joy' in 'nothing', is contingent precisely on his spontaneous and unconditional embracing of what appears to be merely destructive. In order for there to be power, there must be danger, not merely some form of circumscribed and more-or-less tolerated misrule. Precisely such a sense of chaos and destruction as necessary for the production of new meaning may be deduced from several early Shakespearean texts. These include not only comedies, where the contribution of discord to harmony is widely recognized as a formal premise, but also political plays, where the process of renewal, however costly, would appear to deconstruct conservative fears of social instability. In particular, the role played by such agents of disruption as Katherina, the Bastard (in *King John*), Aaron (in *Titus Andronicus*), and Richard III matches Douglas's documentation of the magical potency often attributed to marginal persons, including (but not limited to) those participating in 'the marginal period which separates ritual dying and ritual rebirth' (Douglas 1966: 96):

> To behave anti-socially is the proper expression of their marginal condition. . . . To have been in the margins is to have been in contact with danger, to have been at a source of power.
>
> (97)[14]

This is certainly where the trickster operates – 'at the boundaries of order' (Street 1972: 101); so does the Fool (Willeford 1969: 129–47), though his marginality simultaneously signifies the limits of his power.

IV

Returning my emphasis to the literary sphere, I wish to consider several previous applications of dialectical process to dramatic structure. To take large things first, there is some overlap between subversiveness, in my sense, and Nietzsche's literary-philosophical concept of the Dionysiac, as formulated in *The Birth of Tragedy* (1964). Some of what I will be saying about the trickster's influence and his suppression could be translated into terms of the Dionysiac–Apollonian conflict, although never without distortion. One distorting factor would be the complex and nebulous post-romantic apparatus that comes attached to the dialectic as Nietzsche develops it. But more fundamentally, I am concerned with a dramatic function ranging over a wide spectrum of meanings, not with large abstract forces taken to be the underlying preoccupation of a text.

A second category of dualistic approaches depends on Sigurd Burckhardt's model of poetic process. According to Burckhardt, 'the poet must always be half fool, the corrupter of words' (S. Burckhardt 1968: 44), disrupting structures of meaning, so that his other side – his priest-like function – may re-create them. Burckhardt's practical application of this idea is limited, but he has inspired more extensive studies. Most in line with my own approach is John W. Blanpied's (1983) theory of the 'antic', as he develops it in relation to the English history plays. For Blanpied, the 'antic' functions as a principle of subversion in opposition to the ordering impulse of the 'machiavel'. Like the trickster, he is infinitely 'self-delighting' (14), revelatory, mocking. Moreover, 'he' is a theatrical impulse, not merely a character-type. This point of similarity to my perspective, however, also marks two significant points of difference, both in keeping with Burckhardt's influence. First, Blanpied's ultimate concern is with Shakespeare's personal creative struggle – 'antic' and 'machiavel' are instruments for exploring the challenge of dealing artistically with historical material. Secondly, a thrust towards balance and synthesis tends to colour the subversive process. In analysing Shakespeare's kings as the site of conflict between 'antic' and 'machiavel', Blanpied (83–4) brings to bear the concept of 'wholeness', of balance between order and disorder, which Willeford finds emblematized by the privileged position of the royal fool.

I prefer to invoke, though in a selective way, another theorist whose interest in the disruptive process is less teleological and less concerned with the presence of the artist in the work. There is an obvious fundamental compatability between Pelton's ideas and the literary–cultural analysis of 'grotesque realism' by Mikhail Bakhtin in *Rabelais and His World* (1968), a study that has had extensive impact on the current critical scene, supporting a broad revaluation of the grotesque as fundamentally life-giving and affirmative rather than minatory.[15] In discussing the carnivalesque literary creations of the Renaissance as emblems of endless creation and renewal through their violation of physical and social norms, Bakhtin is effectively dealing with the trickster-archetype in a way that acknowledges its paradoxical nature and ritual function. Moreover, in extending this concept beyond individual characters to what he conceives as the comic spirit of the Renaissance, he opens the door to the analysis of subversive dramatic patterns and plot elements.

Yet my argument does not, like those of Bakhtin and some of those he has inspired, depend on those various 'festive' social phenomena that have come increasingly to be grouped under the rubric of carnival. Certainly, Eliade cites such periods of licence and reversal in terms of a return to chaos for the sake of regeneration (1958: 358–9 and 398–400), but he also makes it clear that the symbolic pattern is an archetypal one, occurring worldwide across an enormous range of cultural practices, rather than historically determined in a narrow sense. This may be just as well, given the difficulty of conclusively documenting and assessing such elements in Renaissance England, apart from the obviously problematic relation between them and Shakespeare's plays. Yet such obstacles have not impeded the tendency within what might be called New Festive criticism to make inflated claims for the political and cultural implications of carnivalesque social behaviour.[16] Peter Stallybrass and Allon White (1986: 6–26) provide a useful critique of this approach, choosing instead to deal with Bakhtin's formulations semiotically – in terms of symbolic inversion and transgression. This returns the authors to the domain of anthropology – Turner and Douglas are invoked, amongst others (18–23) – although it might be argued that, when they exclude the 'celebratory' note in the cause of materialist analysis, they exclude an entire dimension of Bakhtin's thought to which those authorities would surely grant greater legitimacy. Such exclusion reflects the general New Historicist and Cultural Materialist ambivalence towards Bakhtin, whose socialist credentials are sometimes perceived as coexisting uneasily with humanist tendencies. Hence also Dollimore's avowed effort to 'forestall' the application to *Measure for Measure* of a Bakhtinian reading that would grant legitimacy to that play's subversive elements (1985: 73).[17]

As it happens, I agree with much of what Dollimore says about the authoritarian ends served by subversion in *Measure for Measure*; in fact, I go farther than he does, because I extend the concept of authority into the psychological sphere. There seems to me no question, moreover, that at least institutionalized forms of social subversion ultimately serve the established hierarchy, as Barber also pointed out (1959: 205). Still, in general I find it valid and important to recognize 'festive' and carnivalesque elements as embodiments of primal energies, which extend to the impulse to challenge political and social power structures. This is essentially the selective attitude to Bakhtin's thought and influence taken by Umberto Eco:

> Bachtin [*sic*] was right in seeing the manifestation of a profound drive towards liberation and subversion in Medieval carnival. The hyper-Bachtinian ideology of carnival as *actual* liberation may, however, be wrong.
>
> (Eco 1984: 3)[18]

The important fact remains, from my perspective, that there is more to the trickster and trickster-like activities than is comprehended in the concept of the carnivalesque, and it is this 'more' – elusive, inclusive, and inconclusive as it is – that emerges from certain patterns of Shakespearean trickery that often have nothing to do with easily recognizable subversives, such as the fools. Indeed, there is a tendency, even amongst resolutely deconstructionist critics, to attribute an essential and universal significance to fool-figures in Shakespeare's plays – namely, 'undermining the "single" truth', as Malcolm Evans puts it, speaking of Touchstone (1985: 153). This is an assumption that my analysis will, itself deconstruct, offering evidence that some fools of the 'allow'd' (*TN*, I.v.94) kind subvert their own carnival heritage – in ways, moreover, that do not fit neatly into a New Historicist framework.

My approach runs parallel, for varying distances, with much criticism concerned with principles of transformation and metamorphosis in the plays. One of the most insightful treatments I know is that of Ruth Nevo, though I give a different interpretation to the progression she delineates from comedies based on 'twinships, rivalries, ambivalences, tamings and matings' (Nevo 1980: 17) to a 'New Comedy' centring on the witty heroine. In discussing the psychological implications of metamorphosis, William C. Carroll also raises issues of disruptive energy, stressing the mystery and ambiguity, the potential for creation and destruction, inherent in the concept of change. As he sees it, 'the whole idea of metamorphosis is subversive, for it undermines the traditional belief in a stable, fixed, and ordered self' (1985: 25). Such subversion, it should be noted, presumes such a belief, and on this score, while comfortable enough with the postmodern consensus that 'human identity is more constituted than constitutive' (Dollimore 1986b: 54), I part company with those more extreme extrapolators of Foucault who insist that the very notion of a human subject with the capacity to 'identify with the "I" of an utterance' (Belsey 1985: 15) is a product of modern ideologies just beginning to make themselves felt in the drama of the period.[19]

To touch on the 'witty heroine' is to introduce another dimension of subversion in the plays – the issue of gender roles, and in particular the frequent identification of women with forces that threaten or question patriarchal power structures.

There were a number of studies from this perspective in the early years of feminist criticism of Shakespeare, and I shall be drawing eclectically on several of them. What they tend to share, however, is the perception of a binary opposition between masculine and feminine principles as constituted in the plays – witness such titles as *Shakespeare's Division of Experience* (French 1981), *Comic Women, Tragic Men* (Bamber 1982), *Domination and Defiance* (Dreher 1986), and 'The Woman's Part: Female Sexuality as Power in Shakespeare's Plays' (Berggren 1980). These principles of gender occasionally cross the sex boundary, as when women and fools are identified (Novy 1984: 93; Bamber 1982: 39)[20] or when French provocatively presents Falstaff's misrule in terms of the 'outlaw feminine principle' (French 1981: 28, 107). Juliet Dusinberre goes farther, though in a reversion to mimetic critical assumptions, by insisting that Shakespeare 'did not divide human nature into the masculine and feminine, but observed in the individual woman or man an infinite variety of union between opposing impulses' (Dusinberre 1975: 308). Still, much feminist commentary on Shakespeare, especially that which privileges practice over theory, has elicited essentialist patterns, and so reinforced essentialist premises.

My approach, practical though it is, aligns itself with more recent theoretical critiques of such practice,[21] while recognizing, of course, that the texts often cast women in roles that are subversive in one way or another. 'Sexual politics' will figure, explicitly or implicitly, throughout this book, and issues of gender will be seen to govern the form that subversion – and counter-subversion – take in specific dramatic contexts. In keeping with the trickster's traditional sex-changing ability, however, the textual function of subversion will be treated as *essentially* genderless. From such a perspective, Portia has less in common with Falstaff than with Prince Hal – one of several points, incidentally, on which I agree with Marilyn L. Williamson (1986), whose approach to sexuality in terms of power derives from Foucault.[22] Perhaps more controversially, I shall be arguing that, far from entering into a patriarchal conspiracy to suppress Rosalind's 'female vitality' (Erickson 1985: 37), Orlando is the genuine vehicle of subversive energy in *As You Like It*.

This study, then, will concern itself with diverse forms of disruption whose ultimate project, successful or not, and moral or not, is nothing less than to re-create the textual universe. Again and again we find such subversion at least offering the potential of bringing to light what must otherwise elude the understanding. We see certain characters exposed to chaos, emptiness, and death with the result that they discover order, meaning, and life. But more often we witness the forces of deception marginalized, deformed, defeated, or co-opted, with the trickster's characteristic delight converted into a grotesque parody of itself. These are perhaps the patterns that have most to teach us about the plays in which they appear. How characters react to the challenges presented by such deception often proves to be not only a test of their openness and intelligence, but an index of the terms of the play-world itself. For the audience, at least, trickery can be counted on to help render that world intelligible.

V

It remains to consider briefly to what extent the dramatic patterns to be explored are distinctively Shakespearean. I have already mentioned the often-noted presence of the trickster behind two (intertwined) character-types which he inherited – the foolish Clown and the Vice. Shakespeare made far more varied and ingenious use of these figures than did his predecessors, medieval or Renaissance, but he did not alter their basic functions, except in the case of one peculiarly Shakespearean extrapolation, the professional 'wise fool'. Fool-Vice-Clown figures were already well established as linguistic and moral subversives, often with an uncanny aptitude for hitting on or exposing disquieting truths despite themselves, but typically also – and this has significant implications for the development of Shakespeare's tamer later version – with a practical capacity to stir up real trouble. Often, the dramatic package includes a comic servant whose subterfuges thwart and exasperate his master, as in the Wakefield pageant of Cain and Abel, where Cain's boy not only revealingly twists words but also sabotages the farm-work, employing, as one of his tricks, an inversion in the realm of the 'grotesque body': 'Thare prouand, syr, forthi, I lay behynd thare ars' (Cawley, *Mactatio Abel*, line 45).[23]

The self-delighting Machiavel also came pretty well ready-

made, with his trickster-heritage intact, and was not even confined to the stage: we should remember that Shakespeare's
Richard III is also, in essence, Thomas More's. A case can be
made, moreover, that Marlowe's Barabas (though not, say,
Lorenzo in *The Spanish Tragedy*) performs much the same sort
of trickery as Richard – that is, trickery that carries meaning for
its political and social milieu and to this extent is paradoxically
affirmative.[24] This perspective naturally takes us back, as Shakespeare himself went back, to the boisterous comic villains of the
Corpus Christi plays – the Cains, Pharoahs, Herods, and Pilates
– who undoubtedly influenced the development of Vice characters. The one that contains them all is Satan himself, the
founder at once of evil and of guile, who renders intelligible, and
so in a sense completes, God's goodness, as it is expressed in the
creation and redemption of man. Here is a precedent, albeit in
decidedly non-materialist terms, for the New Historicist paradigm. Satan's is a subversiveness permitted, exploited, and so
ultimately, despite his free will, produced. The principle is
clearly articulated by Jean Bodin – a formidable Renaissance
expert on matters related to creation, thanks to his impulsion to
reconcile divinity and history:

> He Himself is said to have created for Himself Pharaoh,
> whom the Hebrews interpreted as the prince of darkness, so
> that He might reveal His own glory in him by restoring
> Himself whatever things he would overthrow and destroy.
>
> (Bodin, *Method*, 316)

This view is at least more respectful of the multivalence and
power of the archetype than is the common modern perception of
what Richard L. Levin calls a 'tendency to reduce the power and
frightfulness of evil – especially supernatural evil – by treating it
in comic terms' (R. L. Levin 1971: 141).[25]

On the other hand, the providential context – the theological
counterpart of terrestrial 'authority'[26] – can itself be overvalued.
Perhaps too much has been made of the concept of the 'scourge of
God' in dealing with certain indirect Elizabethan descendants of
such villains, including Richard III. First, it needs to be
recognized that the scourge idea, however commonplace, was
hardly monolithic in Renaissance historical thought. Neither
was the determinism it implies, as Myron P. Gilmore (1956)
demonstrates by way of Bodin himself: Machiavelli, however

stigmatized as subversive, was far from alone in making human-kind historically responsible. More important, such a displace-ment of evil from intrinsic to extrinsic, in effect from indetermi-nate to overdetermined, is too confining even for the medieval originals of the character-type. There the role of providence is beyond dispute, yet the subversive powers of such villains, which are inextricable from their comic energy, somehow coexist with the very elements that defeat and contain them, perhaps because such will be the case until the real 'promis'd end', not merely the 'image of that horror' (*Lr*, V.iii.264-5). Cain is doomed to wander, Herod to rage in impotent fury, but all of the pageants till the crack of Doom leave such villainy indeterminately abroad in the world. To return to the later drama, the model of the scourge seems even less adequate aš a container for the archetype of the trickster where the moral context is more problematic than in Richard's case. If Barabas, for instance, is inflicting punish-ment on a society of hypocritical Christians, what do we make of the final triumph of that society, hypocrisies intact, despite its casualties? Nor should we forget that Marlowe actually used the sobriquet, Scourge of God, not for Barabas but for Tamburlaine, who bears no resemblance to trickster or Vice.

Clearly, to gather evidence that trickster-figures are abundant and prominent in Shakespeare's artistic heritage is to be reminded that the heritage was hardly his alone. More broadly, we must again acknowledge that deception, fooling, and subver-sion of various kinds are Renaissance drama's stock-in-trade. And in plenty of cases – from the comedies of Jonson to Marston's tragicomic *The Malcontent* and Tourneur's (Mid-dleton's?) *The Revenger's Tragedy* – there are obvious impli-cations of exposure and affirmation beyond the immediate context. All of this yet again threatens to blur the outlines of the present topic. Certainly, it constitutes a caveat against making claims for the uniqueness of Shakespeare's management of dramatic trickery. It does not at all impinge, however, on the unique position among the dramatists of his time which he continues to possess, however rigorously we demythologize his achievement, by virtue of the kaleidoscopic intertextual reso-nances within his *oeuvre*. And this fact, too, has implications for a study of the uses and abuses of subversion. This book, I hope, will finally justify itself not only by demonstrating that the dramatic practices described are pervasive and central in the canon, but also by opening yet another avenue of access to the infinite interplay among texts that gives Shakespeare's roughly twenty years of writing for the stage an (inter)textual status of its own.

2

THE CREATION
ACCORDING TO KATE

Such apostles of transformational comedy as Barber and
Northrop Frye, succeeded by numerous disciples, have effectively
promulgated the principle that Shakespeare's comic achievements of order and resolution resound with communal renewal.
For most members of this school, however, *Taming* is not a
major text, presumably because any transcending of its farcical
mode depends heavily on Katherina's notoriously problematic
disquisition on the very institution that is usually taken to
vibrate with higher harmonies. Critics who are determined to
treat the taming as a creative metamorphosis must either posit a
submerged level of 'playful' communication between husband
and wife or make parenthetical excuses for Elizabethan
backwardness.[1] Fortunately for some criticism, Shakespeare's
comic 'copulatives' generally neglect, in their winsome heedless-
ness, to discuss the ideology of matrimony.

I should like to take a different approach to integrating the play
into the comic mainstream – indeed, I wish to place it squarely at
the troubled fountainhead ('A woman mov'd is like a fountain
troubled' (V.ii.142)) – by giving due recognition to the catalytic
value possessed by shrewishness itself despite, or rather in
conjunction with, its presumed moral marginality. In so far as the
play qualifies as a comedy of transformation, it does so precisely
because of, not despite, Katherina's initial resistance to socialization. Yet the resulting stability comes at the cost of the very energy
needed to produce it. Joel Fineman has germanely posed the
paradox in terms of language and power, asking how 'a discourse
of subversiveness, explicitly presented as such, manages to
resecure, equally explicitly, the very order to which it seems, at
both first and second sight, to be opposed' (Fineman 1985: 138).

24

For him, the process is merely circular, and the question is as rhetorical as its answer: the 'order' is simply patriarchy, with which language itself is inevitably in complicity. Still, Fineman's own language ('manages') concedes an element of power successfully exercised, and when one allows that, at least at the level of textual organization, a form of order is produced that did not exist before, the paradox even more stubbornly resists erasure. Moreover, I shall be making use of that anonymous play, *The Taming of a Shrew* - whose relation to Shakespeare's I hope to render more productive, though no less problematic[2] - in order to argue that Katherina internalizes the patriarchal silencing of an intertext authorizing her disruption. The consequence is that *Taming*, beyond any other work in the canon, has value as a tensely poised paradigm of subversion's power and its suppression.

I

At the simplest level, doing justice to the power of shrewishness means appreciating its structural and imaginative centrality: by standing between Bianca and her suitors, deferring romantic consummation, Katherina provokes the plots that comprise the plot. The very title locates the struggle of Katherina and Petruchio, not the conventionally romantic wooing of Bianca, at the dramatic core. Moreover, we are brought to this core by a series of palpable displacements, as the Sly plot yields to Lucentio's passion for Bianca, which in turn is pushed aside by the claim of Katherina - the claim, that is, to be heard, to take precedence over her sister, not only in age, but in textual prominence. By this means Petruchio, at first supplementary to the action, is drawn into its centre. Next, the theme of shrew-taming is centred within him. The detached quality of Petruchio's original motive – 'gold's effect' (I.ii.93) - is usurped (though it is never totally effaced) by an intense sense of personal challenge. Even before he meets her, Petruchio's imagination is possessed by Katherina's ferocity, which daunts his fellow males and goads his masculine self-image (he is, among other things, the first of Shakespeare's woman-threatened warriors):

Think you a little din can daunt mine ears?
Have I not in my time heard lions roar?
Have I not heard the sea, puff'd up with winds,

Rage like an angry boar chafed with sweat?
Have I not heard great ordnance in the field,
And heaven's artillery thunder in the skies?

(199–204)

Comparisons here and elsewhere make Katherina's wildness elemental: it is like air; it is like fire; above all, of course, it is animal-like. As Coppélia Kahn points out, Petruchio is harnessing his male social position to the larger role of 'lord over nature' (1981: 107). The forces involved are not merely exemplary but mythic in a way that goes deeper than the facile archetype of the 'battle of the sexes'. And yet that battle finally contains the mythic structure within socio-political realities. Their triumph is Katherina's submission.

It is worth trying to respond to Katherina's controversial lecture on marriage undefensively – that is, neither imputing to Shakespeare a covert progressiveness, located in Katherina's 'private' thoughts, nor insisting on his right to reflect the benighted values of his age. To withhold such projections is to recover the signifying potency of Katherina's figures of speech, which derive from the topos of hierarchical marriage as a microcosm of political hierarchy. However commonplace these concepts, or conducive to consoling perceptions of a 'reciprocity of duties' (Bean 1980: 68), their appearance and form of expression here have a radical force. For they conspicuously fulfil a political discourse originating with Petruchio – a discourse imposed on his wife as surely as the test of obedience itself. Both the fact of Katherina's submission and its manner signal the acceptance of someone else's scripted reality. The speech thus recapitulates another peremptory lord's imposition – similarly unresolved – upon an equally recalcitrant figure of social disorder, Christopher Sly. In fact, it is easier to appreciate from this perspective the ending as it stands in the First Folio – that is, without a return to the framing device: reality has been transformed not only for, but with, Katherina; the audience, too, is implicated in her manipulation – after all, how can we ever, in the Elizabethan theatre, know the sun from the moon without on-stage authority? – and there is no going back to the comfort of reality and illusion 'right-side-up'. The failure to ease us out of the dramatic experience through the Sly framework, or even an epilogue, paradoxically functions much as does Puck's concluding address to the audience, which, by suddenly opening the option of dismissing a play as a dream, implants it more deeply in waking consciousness. There, too, dream makes itself reality; for its spokesman to invite us to escape by way of Theseus' self-discrediting rejection – 'I never may believe/These antic fables, nor these fairy toys' (*MND*, V.i.2-3) – is a fitting final act of constructive mischief.

As a homiletic set-piece expounding the most conservative Renaissance ideas of social order – ideas most accurately envisaged as comprising *one* Elizabethan world-picture, prescriptive rather than descriptive – Katherina's speech stands by itself in the early work of Shakespeare. The generic resemblance to Luciana's plea for wifely obedience in *The Comedy of Errors* (II.i.16-25) merely throws into relief telling points of contrast. Not only is that speaker's authority comically undercut by her confessed fear of 'troubles of the marriage-bed' (27), but her argument eschews the political in favour of the natural, appealing to the basic creationist justification for hierarchy: 'The beasts, the fishes, and the winged fowls/Are their males' subjects and at their controls' (18-19). For the closest parallels, suggestively, we must wait for Canterbury's lecture on the honeybees in *Henry V* (I.ii.183ff.), Ulysses' disquisition on degree (*Tro.*, I.iii.78ff.), and Menenius' Fable of the Belly (*Cor.*, I.i.96ff.) – speeches that belong to toughly political plays, hardly farcical comedies, whose complex ironies they help to focus. Here, too, the ironies are complex, but they centre on a simple paradox: the moral of the obedience-trial, pointed by Katherina herself – the value of *unconstrained* submission of wife to husband – is at odds with the constraint Petruchio has applied in his 'taming'.

No doubt an Elizabethan audience would have taken wife-beating more in its stride and thought in physically more drastic terms.[3] Certainly, too, the often-compared Noah pageants in the Corpus Christi cycles connect shrew-taming with restoration of the 'natural' relation between husband and wife.[4] However, these pageants also furnish grounds for questioning Petruchio's methods, and such questioning is encouraged here, as it is not in more crudely misogynistic analogues, precisely by his ostensible mildness and by Katherina's philosophical rationale for her submission. The fact is that Noah's attempts to establish the rightful dominance of husband over wife by physical force – that is, by his own strength – are comically futile: Noah's superiority depends on God; his wife's submission, as an aspect of the larger transformation of discord into harmony, is a function of the flood and their deliverance by divine mercy. By contrast, Petruchio does not lay claim to obedience as the privileged mediator of a transcendent truth – 'she for God in him'. He demands the same unquestioning acceptance of his inscrutable will for its own sake as God does of Noah – or as the prince does of his subjects, to apply Katherina's political terms. Yet Petruchio's tactics pointedly recall divine prerogatives. He claims for his *logos* power over time – 'It shall be what a' clock I say it is' (IV.iii.195) – and Hortensio's admiring prophecy that he 'will command the sun' (196) is resoundingly fulfilled. Kate (never 'Katherina' or 'Katherine') in *A Shrew* is made to yield merely by echoing her husband's pious exclamation, 'Jesus save the glorious moone' (xv.11). Katherina, faced with a husband who will swear only 'by my mother's son, and that's myself' (IV.v.6), delivers a prayer-like tribute to the creative force of his language, his right to fix (and unfix) the relation between sign and signified in a way that overrides the principle of truthful recognition embodied in adamic naming:

> Then God be blest, it is the blessed sun,
> But sun it is not, when you say it is not;
> And the moon changes even as your mind.
> What you will have it nam'd, even that it is,
> And so it shall be so for Katherina.

> (IV.v.18–22)[5]

In this context, Katherina's final credo carries overtones of idolatry likely to have disturbed the very segment of an audience to which her orthodox posture would have appealed. Her failure to extend the argument to the divine basis of all human authority – as if a husband's power were self-engendered and self-justifying – is conspicuous, when her speech is set beside conventional Christian arguments, such as the discourse of Canterbury, mentioned above, or the Bishop of Carlyle's defence of Divine Right in *Richard II* (IV.i.114ff.). Even the pagan Ulysses appeals to the governing principle of the universe, while Katherina appears to see no power higher than that of the earthly prince. As has been pointed out, the equivalent speech in *A Shrew* (xviii.15–43) does contain a metaphysical justification, in terms of the first woman's responsibility for disrupting the order God had created.[6] There, indeed, it is the political rationale that is conspicuously absent, while Kate particularly stresses God's governance of time: 'For all the course of yeares, of ages, moneths,/Of seasons temperate, of dayes and houres,/Are tund and stopt, by measure of his hand' (xviii.20-2). The husband may do God's work, but he certainly does not take God's place.

Ultimately, then, Petruchio's confrontational tactics work, where Noah's do not, because he establishes himself as a creator-figure of transcendent authority, as Noah cannot. The enormity of this imposition, couched in terms that would make it difficult for a Renaissance audience to dismiss as frivolous, throws into relief the degree of hidden violence involved. Precisely because it downplays the trivializing mode of slapstick, working against the mitigating framework of farce, the text exposes Petruchio as a master of more advanced forms of torture: brainwashing, sensory deprivation, and humiliation (another case of Shakespeare's being ahead of his time).

This alienating brutalization, too, culminates in Katherina's final speech. After all, as various critics have noted, the shrewish stereotype – the interpretation of Katherina imposed on her by other characters – is in constant tension with elements that humanize her, apart from the humanizing effect of her victimization itself. A brief but resonant sequence – our only glimpse of the family without outsiders – sketches her shrewishness as a psychological response to her position. Katherina is shown to be resentful not so much of her sister's suitors as of her father's favouritism: 'She is your treasure, she must have a husband;/I must dance barefoot on her wedding-day,/And for your love to her lead apes in hell' (II.i.32-4). For her part, Bianca, in both name and nature, suggests the 'fair' Helena, whose sense of victimization by her sworn sister Hermia is similarly inextricable from a smug and taunting sense of superiority:

> Let her not hurt me. I was never curst;
> I have no gift at all in shrewishness;
> I am a right maid for my cowardice.
> Let her not strike me. You perhaps may think,
> Because she is something lower than myself,
> That I can match her.
>
> (*MND*, III.ii.300-5)

Bianca's chief skill is in making herself one-dimensional, giving men what they want – mildness, modesty, aesthetic sensitivity, deference – until she gets what she wants. By contrast, Katherina's multidimensionality is never in doubt when her speech and behaviour are subversive and anarchistic. Only when she embraces the patriarchal régime, submerging her voice in its ideology, is she reduced to caricature.

In this way, Katherina's concluding expression of her current position in the lexis of political power – the centrifugal movement of her language towards terms such as 'lord', 'king', and 'governor' – calls attention to the process of the play as the triumph of the collective and social over the individual. In the speech's retrospective light, Petruchio appears outlined, not merely as the conventional mercenary suitor, but as the instrument of a civilizing mission. It is not surprising to find him anticipating that other arch-opponent of a simultaneously attractive and threatening anarchy, Prince Hal. Like Hal, Petruchio concludes a role-playing scene with a soliloquy proclaiming the political method in his seeming madness: 'Thus have I politicly begun my reign,/And 'tis my hope to end successfully' (IV.i.188–9). But this revelation comes in the fourth act of *Taming*, not in the second scene. Now we have known from the start that Petruchio intends to tame the shrew, but we have also been encouraged to suppose that he possesses disruptive impulses making him Katherina's match in a more sympathetic sense. Coming where it does, the soliloquy shocks us into recognizing, in effect, that this couple is not Beatrice and Benedick, with interlocking vulnerabilities and offensive tactics that are really defensive. This game is about power, and it is one-sided. If there is a 'real' Petruchio behind the mercenary egotist, it is evidently not the madcap we have wanted to believe in – and we will see no other side of him.

Perhaps the ultimate indication of Katherina's submission to the discourse of political order as the social projection of male power is her sympathetic picture of the burdens and cares of the husband:

> thy lord, thy life, thy keeper,
> Thy head, thy sovereign; one that cares for thee,
> And for thy maintenance; commits his body
> To painful labor, both by sea and land;
> To watch the night in storms, the day in cold,

Whilst thou li'st warm at home, secure and safe.

(V.ii.146–51)

This is a striking anticipation of the complaint of Henry V, when, on the eve of the battle he has brought about, he speaks of the unappreciated burdens of Ceremony:

The slave, a member of the country's peace,
Enjoys it; but in gross brain little wots
What watch the King keeps to maintain the peace,
Whose hours the peasant best advantages.

(*H5*, IV.i.281–4)

This governor, ironically, specifically resents being expected to bear responsibility for 'careful wives' (231). It is ironic, too, that the value placed on sleep – by Katherina, by Henry V, and for that matter by his insomniac father (*2H4*, III.i.4ff.) – corresponds with Petruchio's recognition, as he concludes his key soliloquy, of the power to be gained by keeping Katherina awake.

Challenging questions, then, are opened precisely by the play's rigorous closure: exactly what has Katherina's shrewishness, now itself put to sleep, accomplished, and at what cost? It is possible to argue that, if plays like *The Comedy of Errors* and *A Midsummer Night's Dream* enact a renewal of the social order, *Taming* shows that order in the very stages of formation. After all, by way of the recurrent motifs of railing, brawling, and discord, Katherina, the elder sister, reincarnates, in familiar Renaissance terms, the very elemental chaos which preceded the divine creation of the world. This is the account of Du Bartas in his epic of creation, *La Première Sepmaine* (first published in 1578):

Ce premier monde estoit une forme sans forme,
Une pile confuse, un meslange difforme,
D'abismes un abisme, un corps mal compassé,
Un chaos de chaos, un tas mal entassé
Où tous les elemens se logeoient pesle-mesle.

(1.223–7)

The image of chaos is implicit throughout Shakespeare's play, but in *A Shrew* a translation of Du Bartas's lines, omitting the one naming chaos,[7] actually forms the core of Kate's final speech,

31

as she depicts God's creation of the order that a shrewish woman threatens:

> The first world was, a forme, without a forme,
> A heape confusd a mixture all deformd,
> A gulfe of gulfes, a body bodiles,
> Where all the elements were orderles.

(xviii.23-6)

Indeed, the speech is nothing more than a rough botching of Du Bartas – until those lines about the creation of woman that actually situate Kate within what Dusinberre aptly terms a 'theology of subjection' (1975: 78).[8]

As the only shaper and controller of inchoate matter that Shakespeare gives us, Petruchio takes it upon himself to implant the contrasting (and convenient) virtues of the younger daughter, whose 'mild behavior and sobriety' (I.i.71) and attraction to 'music, instruments, and poetry' (93) qualify her as '[t]he patroness of heavenly harmony' (III.i.5). This opens the way for Lucentio's love-match to justify his initial vision of '[t]he pleasant garden of great Italy' (I.i.4) and for the conclusion of all 'jarring notes' (V.ii.1) at the final communal feast. Yet, as Bianca's disobedient coda reminds us, the teleological momentum of this creation myth never ceases to be subject to ironic questioning. A Shrew's pointed portrayal of God as tamer of chaos makes it all the clearer that Petruchio's arrogation of divine prerogatives sits uneasily on his human frame.

Moreover, the chaos that is Shakespeare's Katherina cannot be decontextualized. It is not as if, at the beginning of the play, all is right with this world: Bianca is not only false in herself, but in love with neither of her original suitors; conflicting forces are converging on Padua and on Baptista's house, but no resolutions are in prospect. Kahn (1981: 105-8) and Karen Newman (1986: 93-4) have written persuasively of Katherina's obstructive temperament, her defiance in particular of her father's authority, as her only possible form of protest – deformed, to use Du Bartas's term, by desperation and impotence – against a sterile family situation and the mercenary distortion of human values. It is through Katherina's provocative intervention, however negative in form, that characters are precipitated into the multiple confusions, mistakings, and suspensions of identity, as usual marked by disguise, that lead to renewal. The familial and social order is thoroughly reconstituted in harmonious terms, while Bianca at least actually makes a love-match.

Somewhat improbably, these aspects of Katherina's role look forward to Cordelia. And indeed, from Lear's point of view, Cordelia's challenge to his vision of order – a vision which is similarly based on doubtful professions of love, a mercenary reality, and sibling rivalry – appears precisely shrewish, that is, perversely and stubbornly resistant to 'natural' patriarchal authority, though her offence is saying too little, not too much. There are, according to Willeford, 'two ways of expressing folly, through silence and babbling' (Willeford 1969: 29). Lear chooses to misread the spoken and unspoken text of Cordelia's love as aggressive hostility: 'So young, and so untender?' (I.i.106). As in *Taming*, a favoured sibling, Goneril, makes a virtue of conspicuous compliance: 'You have obedience scanted,/And well are worth the want that you have wanted' (278–9). Newman (1986: 93–4) points out that the 'silence' (I.i.70) that attracts suitors to Bianca is an intolerable sign, for Katherina, of acquiescence in the *status quo*: 'Her silence flouts me, and I'll be reveng'd' (II.i.29). This makes it the inverse equivalent of Goneril's and Regan's hypocritical effusiveness. Baptista, like Lear, clearly considers a low voice 'an excellent thing in woman' (*Lr*, V.iii.274), while his sense of his wrongs at his daughter's hands – 'Was ever gentleman thus griev'd as I?' (II.i.37) – comically anticipates that tragedian's huge paternal agonies.

Such a comparison underlines the issues in the comedy too of loss and sacrifice. Our response to Katherina's sufferings may remain this side of pathos, but our sense that order comes at the expense of her fullness as a character is strengthened by the ironic triumph of the mercenary motive in the case of her own marriage. (If we choose to read affection into Petruchio's words or actions, after all, we do so without benefit of evidence.) To the point here is Cordelia's virtual sacrifice not only of her life but of her original stubborn realism. When she cares for the mad and broken Lear, her ministrations are notable for her withholding of truth, when truth-telling has been her stock-in-trade: 'No cause, no cause' (IV.vii.74). This is hardly to claim for Katherina the status of either wise or tragic heroine. But it is to suggest that her rebellious energy, however poorly directed, carries a value with its power, and that its elimination, while marking the imposition of closure on the play, itself imposes closure on the future possibilities of the play-world.

Katherina's violent repudiation of her world as she finds it expresses not only the claims of deformed matter itself to be fashioned anew, but also the potential for such refashioning. Lear is notoriously denying the premise of the Christian creation when he warns Cordelia, 'Nothing will come of nothing' (I.i.90); in fact, it is precisely Cordelia's 'nothing' that offers, fleetingly, the potential for a recreation that might obviate tragedy. Lear finds the threat of chaos in the challenge of flux and the demand to 'see better' (158). Similarly, Othello mistakes the nature and locus of chaos – 'when I love thee not,/Chaos is come again' (III.iii.91–2) – identifying Desdemona with the same destructive parody of creation ('a cestern for foul toads/To knot and gender in' (IV.ii.61–2)) that he himself enacts when, god-like, he imports ordering justice into the world by killing her ('It is the cause' (V.ii.1)). What he actually kills with her, as when Lear disowns Cordelia, is the potential for on-going creation within the framework of change, time, and mortality: 'The heavens forbid/ But that our loves and comforts should increase/Even as our days do grow!' (*Oth.*, II.i.193–5).

The paradox, then, is that while Katherina's shrewishnesss must be vanquished if a stable and harmonious world is to be created, it is also the raw material, hence the essential precondition, of that creation. The paradox is familiar to anthropology – witness Eliade's analysis of initiation rituals:

> If the world was restored to the state in which it had been at the moment when it came to birth, if the gestures that the Gods had made *for the first time* in the beginning were reproduced, society and the entire cosmos became what they had been then – pure, powerful, effectual, with all their possibilities intact. . . . In order to be created anew, the old world must first be annihilated.
>
> (Eliade 1965: xiii)

In theory, anthropologically oriented critics would agree; hence, the value placed by Sherman Hawkins on the 'topsy-turvy' – as managed, however, by Petruchio. The assumption that such re-creative disorder is Petruchio's prerogative rather than Katherina's may reflect a residual attraction to Paduan ideas of harmony. More fundamental, however, is the teleological bias thus revealed. Petruchio's disruptive energy, it seems, is valid because it is visibly in service to order; it is also narrowly focused and reassuringly temporary, put on for the occasion. By contrast, Katherina's chaos accepts no boundaries and makes no promises; it leads nowhere that one can see. In short, it is the real thing in being, in itself, nothing. And this is precisely the key to its potential to give birth to a new world.

II

On this point too, Du Bartas's account of the creation furnishes a revealing intertext, in lines that are certainly *not* incorporated in *A Shrew*:

> Ce lourd, dy-je, Chaos, qui, dans soy mutiné,
> Se vid en un moment dans le Rien d'un rien né,
> Estoit le corps fecond d'où la celeste essence
> Et les quatre elemens devoient prendre naissance.
>
> (2.43–6)

As in several other key images, Du Bartas presents the production of order from chaos in terms of maternity. Primeval discord here, though destined to be harmonized by the divine will, is itself actively fertile – and pointedly female. This view, though opposed not only to the standard Christian reading of Genesis, but also to Plato's portrayal in the *Timaeus* of primordial matter as inert, if evil (because of its resistance to the Demiurge), is common in Neoplatonic thought.[9] Thus Paracelsus portrays the primeval chaos as a matrix containing all the beauties of creation *in potentia* and compares to this the ongoing creative power of woman (*Selected Writings*, 13–26). Plutarch, in his 'Commentarie' on the *Timaeus*, limits God to the organizing of a '*chaos*' understood as not 'without a bodie, without motion, or without soul' ('Commentarie', 1032), while his essay on Isis and Osiris (to which I shall return in connection with *Antony and Cleopatra*) makes matter 'the feminine part of nature' ('Of Isis and Osiris', 1309), endlessly generative in itself, though inclined to 'the first and principall essence, which is nothing else but the sovereign good, . . . as to a subsistance and being' (1309–11).[10] The Hermetic *Asclepius* goes farther in exalting matter's claim, as an independent co-creative entity, to 'original fecundity': 'In the beginning were God and Matter. . . . [Matter] undoubtedly contains in itself the power of generating all things' (Scott, ed., *Hermetica*, 1: 312–13 (14b)).[11] Now Du Bartas is careful to provide a context of creation *ex nihilo*, but for Bodin, for instance, the very attribution of creative power to matter, an idea which he attacks vigorously (307–9), clearly posed a threat to fundamental concepts regarding God's relation to his creation, the status of the world, and the nature of time. Amongst modern commentators on Du Bartas, Luzius Keller has perhaps been most alert to this subversive subtext, concluding, after a thorough analysis of the poet's treatment of chaos, 'Tout nous fait croire que Du Bartas est tenté d'attribuer à la Matière un prestige semblable à celui qu'il attribue à Dieu' (Keller 1974: 130).

I suggest that this subtext, suppressed in *A Shrew*'s appropriation of Du Bartas for Kate's final speech, is effectively released into Shakespeare's multiplicity of meanings by his presentation of Katherina and Petruchio, including her conspicuous failure to invoke a creationist sanction for her submission. Liberated, too, are the power and value assigned by Du Bartas, not only to the female creative function in the abstract, but to women in relation to men. The anonymous play uses its borrowings to authorize Kate's anti-feminist conclusion, the divine sanction for women's subordination:

Then to his image he did make a man,
Olde *Adam* and from his side asleepe,
A rib was taken, of which the Lord did make,
The woe of man so termd by *Adam* then,
Woman for that, by her came sinne to us,
And for her sin was *Adam* doomd to die.
As Sara to her husband, so should we,
Obey them, love them, keepe, and nourish them.

(xviii.31–8)

Yet not only do these lines suddenly break the pattern of translation from Du Bartas – they also sharply contradict that poet's portrayal of the creation of woman. 'Le Sixiesme Jour' makes no mention of the sin to come or of woman's inferiority. Rather, man is spiritually completed, even redeemed, by woman,

Sans qui l'homme ça bas n'est homme qu' à demy:
Ce n'est qu'un loup-garou du soleil ennemy,
Qu'un animal sauvage, ombrageux, solitaire,

Bigarre, frenetique, à qui rien ne peut plaire
Que le seul desplaisir, né pour soy seulement,
Privé de coeur, d'esprit, d'amour, de sentiment.

(6.949-54)

And so God approaches Adam '[c]omme le medecin, qui desire trencher/Quelque membre incurable' (6.961-2), and '[p]our sauver l'homme entier, il en coupe une part' (6.966). As the crowning glory of creation, Eve forms, with Adam, the Edenic 'amoureux Androgyne' that continues to serve, in this fallen world, as '[s]ource de tout bon heur' (6.987). This intense idealization of marriage, though premised on a concept of female supplementarity that hardly qualifies as feminist in the modern sense, nevertheless indicates what is most basically missing from the conjugal vision, not of Kate in *A Shrew*, but of Shakespeare's character. The former mechanically substitutes a metaphysics of sin for one of redemption. Shakespeare subtly recuperates Du Bartas as intertext by having Katherina exclude the spiritual dimension of marriage entirely in favour of a rigorously political reading from a position of subjection.

Given the instability of Petruchio's claim to creative hegemony, even a partial recuperation of Katherina's chaos as itself creative has radical consequences for our perception of the civilizing force he represents. Petruchio's energy is relegated to the status of reaction and imitation. We are reminded that, in a sense, Petruchio comes into dramatic existence only through the potently marginal Katherina. He derives his shrew-taming purpose from her. But most significantly, he mimics her behaviour in order to subdue her. The displacement we experience on learning, from the Act IV soliloquy, that we have not been seeing the real Petruchio is partly the shock of discovering the ability of a crafty intellect to simulate such spontaneous energy. The trouble-maker succeeds in provoking the renovation of her world but is in turn neutralized by the appropriation of her own behavioural sign. A false shrewishness conquers a true and somehow derives from its conquest, sealed by the parading of Katherina as living trophy, the aura of her creative force. It is a process analogous to *A Shrew*'s conscription for repressive purposes of the poetic voice of creation itself. Thus are cannibals supposed to assimilate the strength of their vanquished enemies. Thus does Prince Hal promise his father that the accumulated honours of Hotspur, another shrew to be tamed for the sake of the socio-political order, will accrue to him; and thus, in a sense, does Hal assimilate and transform into a precision instrument of policy the jesting of Falstaff – the ultimate fulfilment of that character's function as 'the cause that wit is in other men' (*2H4*, I.ii.10).

Not only, then, does *Taming* present an even more primitive stage of community- (or indeed cosmos-) formation than do the 'festive' comedies, but it also illustrates – without resolving – basic principles of trouble-making and counter-trouble-making that repeat themselves, with variations, throughout Shakespeare's work. Again and again, we are drawn into measuring and balancing the creative and destructive impact of centres of subversive energy. Consistently, we find our judgements, made according to conservative Elizabethan principles, treated deferentially but our sympathies divided. At least we have our warning that, however *sly* an audience may think itself, deferential treatment is no guarantee of truth: we may be sleeping.

3

CATALYTIC CHAOS: TROUBLE-MAKERS MAKING HISTORY

There are, I think, more shrews than meet the casual eye in Shakespeare's early work. In addition to Katherina, three important characters – Richard III, Aaron in *Titus Andronicus*, and Philip the Bastard in *King John* – are similarly dominated by what may be thought of as the impulse to outrage, and they similarly bring that impulse to bear on their respective play-worlds. It is important, for my purposes, to insist on the contingent nature of their subversiveness, as opposed to a purely 'antic' function such as Blanpied (1983) finds exemplified by Richard and the Bastard. When Blanpied isolates this function in terms of 'the fool, materialized from a blurred background of anarchic energy, of the chaos always just a little beyond the human clearing' (14), he seems to have touched the trickster indeed. But I do not believe that the subversives in the histories, any more than subversiveness in Padua, can be thus decontextualized. It does not follow from their 'self-delighting' quality that they '[play] for the sake of playing' (14). The essential sign of the disruptive impulse in all these characters is behaviour that asserts, and so constructs, the self by discomfiting others; shrewishness is not a private, 'neutral' state of being but a role socially defined and produced – hence its political potency. In the case of the Bastard, this disruption is overtly directed by constructive values, but the impulse itself remains traceable as such – at least until the final scenes. There, as I hope to show, its metamorphosis resembles the ambiguous transformation of Katherina.

First, however, the connection of all three figures with Katherina needs to be established on a broader base. Their most often-noted association is with such obvious off-shoots of the Vice-tradition – a male tradition – as Edmund and Iago. Among more nearly contemporaneous characters, one perhaps thinks first of Mercutio and Puck. Though Mercutio is hardly a villain, and though the province of the fairy may be a harmless sort of mischief, both have their darker sides;[1] moreover, the very premise of the self-delighting energy all of them have in common is precisely that it collapses the distinction between darkness and light. What the disruptive drive of Richard, Aaron, and the Bastard most distinctively shares with Katherina's relates to dramatic form: by, in effect, hijacking their respective texts, they too serve to realize the structurally determined destinies of those texts despite themselves and, more or less drastically, at their own cost. The defeat of the two villains follows directly from their power and should not obscure their impact. Nor should the eventual exhaustion of the subversive identity itself – the fact that Richard 'subsides into the historical world he has been busy mocking down' (Blanpied 1983: 15), or that Philip loses his own language (S. Burckhardt 1968: 135–9) and 'cannot possess the center of the play and positively reform it' (Blanpied 1983: 117). As with Katherina, such exhaustion contradictorily signals both the end and the fulfilment of creative potential – a doubleness that intrinsically sets limits to the sense of resolution.

Ultimately, then, all of these characters function, in their different ways, as successful catalytic agents of order by means of the very impulse to disorder that ensures their victimization. This is true neither of Mercutio, given his decisive early exit from *Romeo and Juliet*, nor even of Puck, who, while he revels in mortal preposterousness, serves Oberon's desire for amorous reciprocity. But if, like Katherina, the three shrews-in-disguise open up their texts to transformation, the structures they affect are explicitly, not just implicitly, political from start to finish. This can be so, of course, because all of them are male.

The term 'shrew' thus becomes untenable, according to modern, though not necessarily Renaissance, usage,[2] but before replacing it with, *faute de mieux*, the gender- and colour-less 'trouble-maker', we might consider what goes with it: first, the implication of animal vitality; second, the link between disruption and femaleness; and, finally, the reassuring confinement of that disruption within an inherently powerless role. (Shrews, like vixens, though they be fierce, are but little – see Helena's shrewish branding of Hermia (*MND*, III.ii.324–5)). Of these ideas, the element of animality continues to figure in much the same way; in fact, it receives more pronounced presentation (with a vengeance, in two of the three cases). On the other hand, in the change from female to male may be traced a movement from an energy focused on relatedness and linked with fertility to a power exercised through violence and at the expense of personal ties.[3] The world of history and politics, characteristically masculine in Shakespeare's work as in his world, subsumes the domestic milieu of comedy. Richard's wooing of Lady Anne makes a virtual emblem of this process, horrifically epitomizing the appropriation of the discourse of love by the cause of hate. The Bastard's disruptiveness, too, pointedly begins at home, before, in taking on his broader textual responsibilities, he repudiates the domestic sphere. (A curious vestige of the domestic in Aaron's villainy is his quasi-maternal feeling for his child.)

Something the three male figures conspicuously share with their female counterpart is at least an initial position outside the established structures that they act upon. The cripple, the black, the bastard: all are by definition cut off from socially sanctioned sources of identity formation. The advantage their sex gives them (if advantage it necessarily proves) is the capacity to respond to exclusion through action, rather than merely through resistance. Nevertheless, the essential contingency of their existences links them with Katherina rather than Petruchio, with the silent Cordelia rather than the blustering Kent. Equally to the point, they are allied, not with the fugitive Edgar, but with his bastard brother. The temporary deprivation of identity imposed on Gloucester's loyal and legitimate son does not alter the parameters of selfhood. Names may have to change – 'poor Tom!/ That's something yet: Edgar I nothing am' (*Lr*, II.iii.20-1) – but Edgar always knows who he is, even if the world does not. By contrast, the world is quite certain as to Edmund; his manipulations of that world express the drive to resolve his own uncertainty: after all, the dominant mode of his self-defining soliloquy – fourteen out of twenty-two lines – is interrogative ('Why bastard? Wherefore base?' (I.ii.6)).

I

That Richard III and Aaron share the same character-type as Edmund is critical common knowledge. The main reason for making the comparison here is to bind more firmly the problematic member of the early shrewish trio, who is significantly set apart by virtue of his virtue. As one of three Shakespearean bastards (the third being the malcontent Don John), Philip is indissolubly linked with Edmund by the very basis of his existence. Moreover, he is the object of a legitimate sibling's attempt to dispossess him of identity and property – precisely the way Edmund sees his relation to Edgar (he is, in his own view, retaliating in kind). By eschewing vindictiveness – and indeed developing into a paragon of virtues otherwise scarce in his world – Philip effectively subverts the popular prejudice against bastards, even as, with his confident, 'I am I, howe'er I was begot' (I.i.175), he anticipates Edmund's more defensive self-determinism: 'I should have been that I am, had the maidenl'est star in the firmament twinkled on my bastardizing' (*Lr*, I.ii.131–3). (We should also compare Richard III's early declaration, 'I am myself alone' (*3H6*, V.vi.83), echoed by 'I am I' (*R3*, V.iii.183) at the end of his career, when his sense of self is collapsing in isolation, guilt, and despair.)

Shakespeare's audience would hardly need Edmund's example to recognize in this earlier bastard traits recalling the same type of stage villain: the self-conscious opportunism, the addiction to scorn and mockery, and, underlying these, the position of at once participant and commentator. Philip's failure to apply these qualities for the usual evil purposes focuses attention on the factors that enable the energy of alienation, the impulse to create a self in the face of denial, to express itself positively in his case. Most obviously, he has the good fortune to be offered an alternative identity almost before he knows he needs one, and the offer comes in a form that more than compensates for his losses. First, Queen Elinor, disconcertingly echoing Christ's call to his disciples, exhorts him to become a New Man, sacrificing material for spiritual gain: 'Wilt thou forsake thy fortune,/Bequeath thy land to him and follow me?' (I.i.148–9). Then it is the King's turn to new-baptize him, richly supplying that lack of a name which is the traditional bane of illegitimacy: 'From henceforth bear his name whose form thou bearest:/Kneel thou down Philip, but rise more great,/Arise Sir Richard, and Plantagenet' (160–2). This adjustment of the name to suit the evident fact amounts to a conferring of legitimacy. Fortunately, there is no necessity for this bastard actually to appeal to his father, as Edmund must do, or to ennoble himself at someone else's expense. As it happens, his presence as a living symbol of King Richard's glory suits the interests of the régime: the gods need not 'stand up for bastards' (*Lr*, I.ii.22) if a king will do so. It is an ironically appropriate way of gaining moral sanction for a political cause that itself is doubtfully legitimate. The irony is compounded by John's conspicuous lack of affection for Arthur Plantagenet, the all-too-lawful son of his other brother Geffrey.

These ironies, however, eventually come home to roost. For having got his foot in the door, the Bastard begins to make himself at home. The play comes to be largely controlled by his transformation of the political structure, which eventually becomes the reflection and embodiment of his identity. And as this happens, the rhetoric of disruption that previously comprised that identity is converted by stages into the discourse of the re-established order, determined to maintain itself in its new form:

> Now these her princes are come home again,
> Come the three corners of the world in arms,
> And we shall shock them. Nought shall make us rue,
> If England to itself do rest but true.
>
> (V.vii.115–18)

These lines set the seal on the union of the individual and the political quests. Philip has progressed from eccentric spokesman for the commonsensical but patriotic Englishman to the exalted voice of England as a polity. It is a unique destiny, for this sort of trickster–outsider, in Shakespeare's *oeuvre*.

It may be surprising that the Bastard maintains his disruptive momentum as long as he does, given his warm reception by the establishment and the premise of his loyalty and honesty. Yet, as he is introduced to the appalling milieu of political power-broking, his irrepressible subversiveness and cynical detachment keep such questions firmly at a distance, so strongly redolent are they of the Vice-stereotype. There is no mistaking his delight in bloodshed and discord when he urges the princes back to battle in Act II, Scene i, or his pleasure in the unsavoury strategem of uniting to subdue 'contemptuous' (II.i.384) Angiers – pleasure all the greater because 'Austria and France [will] shoot in each other's mouth./I'll stir them to it' (414–15).[4] Even more squarely in the tradition are his two soliloquies. In the first, he mocks the manners of 'worshipful society' (I.i.205), yet accounts himself a 'mounting spirit' (206) with 'the inward motion to deliver/Sweet, sweet, sweet poison for the age's tooth' (212–13). He has no choice, he argues, 'For he is but a bastard to the time/That doth not smack of observation – /And so am I, whether I smack or no' (207–9). The resemblance to Edmund's rationalizing is strong, though Philip appends a most un-Edmund-like disclaimer of any intention to deceive (he will merely learn deceit in order to avoid it). The second soliloquy similarly moves from contemptuous but disinterested moralizing, here more in Thersites' railing vein ('Mad world, mad kings, mad composition!' (II.i.561)), to frank self-interest: 'And why rail I on this commodity?/But for because he hath not woo'd me yet' (587–8). This time the conclusion is an unqualified anticipation of Edmund's quasi-religious dedication to his own advancement: 'Since kings break faith upon commodity,/Gain, be my lord, for I will worship thee' (597–8).

Before the trouble-maker's role begins its assimilative metamorphosis, then, it actually becomes more sharply defined. The increasingly radical alienation evident in these speeches spills over into moments in Act III when the Bastard is on the verge of overstaying his welcome, giving his well-wishers (perhaps one should say his handlers) too much of a good thing. In contrast with, say, Kent–Caius, that later 'good blunt fellow' (John's words at I.i.71) who puts on the character-type selectively, Philip does not always keep his sauciness within bounds acceptable to his master. The king's rebuke, 'We like not this, thou dost forget thyself' (III.i.134), when the Bastard continues to taunt Austria despite the cessation of hostilities, reminds us that it is precisely such flouting of constraint that constitutes selfhood for such a character; it is the socially and politically determined self that he is 'forgetting', and his provocation is telling: corruption and duplicity, the evasion and suppression of truths that cry out for honest confrontation. Even when he is behaving himself, in John's terms, the constant thrust of his commentary is to say the unsayable, to expose rotten façades and hypocritical accommodations masquerading as statecraft in a world where Pandulph's words (like Petruchio's) usurp creative power: 'All form is formless, order orderless,/Save what is opposite to England's love' (III.i.253–4). It is natural, then, that he, once the victim of false naming, becomes more Vice-like – not merely more bitterly outspoken, but more subject to the pure impulse to 'stir' stasis into action – in proportion to his sense of the moral stagnation that most fundamentally endangers the realm.

The effect is to present Philip as having arisen, like the veritable ghost of his father, in response to the state of the kingdom and the kingship. Despite his position as outsider, then, he is hardly 'blessedly unimplicated' in historical process (Blanpied 1983: 101): to be 'a bastard to the time' signifies belonging as well as detachment. In fact, the shifting significance of 'time' helps to gauge the transformation of the Bastard himself. From using it as a virtual synonym for 'commodity' in his mocking vocabulary – 'Old Time the clock-setter, that bald sexton Time!/Is it as he will? (III.i.324–5) – he comes to invest the word with a high seriousness reflecting his committed participation in affairs of state: 'The spirit of the time shall teach me speed' (IV.ii.176). John's comment, 'Spoke like a sprightful noble gentleman' (177), acknowledges the transformation and prepares us for his transfer of authority when Philip spiritedly objects to the 'inglorious league' (V.i.65) with Pandulph: 'Have thou the ordering of this present time' (77). When the Bastard appears on the battlefield, he at once appropriates and is appropriated by the king's voice: 'Now hear our English King,/ For thus his royalty doth speak in me' (V.ii.128–9). That voice now speaks like royalty indeed.[5]

We get our last glimpse of Philip in true Vice-like form when he heads off at John's behest to plunder the monasteries, full of a contempt for Roman ritual that the audience would doubtless have relished: 'Bell, book, and candle shall not drive me back,/ When gold and silver becks me to come on' (III.iii.12–13). Much important action ensues in his absence – his longest in the play. This includes the king's cold-blooded plot, and Hubert's compassionate failure, to murder Arthur – the nadir, that is, of John's moral degeneration and the turning point in his fortunes, since it is Arthur's death (first the rumour, then the fact) that turns many of the lords against him. The Bastard, of course, is not one of these, but Arthur figures in his urgent report, when he returns, of the disorder and discontent that are spreading through the kingdom. The social consequences of John's leadership have thrust into the background his success as a bag-man:

How I have sped among the clergymen

45

The sums I have collected shall express.
But as I travell'd hither through the land,
I find the people strangely fantasied,
Possess'd with rumors, full of idle dreams,
Not knowing what they fear, but full of fear.

(IV.ii.141–6)

While Philip's loyalty will not allow him to challenge the king, whose cause he identifies absolutely with that of the nation, his discovery of the dead child strips away the last vestiges of shrewishness, completing the conversion of his outlook on the world from bemused detachment to desperately anxious involvement:

I am amaz'd, methinks, and lose my way
Among the thorns and dangers of this world.
. . .
The life, the right, and truth of all this realm
Is fled to heaven; and England now is left
To tug and scamble, and to part by th' teeth
The unowed interest of proud swelling state.
. . .
Now happy he whose cloak and center can
Hold out this tempest.

(IV.iii.140–56)

The cynicism defined and maintained by the status of outrageous outsider has been lost, and with it, paradoxically, a form of innocence derived from freedom from responsibility. This is, then, a re-enactment of the Fall, and accordingly it opens the way to the emergence of the heroic self. This process is emblematized in Act V, Scene vi, where the Bastard and Hubert grope for each other's identities in the dark, and from 'Who thou wilt' (9) the former emerges as Hubert's '[b]rave soldier' (13). And because this is not his tragedy, that heroic self can become the cornerstone of the patriotic renewal and affirmation with which the play concludes. There is a final reminder of his former impulsiveness. The news of John's death momentarily provokes him to wild thoughts of revenge and desperate action; however, as soon as he learns that peace, not war, is the consequence, his loyalty becomes forward- rather than backward-looking, as he vows to Prince Henry 'my faithful services/And true subjection everlastingly' (V.vii.104–5).

The Bastard's catalytic function has been triumphantly fulfilled; the measure of its success is his integration into the new order. Yet as with Katherina, though in less obvious ways, the cost of being translated from the margin to the centre of the text contributes to the ironic qualification of the final harmony. In the first place, an audience is bound to have mixed feelings about trading-in disruption and satirical commentary for high-sounding sentiment, even at the point of closure. And behind such reservations surely lies the fact that the trouble-maker's creativity consists, not in its productions, but in its ongoing revelatory potential. Becoming the embodiment of socially sanctioned truth means losing the capacity to keep elusive truths sceptically in view – a dangerous limitation when the forces of history are identified with the destabilizing power of time itself.[6] To write oneself into a text is to become a function of its contexts; to reach the centre of power is to incur 'true subjection'.

II

What qualifies Richard and Aaron as tricksters is the fact that, beneath the calculating deception which displaces the reckless boisterousness of Katherina and Philip, a version of the same impulse to outrage for outrage's sake remains compulsively in charge.[7] Hence, the essential emptiness of achievement as opposed to process: Aaron's goal is criminality itself; Richard's kingship proves a burden when he finally gets it. But the impulse is most apparent from their notorious self-disclosing (yet simultaneously self-withholding) soliloquies – soliloquies that, as has often been observed, by taking the audience into the characters' confidence, establish a potent complicity. Such complicity develops our sense of the villains as standing outside the worlds they manipulate. And there they remain. Commanding and confident as his commentary may be, the glossist's province remains the margins, and it is from the margins that Richard and Aaron proceed to rewrite their texts. Yet as with the less dangerous trouble-makers, the ultimate result is, paradoxically, the renewal of the socio-political order in ways they have hardly intended. (Significantly, this is not a claim that can be made for Edmund or Iago.) Because these revisions have been done in blood, however, the new versions of reality not only have no room for their authors but must actually expel them in order to stabilize themselves, ritually sacrificing the very forces of creative anarchy that have brought them into being. Getting caught in his own web is the inevitable fate of the Machiavel on the Renaissance stage, but in metadramatic terms, with the on-stage plotter considered as stand-in for the dramatist himself, Richard and Aaron pay the price not of failure but of success.[8]

It is easiest to take the measure of the two villains as structural agents by setting the two structures side by side. On the surface, there is a contrast between Aristotelian completeness in the Roman tragedy, a narrative presented from start to finish, and the dynamics of continuum and contingency, history rather than story, in the English chronicle play. Even apart from *Richard III*'s position in its tetralogy, this is to be expected from the different settings, which assume divergent audience responses: on the one hand, a detached fascination with the (presumably edifying) exotic; on the other, an involving sense of self-definition as a national collectivity. Yet closer examination brings the two works more nearly in line as narrative units. The action of *Titus* is not really self-contained – it starts *in medias res* and beneath the looming overhang of preceding events, while *Richard III* concludes, not with a mere pause in the historical continuum, but with an apocalypse: the raising of the curtain on Tudor good times constitutes, in effect, entry into the kind of timeless present normally associated with romance.[9]

It does not imply a simplistic view of Shakespeare as Tudor propagandist that any ironic qualification of the glorious future anticipated in Richmond's final speech must be supplied by the audience: Shakespeare's audience, after all, was certainly in a position to do so. One may even argue that the portrayal of order and authority throughout Shakespeare's treatments of history is calculated to foster a deeply cynical response, whatever use is made of the providentialist perspective by certain characters, or even, as in this case, by dramatic structure.[10] Yet the play does not otherwise smirk at the pious hope that the new dynasty will 'Enrich the time to come with smooth-fac'd peace' (V.v.33). A useful comparison is with the downfall of Macbeth, who, as Shakespeare's only other self-crowning murderer–tyrant, resembles Richard in career if not in character. (Despite his treacheries, Macbeth is notably a man more tricked against than tricking.) In the later tragedy, Macduff's proclamation that 'the time is free' (V.ix.21), together with a supporting romance-like apparatus (the rebirth symbolism, the religious sanction, and so forth), is set off against hints of cyclicality and the nagging fact of time's commitment to Banquo's, not Malcolm's, line. Ultimately, to lay the whole burden of Scotland's miseries upon 'this dead butcher and his fiend-like queen' (35) is to restrict both the evils themselves and the conquest of them to the political level: the mythic pattern is destabilized by an admixture of historical process.[11]

By contrast, Richmond, having disposed of his tyrant physically, makes an equally definitive rhetorical disposition of him with a succinct phrase: 'the bloody dog is dead' (V.v.2). Richard's very name is subsumed by a stock image for brutal violence. In remarkable contrast with Richmond's exhortation to his troops before the battle, which dwelt on Richard as the embodiment of evil, his peroration now contains no reference at all to Richard but presents England's sufferings impersonally, in terms of the years of bloody division that Richmond aims to cure. He leaps over the gory particulars of Richard's reign to fasten, emblematically, on the very essence of civil strife, the concept of bloodshed within a family:

> England hath long been mad and scarr'd herself:
> The brother blindly shed the brother's blood,
> The father rashly slaughter'd his own son,
> The son, compell'd, been butcher to the sire.
>
> (V.v.23–6)

This depersonalizing of history is no doubt politically shrewd for a monarch who needs to reconcile hostile factions – hence the political utility of the so-called Tudor myth itself. But the dramatic effect is to impress upon the audience the radical transformation it is witnessing, the inauguration of an era transcending history itself, as the weight of the entire tetralogy is brought to bear on the moment of transition. Indeed, the patterns of slaughter have recurred so often that the identities of individuals have tended to merge – and not only for undergraduates; witness the reproachful lamentations of Queen Margaret, who, even as she brings the bloody details of the past to bear on the present, universalizes them and makes of her own asserted self a disembodied voice:

Tell over your woes again by viewing mine:
I had an Edward, till a Richard kill'd him;
I had a Harry, till a Richard kill'd him;
Thou hadst an Edward, till a Richard kill'd him;
Thou hadst a Richard, till a Richard kill'd him.

(IV.iv.39–43)

Moreover, Richmond's picture of civil war has been precisely anticipated in the action of *3 Henry VI*. In Act II, Scene v, of that play, the ineffectual king looks on as a nameless son discovers that he has unknowingly killed his father and a father then makes the same discovery about his son. Clumsy by mimetic standards, this scene gains its power from the very boldness with which it breaks through the chaos of confused particular events to emblematize, in the mode of the older allegorical drama, the fundamental issue. In sum, the effect of the resolution of *Richard III* is to make it the resolution of civil discord itself, and to imply that Richard matters more as the incarnation of destructive historical forces than as wilful evil incarnate and self-generated.

This is hardly news in critical terms. The well-established view of the character as a Vice-figure (and therefore a trickster *ex officio*) has always had plenty of room in it for the concept of divine scourge.[12] Nor, if we keep matters secular, are we really doing more than expanding Sigurd Burckhardt's perception that Richard possesses a history (fifteen acts' worth), while Richmond arrives as England's saviour 'from a realm beyond time' (S. Burckhardt 1968: 175). To possess a history is to be possessed by it. It is perhaps Edward Berry who has made the most of this idea: 'It is in one sense time itself that has given birth to Richard, the chaos of civil war breeding the "unlick'd bear-whelp" whose only future is savage destruction' (E. Berry 1975: 71). In using the image of birth, Berry is picking up the signals of the text itself, as a number of critics have done. It is standard practice in the 'tragedies of blood' of the late 1580s and early 1590s to stress the production of the role of revenger or villain in terms of a symbolic death and rebirth;[13] in fact, in *The Jew of Malta*, this process is combined with Barabas' explicit incarnation of the spirit of the age, personified by Machiavelli. But the preoccupation with physical birth that accompanies Richard's birth as a subversive is unique, as is the depth of the psychological dimension thus developed. Ultimately, it is this 'realistic' framework that does most to make visible the creation of Richard as mytheme – a stylistic paradox that supports the suspended contradictions in meaning: the creative dimension of Richard's destructiveness; the essential powerlessness of Richard's domination of his world and of his text.

That domination begins with the play's first words – the soliloquy in which Richard in effect arrogates to himself responsibility for the evil to follow. But, as the audience would have known well and continues to be reminded throughout, the beginning of *Richard III* is far from being the beginning of Richard. Richard's *determination* to 'prove a villain' (I.i.30) needs to be recognized as a statement not only of moral self-expression or even of self-creation but of self-relocation in historical and political terms.[14] It is a declaration of war – war against peace itself, on the grounds that peace, the milieu of the lover, has robbed him of identity. The same complaint was even more explicit in his first self-disclosing soliloquy in *3 Henry VI*:

> since this earth affords no joy to me
> But to command, to check, to o'erbear such
> As are of better person than myself,
> I'll make my heaven to dream upon the crown . . .
>
> (III.ii.165–8)

In effect – and this reveals his royal ambition as an inevitably futile assault on time itself – Richard refuses to relinquish the past, and the past happens to be the colour of blood. As is often the case with accomplished actors, his infinite flexibility is laid on a foundation of inadequacy, yet this inadequacy runs deeper than the sense of deformity that he actually expresses. It involves Darwinian original sin, the inability to adapt. Precisely by failing to make this transition, Richard reveals that the peace of the present ignores unfinished business, as Margaret shrilly insists from a different angle, her curse serving as an expressive metaphor for the absence of reconciliation or atonement. She is not, then, the only ghost abroad.[15]

From the start, Richard has derived his very being from the shedding of blood. Yet what is chiefly remarkable about his initial presentation in *Henry VI* is the fact that he belongs so thoroughly and comfortably to his milieu. Apart from the visual signs of his deformity – and armour, surely, should serve in production as a great disguiser, contrasting with the garments of peace – he is not set apart from his fellow warriors, unless by his superior prowess. There is nothing distinctive about his first appearance when he slays Somerset at the end of *2 Henry VI*. Although a foreknowledgable audience would find it ominous that he enjoins himself, 'heart, be wrathfull still:/Priests pray for enemies, but princes kill' (V.ii.70–1), his speeches are neither more nor less bloodthirsty than those of his peers. He is capable of better than average epic eloquence, as when he relates the exploits of Salisbury:

> My noble father,
> Three times to-day I holp him to his horse,
> Three times bestrid him; thrice I led him off,
> Persuaded him from any further act:
> But still, where danger was, still there I met him,
> And like rich hangings in a homely house,
> So was his will in his old feeble body.
> But noble as he is, look where he comes.

(V.iii.7–14)

Suggestively, it is Richard's father who brings out the heroic bent in him, both in language and in action. The opening of the third part of *Henry VI* shows him winning York's praise: 'Richard hath best deserv'd of all my sons' (*3H6*, I.i.17). The special bond with his father ('Methinks 'tis prize enough to be his son' (II.i.20)) is the route by which he first acquires individuality as a character, so that later in the same scene, when, in an anticipation of Hamlet, he vows revenge for his father's death, his ruthlessness seems all the more justified, not a mere echo of the brutality around him: 'Richard, I bear thy name, I'll venge thy death,/Or die renowned by attempting it' (87–8). His sense of identity here, located in the name that links him with his father, carries no trace of his subsequent alienation from family: 'I have no brother, I am like no brother' (V.vi.80). Such alienation is the precondition for the disruption of bonds of kinship that constitutes, as Edward Berry points out, the final apocalyptic phase of a progressive social dissolution (E. Berry 1975: 72–4). Perhaps unfortunately, Richard's revenge – unlike Hamlet's – is soon accomplished, and after killing Clifford he is left both fatherless and at loose ends – in need of another 'prize'. And so he appropriates, in a form at once mis-shapen and more effective, his father's ambition, which for him, paradoxically, necessitates destroying his family.

52

Richard's subsequent emergence as a monster, and a trickster, is given strong overtones of ritual rebirth – a process which, according to Douglas, involves acquiring the potency of marginal status (1966: 96-7). It begins with his reluctant renaming at his brother's hands. The cessation of wars brings the distribution of honours, and Richard becomes Gloucester – the *real* 'G' that 'Of Edward's heirs the murtherer shall be' (*R3*, I.i.40). In this light, Richard's objection to the title as 'ominous' (*3H6*, II.vi.107), with a foreboding akin to Macbeth's reaction to being named Thane of Cawdor, contains a suggestion of resistance to his own potential for evil. His initial soliloquy of alienation, pointedly occasioned by Edward's smooth wooing of Lady Grey, links sexual jealousy with a Macbeth-like attack on child-bearing in support of his royal rebirth beyond the flux of time:

Ay, Edward will use women honorably.
Would he were wasted, marrow, bones, and all,
That from his loins no hopeful branch may spring,
To cross me from the golden time I look for!

(*3H6*, III.ii.124-7)

Now for the first time Richard dwells upon his actual birth as 'a chaos, or an unlick'd bear-whelp/That carries no impression like the dam' (161-2). Given the ambivalent overtones of chaos, as portrayed by Du Bartas, which illuminate the role of Katherina by way of *A Shrew*'s Kate, it is particularly suggestive that Richard juxtaposes these two images. For in elaborating on the process by which chaos was made to give birth, Du Bartas proposes that God

En formant l'univers fit donc ainsi que l'ourse
Qui, dans l'obscure grotte, au bout de trente jours,
Une masse difforme enfante au lieu d'un ours;
Et puis en la lechant ores elle façonne
Ses deschirantes mains, or' sa teste felonne,
Or' ses pieds, or' son col, et d'un monceau si laid
Son industrie anime un animal parfait.

(11.408-14)[16]

Strangely, this passage moves from chaos, the antithesis of order that is nevertheless a matrix, only as far as a bear – an animal which, for the Renaissance, was savage destructiveness incarnate (witness the 'deschirantes mains' and the 'teste felonne'), though also, in the sport of bear-baiting, the object of play.[17] The process folds in on itself: birth turns to death yet remains birth. Creation and destruction are inextricably intermingled, as in Richard's self-imagery, and incorporated into an on-going natural dynamic beyond moral judgement. (This work might be 'parfait', but how could God see it as 'good'?)

In the same new vein as Richard's first self-examination are King Henry's abusive speech immediately before Richard murders him and the soliloquy of Richard immediately after. In all three cases, the emphasis is on his nativity, including the fact that he was born with teeth, and more particularly on his mother, whose appearance in the subsequent play sustains this perspective. A hateful maternity – intimately linked with his obsessive hatred of women generally – replaces a glorious paternity as the basis of Richard's self-image.[18] He thus becomes a partial precursor not only of Hamlet, but of that fatherless mother-obsessed slaughter-man Coriolanus, and, indirectly, even of Macduff. It is as if he has symbolically redefined himself as the child of the bloody times themselves, asserting the creative prerogative of chaos. From a fear of evil destiny, he comes to invest with ultimate meaning the role of fated scourge and destroyer. Yet at least at first his ambivalence remains painfully obvious. The hatred and the embracing of this destiny unite and explode, as if an emotional critical mass has been reached, when he stabs the taunting Henry: 'I'll hear no more; die, prophet, in thy speech:/For this, amongst the rest, was I ordain'd' (V.vi.57–8).

When Richard is seen against this background, it becomes evident that Shakespeare here takes advantage of the epic scope of the tetralogy to explore more fully than anywhere in his more psychologically complex later drama the process of deforming a human being into a moral grotesque. In technical terms, a simple dramatic representation acquires a numinous quality by flattening into caricature – a process reversed when Richard's conscience at once debilitates him and restores a mimetic dimension on the night before Bosworth field. Like his misshapen body, the stereotype of the trickster-villain is always a part of Richard in the audience's mind – not only his historical but his dramatic destiny is common knowledge. It is knowledge that the text exploits, in a way without exact parallel elsewhere in Renaissance drama, to highlight and to comment on what is usually taken for granted in the Elizabethan theatre: the mixing of realistic and stylized modes. The trickster is showing his roots, and they are not in the otherworldly hell of his Satanic forbears but in the world around him, which is also, *mutatis mutandis*, our world: where we are *is* hell, nor are we out of it.

III

It is worth applying the closing terms of the first tetralogy to the opening of the Roman tragedy. Here the bloody background, first depicted by Marcus Andronicus, then brought to life (if that is the word) by Titus' self-advertisement over the bodies of his newly slain sons, seems to be contained firmly within clear-cut ideals of patriotism, virtue, valour, and honour. These are the keynotes of high-sounding speeches that celebrate a decisive Roman victory after ten years of war and present Titus as a figure of transcendent political authority uniquely capable of reconciling competing factions. As the bodies are laid to rest in the already well-stocked tomb and Titus talks of sheathing his sword at last, we might be witnessing a Richmond-like imposition of closure on historical process. In fact, however, Richmond's theme of slaughter within the family points to the existence of unfinished business, too, in *Titus*. Through the haze of mingled grief and triumph, we catch glimpses of a father whose hunger for honour has actually been consuming his children: they have been sacrifices not only for Rome but to himself.[19]

The buried suggestion of sacrifice instantly proliferates in more problematic forms, beginning with Titus' acquiescence in the ritual slaughter of Alarbus, Tamora's eldest son. That Titus is part of the bloody processes of time rather than above them is confirmed, ironically, by his refusal to accept the empery on the grounds of age, when doing so might help resolve the factional disorder in the state. In a speech that sounds like an early study for *King Lear*, he abdicates responsibility for the sake of freely enjoying his transcendent prestige – prestige purchased, as he proudly reminds his auditors, at the cost of his sons' lives: 'Give me a staff of honor for mine age,/But not a sceptre to control the world' (I.i.198–9). As blindly as Lear, Titus prefers the hypocritical and vicious Saturninus to the virtuous brother Bassianus, betrothed to Lavinia, thus foolishly giving his enemies power over himself. More tellingly, as a mere gesture of loyalty, he offers to sacrifice his loving and dutiful daughter to Saturninus. When his sons join Bassianus in resisting the bestowal of Lavinia against her will, Titus displays a Lear-like quickness to disown his children and, in killing his son, puts Lear's impotent threats and curses into action.

It would be hard to conceive of a background to the ultimate tragedy of Titus more in keeping with Richmond's emblems of civil discord. In particular, the horrors that will confront Titus visually in Lavinia's condition – the overt beginning of the tragic end – have all been broached: mutilation, child-slaughter, even rape and denial of speech in his attempt to make Lavinia violate her plighted troth, though his twisted outlook aligns him with Saturninus' claim that the 'rape' is on Bassianus' side (I.i.404).[20] The key to the process of carving flesh into images that do (retributive) justice to this manifold brutality is, of course, the creative malice of Aaron, though he has plenty of support. But it is Aaron's initially innocent position in the background – the very fact that he has played no part whatever in establishing these moral conditions – that reveals most about the trickster's role both here and in *Richard III*. While the seminal cruelties are taking place, Aaron is a silent on-stage witness, as yet quite unknown to the audience. Only at the end of the first act does he single himself out by remaining behind and delivering a self-defining soliloquy, thus also making himself a sort of structural pivot between major segments of the play, as the tragic forces prepare to zero in on Titus and his family. Now he reveals himself as Tamora's lover and, in view of her advancement, looks forward to high times: 'I will be bright, and shine in pearl and gold' (II.i.19). But he says nothing to diminish his essential mystery. The lack of a history, of an explanation for a Moor's presence among the Goths, above all of a rationale for his malignancy, is in keeping with stage tradition (if in contrast with Richard III), but here it specifically fosters the impression that Aaron is the creature of the play's universe.

In light of this origin, Aaron's entry into the role of manipulator, and so of creator–dramatist, both articulates and sets in motion the destructive cyclicality of the dramatic structure at large. In a more concentrated form than any of the histories, *Titus* presents a spiralling series of character-changes from victim to victimizer and back again. The role of revenger, as

Tamora's disguise suggests and the sequel demonstrates, is eminently transferable – the only hard currency, ultimately, in a world where Goths and Romans are interchangeable. Resolution depends on exhausting the supply of victims, so that revenge feeds on and finally consumes itself. This is the process that Titus literally enacts, imposing his cannibalistic closure on the script without end initiated by Aaron. He thus becomes, in effect, Aaron's collaborator, while he diminishes himself as tragic hero. The ultimate result of Aaron's intervention is a world turned upside down in order to be set right, as the invading Goths of Lucius reimport civilization to the ruins of Rome. Aaron's legacy is truth – not only what he confesses, but what he has exposed – and it seems appropriate, therefore, that his condition for telling his story (as Iago, for instance, vows never to do) should be a form of vicarious survival. It expresses the good left behind by Aaron's evil, despite himself, that Lucius, the righteous redeemer, piously swears to take responsibility for the life of his son, thus extending into the future the Moor's only *redeeming* quality.[21]

This forms part of a remarkable recuperation of nurturing values through the speeches, first of Lucius, then of Marcus, to Lucius' own son, in which they conjure up the memory of a domestic Titus overflowing with warmth of feeling – a far cry from the warrior–patriarch actually presented in the text:

> Many a time he danc'd thee on his knee,
> Sung thee asleep, his loving breast thy pillow;
> Many a story hath he told to thee,
> And bid thee bear his pretty tales in mind,
> And talk of them when he was dead and gone.
> *Marc.* How many thousand times hath these poor lips,
> When they were living, warm'd themselves on thine!
>
> (V.iii.162–8)

This is an image implicitly coded as feminine and specifically incorporating Lavinia's former role as story-teller to the boy (IV.i.12–14) – a role that underwent its own tragic metamorphosis. Ironically, for a frank 'tragedy of blood', in so thoroughly reconceiving itself in androgynous terms, this community of male survivors arguably goes farther than any other Shakespearean tragic universe towards integrating the lesson of its subversion. It has earned the right, in a sense, to bury alive the purely negative traces of subversiveness that remain, as Aaron himself appears to acknowledge, using a significant image: 'I am no baby, I, that with base prayers/I should repent the evils I have done' (V.iii.185).

Aaron's initial translation from background to foreground bears an obvious similarity to Richard's development in *3 Henry VI*. But it may also be compared with Edmund's emergence as a villain after *King Lear*'s crucially influential first scene, though Shakespeare is at pains to take us close to the heart of Edmund's mystery, if not to pluck it out. Lear's behaviour and its consequences help render Gloucester susceptible to his son's scheme; they may also be linked with Edmund's inspiration.[22] Certainly, Edmund too is seen to be partly engendered as a villain – a second birth to undo his first – by social and cultural forces already at work, and not just in the narrowly retributive way described by Edgar: 'The dark and vicious place where thee he got/Cost him his eyes' (V.iii.173–4). The new world Edmund would create is an accurate image, if like himself unacknowledged, of at least one aspect of the old. Albany's belated vision of horror, couched in the metaphor Titus puts in practice – 'Humanity must perforce prey on itself,/Like monsters of the deep' (IV.ii.49–50) – trails lamely behind the predatory realities present from the start.

Apart from these specific parallels, it is hardly surprising, given the standard dramatic paraphernalia of the Machiavel, that Edmund's first soliloquy is so closely anticipated by Aaron's self-exhortation to villainy: 'Then, Aaron, arm thy heart, and fit thy thoughts,/To mount aloft with thy imperial mistress,/And mount her pitch' (II.i.12–14). But the metaphor Aaron uses also points to a difference between Edmund and Shakespeare's early trickster-villains, considered as subversive elements in their respective plays. There may be a sexual innuendo here, but the main burden of the image, which is taken from falconry, is the suggestion of a bird of prey, an animal dangerous by nature, ranging widely and under only a tenuous sort of control. Relevant here is Petruchio's metaphor for his taming of Katherina, the confining and appropriating of her wild energy:

My falcon now is sharp and passing empty,
And till she stoop, she must not be full-gorg'd,
For then she never looks upon her lure.
Another way I have to man my haggard,
To make her come, and know her keeper's call,

That is, to watch her, as we watch these kites
That bate and beat and will not be obedient.

$(Shr., IV.i.190-6)^{23}$

In these terms, the point of Aaron's scenario is the absence of the falconer. It is an idea that, in the anxious hands of Yeats some centuries later, explicitly contains the threat of chaos, there conceived as merely negative, the antithesis of a supposedly humane civilization. And since the control in question is ultimately that of the playwright, who has unleashed this creative-destructive force upon the dramatic universe, but for whom it serves as creative matrix, also implied is a danger to the integrity of the text itself, its status as emblem of meaningful order. The same sense of the destroyer as a threatening rival creator attaches to the master-dramatist Richard III,[24] a self-proclaimed 'chaos' who is constantly and more variously surrounded by the imagery of devouring. Thus the engaging tensions generated by these characters may flow, not only from our own ambivalence, which is moral in origin, but also from the playwright's uneasy wearing of the creator's crown. The first mover of the dramatic universe puts himself in the position of the conspicuously passive God of Marlowe's *Tamburlaine*, who, if he has really set in motion that monomaniac spiller of blood as his scourge, finally seems to be in danger of getting scourged himself.

There is no reason why such anxiety, which may be thought of as inherently textual - the product of the text's confrontation with its own instability - should be confined to Shakespeare. Indeed, it is tempting to see this as a factor in what Calderwood terms the 'overkill' often applied to the Elizabethan stage-villain (Calderwood 1987: 199). Of course, there is the theatrical pressure for a spectacular climax, the moral requirement for exemplary retribution. Still, the degree of ingenious and conspicuous textual consumption of villains tends to vary according to their quotient of subversive energy. Aaron must be seen to be buried alive - 'Some stay to see him fast'ned in the earth' (V.iii.183) - though, as Nicholas Brooke puts it, his vital energy 'cannot be contained within the emblematic pattern of his punishment' (Brooke 1968: 43). Others suffer torments with similar reassuring overtones of degradation and confinement - witness Barabas' cauldron, with its implication that the trickster has been safely destroyed because he has been out-tricked. Even Richard, who must be killed in more or less heroic fashion in order to exalt Richmond, is pointedly brought down doubly: in offering his kingdom for a horse – three times – Richard avows his fall into a humiliating and desperate relativism, as if the text itself requires a parodic epic reversal of his dangerous ambition.

It is remarkable, then, that the two subversive script-writers in Shakespeare's later tragedies, Edmund and Iago, do not similarly destabilize their texts, however much damage they do to their fellow characters. The falconer is palpably in control, as seems to be reflected in Anne Barton's observation that 'the theatrical imagery connected with them as deceivers is not only sparser than that which surrounds Richard III, but stripped of that early conviction of the power of illusion' (Barton 1962: 184). Iago need not die before our eyes, or even before the end of the play; Edmund is allowed a measure of redemption. No doubt this has something to do with the more realistic conventions that govern these figures, clothing their mysterious superhuman energies in vulnerable flesh, as well as with the emphasis on the tragic heroes. But the change also reflects the progressive evolution in Shakespeare's work of the intervening years, especially the comedies and histories, of new strategies of textual self-defence. Subsequent chapters will document this process, showing how the catalytic power of subversive elements is reduced, evaded, or thwarted. Often this is accomplished through the outright authorial loading of the dice – the relegation of such energies to the verbal licence of a fool or the marginality of a subplot. In other cases, a figure of counter-subversion emerges. This is a pattern reminiscent of *Taming*, where Petruchio vanquishes Katherina by imitating her own methods. But Katherina, I have argued, succeeds in provoking the fundamental reshaping of her world, as do Philip, Aaron, and Richard. Increasingly, the characters threatened by subversive energy – they include Prince Hal, Portia, Vincentio, and Prospero – succeed in preserving the terms of their dramatic worlds essentially unchanged. Their ideas of order may be ironically undermined, the subversive elements may retain our sympathies to a remarkable degree, but these characters, theatrical manipulators all, succeed in imposing their scripts to the exclusion of other possible scenarios. It is tempting to explain this phenomenon in thematic terms, reading the plays as weighing the claims of order against the attraction of disorder.

This may be to undervalue the demands of the compositional process itself - what a text needs to keep its meanings in productive ferment in the face of forces that threaten a sterile hegemony. By recognizing that the ultimate danger of the trickster and the anarchy he represents is to the power of the creator to continue creating, it is possible - as a means of forestalling the reckless projection of ideologies upon authors - to posit an intrinsic need for structural baffles and channels, for agents of order to counter the *agents provocateurs*, if the show is to go on at all.

4

'SUCH TRICKS HATH STRONG IMAGINATION'

It has seemed important to stake the territory of this study by way of those pre-1595 plays, representing each major genre, that pivot on a distinctive character's embodiment of the energy of disruption. A more obvious starting point would have been the early comedies in which such energy, while not so sharply defined or so narrowly incarnated, more frankly functions in aid of harmonious resolution. The danger is that this alliance, which in practice is often provisional, uneasy, and reluctant, may be taken for granted as part of the transformational dynamic of comedy itself. That dynamic is usually discussed teleologically, in relation to highly determined structures of meaning having persuasive claims to universality, whether in terms of seasonal myth, festive ritual, social renewal, or psychological development. Nature itself appears to determine the nature of comedy. At the same time, the self-conscious artificialities of the form tend to disarm, by vigorously welcoming, criticism in search of contradiction. Such texts preserve their integrity by being infinitely accommodating. How can a focus on the very mechanisms that produce comic closure hope to open such closed systems?

An answer might begin with the point that, as I hope the previous chapters have illustrated, the terms of trickery go deeper than structure or meaning. Trickery's energy has the potential to generate both, but it remains always itself, like a grammatical function recurring across related languages or a medium of exchange carrying – that is, not just possessing, but transmitting – value in dramatic transactions of various kinds. And as in financial transactions, what really 'counts' is not the nature of the currency but the use made of it: the commodities bought and sold, the element of gain or loss, the possibilities for misappropriation. To define and apply broad comic structures as normative can be productive, as many critics have demonstrated, but it is an enterprise imprisoned in circularity. Focusing on the principle of disruption itself offers access to more complex forms of textual interplay than are permitted by an approach that projects variant effects against a constant background.

For this reason, I think that Nevo, one of the most sensitive recent transformational critics of the comedies, is overhasty in claiming that, because 'the confusions, transformations and disorientations of the *processus turbarum* lead eventually to self-possession and self re-formation',

> Bakhtin can tell us nothing about the protagonists of Shakespeare's romantic comedies, nor of the subtle interrelationship and interplay between the protagonists and the fools, nor of the formal coherences and patterns which also release the powers and energies of imaginative recreation.
>
> (Nevo 1980: 218)

Curiously, this rejection of Bakhtin on essentially teleological grounds has much in common with his appropriation by other critics. Thus for Terence Hawkes the 'green world' of Frye and the 'holiday' mode of Barber are identical with Bakhtin's principle of carnival (Hawkes 1980: 162).[1] Yet simply to hitch Bakhtin to the transformational wagon is to ignore his privileging of subversive process over product – or, perhaps, to justify Geoffrey Harpham's critique of Bakhtin himself for ignoring Baudelaire's claim for 'the satanic origin of all laughter' (Harpham 1982: 72). At any rate, we are thereby returned to the standard view of folly as a temporary means to a stable comic end.[2] As my previous chapters have made clear, the idea of chaos as the generative matrix of order is very much to the point, and not just in a comic context. But it follows that such chaos remains the fundamental and irreducible component of the system, the lowest common denominator, whose disruptive potential must always exist in tension with the 'formal coherences and patterns' it produces, as well as with the characters who repudiate or rise above it. I should like to think it possible, without similarly dismissing all criticism concerned with the 'pattern of release and reintegration', to agree with Malcolm Evans that 'the mode of Holofernes and Launce . . . is not froth to be blown off the top of the text but froth that sits at the bottom, problematizing any comic "spirit" or essential meaning that a theological mode of criticism in quest of the Shakespearean *logos* might wish to recover from the impenetrability of the "letter" ' (1985: 82).

Nevertheless, it is the valuable legacy of years of transformational criticism that, in approaching *The Comedy of Errors, The Two Gentlemen of Verona, Love's Labor's Lost,* and *A Midsummer Night's Dream,* certain shared structural features can be taken for granted. I should like to start by redefining the common ground in terms of trickery. In fact, this is to extend the common ground. For while *Love's Labor's Lost* is a notable exception to the 'festive' pattern, in that it does not end 'like an old play' (*LLL,* V.ii.874), it joins the other four texts in allowing the energy of disruption, here built into both action and characters in multifarious forms, to restructure its dramatic world and reconstitute its leading characters. Even in *Love's Labor's Lost,* trickery gets its way, which is, in essence, the way of revelation and change, regardless of consequences. Yet in all four plays – and this is where the subversive principle resists assimilation into the comic momentum – complications arise from the interplay between this textual impulse towards openness and various kinds of blindness and resistance on the part of those who are propelled by it. In *Two Gentlemen* and *Love's Labor's Lost,* certain characters actually manipulate the energy of transformation in problematic ways – a reminiscence of Petruchio and a glimpse into the dramatic future. For the most part, however, that energy simply produces forms of ironic distance between what is revealed to the characters and what is revealed about them.

This is precisely the distance opened up by Bottom's inability to expound his dream of self-translation, by Demetrius' confidence that his heart has returned 'home' to Helena of its own accord. And this gap – not closed, one might argue, until wonder and understanding unite at the ends of some of the final plays – survives as the visible trace of the realm of mischievous shadows, where a bush and a bear may indeed be the same thing. *A Midsummer Night's Dream* articulates, through the mediation of the fairies, the operations of forces elsewhere hidden behind the scenes. It seems appropriate that the very play which in all likelihood concludes the early comic series should make visible, by means of the invisible, the machinery of a mode that will give way, over the next several years, to versions of comedy in which such charms have lost their power. What 'cool reason . . . comprehends' (*MND*,V.i.5-6), it can control.

I

If *A Midsummer Night's Dream*, by metadramatically displaying its deceptive mechanisms, takes a position at one end of the representational spectrum, *The Comedy of Errors* seems to situate itself firmly at the other. The distinction is all the more evident because of the strong thematic links between them, and all the more significant for this study because the most conspicuous such link is the central paradox that folly begets wisdom, that illusion and dream may be truer than 'reality', and that losing the self is a precondition of finding it. Both in terms of this paradigm, which is historically supported by the well-established heritage of Christian folly, and in terms of the 'festive' potency of play itself, the creative function of trickery in these plays has received ample critical recognition. To take this function for granted, however, is to risk obscuring the unstable relation between means and ends.

The Comedy of Errors is unique in the canon for its defiant unconsciousness of its own methods. Rather as Bottom might do, the text naïvely embraces the often-cited absurdity of its premise – two sets of twins, not one as in Plautus – and the naked improbability of the ensuing complications. The title pointedly implies, not two possible forms of consciousness, dream and waking, but a self-contained world made up of errors and so created by the very principle of error – trickery in its purest form.[3] Thus, too, its setting is a single place, one that, like the fairy world, is less a matter of place at all than of suspended time, with Shakespeare exploiting the magical associations of Ephesus. It is up to the Abbess finally to give solidity and meaning to place and time at once, as well as to call attention to the formal unity of both:

> And all that are assembled in this place
> That by this sympathized one day's error
> Have suffer'd wrong, go keep us company,
> And we shall make full satisfaction.
>
> (V.i.397-400)

As in *The Winter's Tale*, time itself 'makes and unfolds error'

(*WT*, IV.i.2). And as the example of Hermione might suggest, there is ultimately more truth in Syracusan Dromio's jest about time's going backward (IV.ii.54ff.) than in old Egeon's fear that 'time's extremity' (V.i.308) has made him unrecognizable. Here too 'things dying' are redeemed by 'things new-born' (*WT*, III.iii.114): 'After so long grief, such nativity!' (V.i.407).

The power and pervasiveness of the tricking impulse do not imply a world of 'pure play' – a figment of some critical imaginations. On the contrary, the resistance of the very characters who enact the impulse – their attempts to cling, in different ways and degrees, to a rational equilibrium – works like a pressure-vessel to generate an especially intense transformational energy. This energy is manifested in the increasingly violent contortions of the action, and it issues in a notably radical resolution. The fundamental transmutation achieved is of Plautine lead – the slapstick, stereotypes, and petty farce of the *Menaechmi* – into the golden fulfilment of romance, a fulfilment that Shakespeare already associated, at least fifteen years before *Pericles*, with Apollonius of Tyre, and with John Gower.[4] The audience, too, is implicated: our knowledge of the secret of the two sets of twins makes it all the more shocking when the final revelation is sprung on us unawares.

Clearly, the twin twinning, with its chiastic potential, is a valuable device if characters are to serve as both instruments and objects of trickery's transmutation. By contrast, *A Midsummer Night's Dream*, whose subversive engine runs on fairy love-juice, can displace the lower-class buffoonery of the Dromios onto a parodic subplot. Still, the later play indirectly exploits the twin device. To start with, there is the suggestion, supported by the probable doubling of parts, that Oberon and Titania are shadow-selves, in some sense, of Theseus and Hippolyta. Then there are the rivals for Hermia. Egeus' introduction of Demetrius and Lysander, though intended to distinguish them ('Stand forth, Demetrius', 'Stand forth, Lysander' (I.i.24,26)), leads at once to demonstrations of their resemblance that throw his arbitrariness into relief. As the action unfolds, the bland similarity of the men is made a foil to the pointed contrasts revealed between the two young women – the breakdown of their naïve childhood unity ('a double cherry' (III.ii.209)) in order, ultimately, to create a true 'union in partition' (210).[5] This is the same pattern that Shakespeare will employ in far more serious terms with Leontes and

Polixenes, whose 'affection', according to an image that identifies natural growth with growing apart, 'cannot choose but branch' (*WT*, I.i.24). More immediately, the sister-like childhood of Hermia and Helena confirms their structural equivalence to the sisters Adriana and Luciana, also the victims of unaccountably fickle men, behaving as if they were mad.

The attenuated motif of twinning in the later play serves, obviously, to lubricate the machinery of farce, a form whose invariable premise is precisely the trickster-in-chief's view that human beings are pretty well interchangeable: 'Lord, what fools these mortals be!' (*MND*, III.ii.115).[6] But beyond this, and beyond the fun at the expense of love at first sight, lies the implication of incomplete or undifferentiated identity, with a need for supplementation. In order to impose the symmetrical love-quadrangle, whose restoration is a foregone conclusion, it would be necessary merely to redirect Demetrius' affections to Helena. But in order to construct identities that will earn the blessing of the agents of transformation, the artificial, self-centred, and petty attitudes initially displayed by all the lovers must be disrupted by a strong dose of what the play frankly presents as imagination.[7] And the ultimate expression of imagination in human relations is not what Theseus ridicules, the mistaking of bushes for bears, but what he conspicuously lacks when he appoints his wedding-day as the day of judgement for Hermia: the capacity to put oneself in another's place. It is by making the lovers see and feel things from each other's points of view that the fairies put them in touch with the hidden significance of their roles. More precisely, this is the result of Puck's non-teleological mistaking, his subversion of the direct course intended by Oberon. The lovers are not merely liberated from, but made to live through, the tragic implications of the love conventions to which they have blindly subscribed.[8] Hermia must experience what it means to be betrayed and abandoned for an old friend; Helena must become the object of unwelcome pursuit, even if it is her martyr-like self-image that makes it unwelcome; both the two men and the two women must be confronted with the destructive implications of their rivalry. Under this pressure, the possessiveness, self-indulgence, and shallow posturings of the opening scene break down. There is, literally, a world of difference between Hermia's fond embracing of adversity – 'As due to love as thoughts and dreams and sighs, /

Wishes and tears, poor fancy's followers' (I.i.154-5) – and the nadir of her despair: 'Never so weary, never so in woe, / Bedabbled with the dew and torn with briers, / I can no further crawl, no further go' (III.ii.442-4). In the end, the legacy of the dream-world is imperfectly recalled by its beneficiaries and less well understood, but the filling-in of the blank spaces defined by the dynamic of twinning has accomplished more than any of the characters realize.

The fifth act, redundant in terms of plot, is irresistibly seen as celebrating multiple 'translations' – of potential tragedy into farce, of the slain Pyramus and Thisby into living mechanicals, of the couples, through the promise of posterity, into infinitely self-renewing images of themselves. But in giving the last word to the fairies, and the final responsibility to the audience, Shakespeare marks the primacy of process over product. And in fact the final scene is as dynamic as it is celebratory, extending process to another level of the social – and of the dramatic – structure. When, in Act IV, Theseus, abroad in search of 'musical confusion' (IV.i.110), responds instead to the 'gentle concord' (143) of the lovers, he echoes Oberon's decision to have mercy on Titania and so effectively integrates into his outlook the spirit of his shadow-self. The fairy king and queen are the 'parents and original' (II.i.117) of infertile disorder in the mortal realm; it is fitting that their reconciliation should resynchronize the natural and human cycles: May-day – for so Theseus is now impelled to designate it, whatever the 'actual' time of the year[9] – is properly an occasion for love-games, not, as Egeus insists it is, for making a decision against the principle of life itself. And so Theseus' further exercise of transformative power – his overturning, earlier proclaimed impossible, of Athenian law when he 'overbear[s]' Egeus' 'will' (IV.i.179) – is less an act of his own will than he assumes.[10]

The assimilation of the self-consciously rational Theseus to the world of moonlight is made visible by his response to the play-within-the-play. '[T]he wall is down that parted their fathers' (V.i.351-2), Bottom solemnly assures his audience, and in doing so he confirms the collapse of a larger partition the mechanicals had never believed in anyway – that between audience and spectacle, or between the worlds of reason and imagination. To dream of playing all the roles at once, to fear that an actor may be taken for a lion, to assume the plausibility of presenting Moonshine and Wall – these are not crass stupidities but the forgeries of unrestrained imagination. And as Theseus has dismissively pointed out to Hippolyta, this faculty – the source of energy for lunatic, lover, and poet alike – operates by means of creative deception: 'Such tricks hath strong imagination' (V.i.18). Notoriously, his dismissal is flawed by our better knowledge and will again be undercut by the fairies' re-appearance. But the immediate source of irony is his own imaginative participation in the mechanicals' spectacle. Under the cover of witty detachment and aristocratic superiority, the on-stage spectators unwittingly take their cue from the players' own assault on the barrier between reality and illusion, sense and nonsense.

The process begins with Quince's Prologue, whose linguistic self-subversion implicates its auditors in an act of interpretation. By this 'tangled chain; nothing impair'd, but all disorder'd' (125–6)[11] – an emblem of ambiguous experience in the forest that recalls the complicating chain of *The Comedy of Errors* – Theseus is drawn willy-nilly into the subversions of another sort of 'shadows', to the point where he finds himself in the position of defending imagination against Hippolyta's 'cool reason': 'The best in this kind are but shadows; and the worst are no worse, if imagination amend them' (211–12). Yet Hippolyta was no foe of imagination earlier, and in fact her objection here – 'It must be your imagination then, and not theirs' (213–14) – insists on his taking responsibility for imaginative response. The Duke's reply is not only a tacit acknowledgement of this role, but a recognition of imagination, as opposed to mere silliness, as the players' stock-in-trade: 'If we imagine no worse of them than they of themselves, they may pass for excellent men' (215–16). He intends merely to jest and mock, but it is precisely this function that links him with the objects of his mirth in a dynamic of creative confusion.

It is instructive to compare the mocking spectators here with the courtiers who jeer the pageant of the Nine Worthies in *Love's Labor's Lost*. There the effect is to sharpen the division between audience and performers, and, by eliciting sympathy even for the exposed Armado, to make the onlookers seem mean-spirited and closed-minded. As Alexander Leggatt points out (1974: 113), the Worthies do not even get to bring their pageant to its intended conclusion; neither, one might add, do their mockers. At the same time, Bottom and his colleagues do not react with resentment or plead to keep their play intact, as Armado does: 'Sweet Lord Longaville, rein thy tongue' (*LLL*, V.ii.656). Instead, they reach out spontaneously, across the barrier that after all does not exist for them, to welcome their audience into the play-world:

> *The.*: The wall methinks, being sensible, should curse again.
> *Pyr.*: No, in truth, sir, he should not. 'Deceiving me' is Thisby's cue. . . . You shall see it will fall pat as I told you.
>
> (182–7)

In *A Midsummer Night's Dream*, the trick is on the mockers. The 'festive' implications of the death and revival of Pyramus and Thisby, supported by a reminiscence of the ritualistic St George plays,[12] are thus firmly harnessed to the broader processes of trickery. It is Theseus himself who, having first insisted on hearing the play that Philostrate discounts as 'nothing in the world' (78), now predicts the resurrection, from Lysander's 'nothing', of Pyramus as Bottom, complete with his fairy-bestowed (or revealed) identity:

> *Lys.*: . . . he is dead, he is nothing.
> *The.*: With the help of a surgeon he might yet recover, and yet prove an ass.
>
> (309–11)

Language and context combine to recall Pelton's characterization of the 'force driving the ironic dialectic of the imagination':

> In touching nothing and finding joy the trickster reveals that this most supple energy of all is by its very adaptability the ultimate holiness made the moving power of ordinary human life.
>
> (Pelton 1980: 283)

The exchanging of partial experiences is also part of the twinning motif in *The Comedy of Errors*.[13] We witness, not simply two brothers imposed upon by circumstances, but two contrasting attitudes towards those circumstances. Their very different starting points – one is a self-assured native of Ephesus, one a baffled stranger – support this contrast.[14] One brother struggles vainly to oppose reason against the energy of trickery; the other, despite his recurrent impulse to flee the city – despite what he thinks of as himself – displays a remarkable openness.

These attitudes are expressed partly through their relation to the feminine: one becomes alienated from his spouse; the other falls in love. Yet the identity of their names promises the eventual creation of a single self out of rational and emotional elements – a psychic marriage. There is truth in the Duke's exclamation and more than literal sense in his question: 'One of these men is genius to the other:/And so of these, which is the natural man,/ And which the spirit? Who deciphers them?' (V.i.333–5).

Not that all the loose ends of the human situation are tied up – Leggatt notes the absence, for instance, of any reconciliatory words between Adriana and her husband (1974: 9). Yet there is a radical shift of perspective, the bringing to birth of an undreamt-of dimension of the dramatic universe that gathers even such reservations into its atmosphere of achieved wonder. This structural 'nativity' coincides with the framing family restoration, which includes the redemption from death of a husband through the rediscovery of his wife. That husband has himself 'hazarded the loss of whom I lov'd' (I.i.131) – an anticipation of the hazarding in *The Merchant of Venice* – in a spirit of despair that proves as fertile as Hermia's: 'Hopeless to find, yet loath to leave unsought/Or that, or any place that harbors men' (135–6).

If the force of imagination has no fairy-world 'objective correlative' in this process, it is none the less powerfully present. The play does not feature poets, as *A Midsummer Night's Dream* abundantly does, at least allusively; it deals only secondarily, albeit significantly, with lovers. Lunacy, however, is its stock-in-trade. Antipholus of Ephesus, like Malvolio, has madness thrust upon him; the Syracusans, master and servant, suppose that they have achieved it. In a rare moment of correct matching, they exchange notes, with Luciana's abettance, in a virtual sketch for the later play:

> S.Dro.: This is the fairy land. O spite of spites!
> We talk with goblins, owls, and sprites.
> . . .
> I am transformed, master, am not I?
> S.Ant.: I think thou art in mind, and so am I.
> S.Dro.: Nay, master, both in mind and in my shape.
> S.Ant.: Thou hast thine own form.
> S.Dro.:   No, I am an ape.

Luc.: If thou art chang'd to aught, 'tis to an ass.

(II.ii.189–99)

In other respects, too, the world of imagination is actually entered, however reluctantly, by Antipholus of Syracuse, while the consequences of ignoring it are brought home to his brother. Ephesian Antipholus undergoes first exclusion (from his house), then confinement (as debtor and later as madman): the two motifs recur insistently as the play draws towards its conclusion. He is forcibly cut off from the domestic happiness he has been helping to impair and compelled to take upon himself his wife's 'mad jealousy' (II.i.116). It is obviously ironic that his unwillingness to acknowledge a chain, the one made for him by the jeweller, leads to his confinement. By contrast, the Syracusan receives inexplicable invitations and proffers of liberty, if not licence. The alienation and deprivation that mark his approach to Ephesus, cut off from family as he is – 'So I, to find a mother and a brother,/In quest of them (unhappy), ah, lose myself' (I.ii.39–40) – give way to an embarrassment of domestic riches, much as his servant Dromio is suddenly endowed with the 'grotesque body' of the kitchen wench, who 'claims', 'haunts' (III.ii.82), and fragments him ('I am an ass, I am a woman's man, and besides myself' (77–8)). When this Antipholus accepts the 'offer'd chain' (181), he puts himself in the way of ultimate freedom from inward bondage.[15]

This act of acquiescence in what seems – rightly, as it turns out – a magical world of 'golden gifts' (183) is linked, by juxtaposition, with the 'mermaid's song' (164) that threatens to make Antipholus 'traitor to myself' (162) by leading him to act against reason. He professes to know better – ' 'Tis time, I think, to trudge, pack, and be gone' (153) – and Dromio agrees, expressing himself in terms that anticipate Theseus' scorning of imagination (as well as the actual fate of Antigonus in *The Winter's Tale*): 'As from a bear a man would run for life,/So fly I from her that would be my wife' (154–5). Yet Antipholus' sense of what the time requires has from the start been the target of successful subversion by trickery. His first encounter with the wrong Dromio leads him to pummel the hapless servant, '[t]hat stands on tricks when I am undispos'd' (I.ii.80). These are not, of course, Dromio's tricks, but those of the play itself – the town is indeed 'full of cozenage' (97) – and they do their job precisely by being mistimed. Antipholus later avers – to the proper Dromio – that he enjoys his servant's role as fool when it matches his mood, but cautions him, 'learn to jest in good time – there's a time for all things' (II.ii.64–5). Yet as *King Lear* illustrates, it is just when fools speak out of turn that they accomplish most, and the subsequent formulaic jesting about time, which seems to be reassuring for Antipholus, does nothing to put him in touch with the suspended reality of the play-world.

The decisive jolt comes with the entrance of Adriana and Luciana a few lines later. In allowing Adriana's accosting of him to open up a new dimension of consciousness, Antipholus responds positively to the creative energy of error:

What, was I married to her in my dream?
Or sleep I now and think I hear all this?
What error drives our eyes and ears amiss?
Until I know this sure uncertainty,
I'll entertain the offer'd fallacy.

(182–6)

We cannot ourselves be sure of the word 'offer'd' (Capell's emendation of the First Folio's intriguing 'free'd'), but the readiness to entrust himself to deceptive appearance rings out clearly in either case. It is even more striking at the end of the scene, where questions of madness and identity are attached to the problem of consciousness:

Am I in earth, in heaven, or in hell?
Sleeping or waking, mad or well-advis'd?
Known unto these, and to myself disguis'd?
I'll say as they say, and persever so,
And in this mist at all adventures go.

(212–16)

Such blind commitment is suggestive of quest-romance: like the knight who inevitably accepts the challenge of the miraculous, Antipholus passes a spiritual test in trusting himself to the mystery simply because it speaks to him.

The Syracusan is right in intuiting that the women can reveal to him a disguised aspect of himself. But he is wrong in assuming that the '[d]ark-working sorcerers that change the mind' (I.ii.99) know what they are doing – or that he is not one of them. Only the text knows, and by failing to display even the semblance of a motive, Antipholus shows himself to be very much the text's creature. What might be written off as a mere concession of character to plot actually shows the origin and working of the 'tangled chain' that draws him, Theseus-like, into the realm of the fantastic – an inner world that amounts to a play-within-the-play. The barrier between stranger and Ephesian – the very barrier that threatens to cost Egeon his life – proves no more substantial than that between spectators and actors in the play of Pyramus and Thisby. So does the underlying identity of names – Antipholus, Dromio – at last assert itself to erase spurious distinctions: 'of Syracuse', 'of Ephesus'.

The 'mermaid's song' that tempts Antipholus is, most immediately, the attraction of Luciana, 'Possess'd with such a gentle sovereign grace,/Of such enchanting presence and discourse' (III.ii.160–1). So described, her magic appears very much down to earth. His developing emotional involvement, however, makes love, as in *A Midsummer Night's Dream*, a matter of imaginative subversion:

> Sweet mistress – what your name is else, I know not,
> Nor less by what wonder you do hit of mine –
> Less in your knowledge and your grace you show not
> Than our earth's wonder, more than earth divine.
> Teach me, dear creature, how to think and speak:
> Lay open to my earthy, gross conceit,
> Smoth'red in errors, feeble, shallow, weak,
> The folded meaning of your words' deceit.
> Against my soul's pure truth why labor you,
> To make it wander in an unknown field?
> Are you a god? Would you create me new?
> Transform me then, and to your pow'r I'll yield.

> (29–40)

This is, remarkably, the closest analogue in the canon to Ferdinand's initial address to Miranda in Shakespeare's last play (*Tmp.*, I.ii.422ff.). Less surprisingly, it participates in the Petrarchan convention of love as worship, as well as in the romance tradition of the seductive enchantress – to the point of bringing out, more fully than elsewhere in the play, the rich implications, in that tradition, of error and wandering.[16] But the most striking feature of the speech is its portrayal of Antipholus' erotic desire – desire for a creature who, for him at that moment, is deception incarnate – as also the desire for renewal, even if this means

74

abandoning the unitary self as he has conceived it, 'my soul's pure truth'.

The irony is that Luciana works her transforming magic even as she repudiates his advances and despite his increasingly desperate efforts to return to the world of common sense. For as part of the pattern of exposing one-sided characters to the hidden implications of their attitudes, she too is made the victim of a disturbing reversal: the seemingly illicit attentions of her sister's supposed husband confront her with the practical effects of the absolute male liberty and dominance she has preached (II.i.15ff.) from a position of sheltered detachment. The 'troubles of the marriage-bed' are brought home to her as a preparation for her own marriage. Consistently, in the play's terms, to shun experience is to invoke it.

If there is any figure who embodies, rather than merely transmits, the omnipresent energy of transformation, it must be the Abbess Aemilia, who provides the answer to the Syracusan's prayer: 'here we wander in illusions:/Some blessed power deliver us from hence! (IV.iii.43-4). According to the method of trickery, that prayer must first be mocked by the entrance of the Courtezan, whose talk of the chain makes her seem diabolic: 'Sathan, avoid. I charge thee tempt me not' (48). Desperate as he is, Antipholus falsely separates dark and evil forces from those that conduce to blessing and revelation. But when the prayer is finally answered, Aemilia's language joins with the miraculous effect of her knowledge to identify her with time's own discharge of its debt to the principle of creation: 'Thirty-three years have I but gone in travail/Of you, my sons, and till this present hour/My heavy burthen ne'er delivered' (V.i.401-3). In cutting the Gordian knot woven by the plot's crossing and recrossing, and reinforced imagistically with real chain and rope, she speaks with the voice of redemption, as she singles out that victim whose confinement under sentence of death emblematizes the predicament of the others: 'Whoever bound him, I will loose his bonds,/And gain a husband by his liberty' (340-1).

In fact, it is the Abbess's own application of the disruptive principle that brings her face to face with Egeon; for by refusing to release (the wrong) Antipholus to be bound by Adriana ('Let us come in, that we may bind him fast' (40)), she provokes the wife to seek redress from the Duke. Precisely in not foreseeing the consequences of her action, Aemilia behaves like subversiveness itself. Her aim and method are merely to confront Adriana with the implications of her conduct. She deliberately tricks the woman into admitting and regretting her jealous persecution of Antipholus, but Adriana still objects, 'ill it doth beseem your holiness/To separate the husband and the wife' (110-11). By insisting on this separation – again, on principle rather than on purpose – the Abbess recapitulates both the divisive means of the play at large and the 'holy' end which those means mysteriously accomplish. She emerges from the hidden inner region of the play to take charge of it at the end, combining, as does the play's dramatic practice itself, the functions of Paulina and Hermione, the transformer and the transformed. In this double capacity, she can relegate the Duke, male ruler of the rational world, to the typically female role of 'gossip' (408) at the feast she calls to celebrate the wondrous rebirth of that world through trickery.

II

If *The Comedy of Errors* seems intent on collapsing distinctions between agents and objects of trickery, while *A Midsummer Night's Dream* projects them, as it were, on a large screen, *Two Gentlemen* and *Love's Labor's Lost* more typically divide creative deception variably between the play-world itself and certain of its inhabitants. The element of subversion thus enters the play of structural tensions inherent in the genre between the collectivizing determinism of comic form and the centrifugal tendency of character production. After 1595, such tensions become increasingly insistent in Shakespearean comedy, to the point where, in the Problem Plays, characters resist, on the deepest level, assimilation into the plot processes that enfold them. By then, those processes have come to be 'successfully' managed by monopolistic appropriators of creative trickery – the paradigm established by *Taming* – but at the expense of its capacity to provoke the restructuring of a textual world.

The two texts at hand point towards these and other later plays by setting off subversion against attempts to oppose it with its own tactics. However, as yet the power of trickery, though it may be exercised at considerable cost – the disruptive energy of the marginalized is conspicuously self-consuming – continues to receive recognition through the shaping of action. In both *Two Gentlemen* and *Love's Labor's Lost*, the trickster-principle explodes the schemes of would-be internal dramatists, disrupts hollow assumptions about identity and values, and generally takes control of events. Yet it is a sign of things to come that Valentine, whose unlikely victory appears to mark him as subversion's chosen vehicle, enacting the triumph of love in the face of machinations and repression, is actually less chosen than choosing.

The more problematic status of trickery in these plays, as opposed to *A Midsummer Night's Dream* and *The Comedy of Errors*, is reflected in its lower profile. Neither work is *about* disruption in an obvious way. Apart from the clowns – who deserve special attention – there are no equivalents here of the active mechanisms of subversion so prominent in the other two comedies. Rather, such deception shifts into the passive mood, becoming chiefly the upsetting of plans. And if it sometimes seems, as with the interruption of comic process by Marcade's message of death, that mere circumstances are themselves conspiring to frustrate human endeavour, the effect is to extend yet again the boundaries of trickery. In the universes of these plays, merely to attempt to control the uncontrollable is to conjure the surprising spirit of contravention. The trickster is equally at work, and equally unseen, when he trips characters in their blinkered courses as when he approaches in their sleep to alter their way of seeing.

III

In *Two Gentlemen*, the plot confusions typical of Shakespeare's comedy of transformation arise from conflicting schemes on the part of the title characters. Proteus plots to displace Valentine in Silvia's affections, while Valentine aims at deceiving her father by an elopement. Yet there is no mistaking either Proteus (despite his name) or Valentine for a trickster-figure. Far from delighting in disruption, they employ duplicity in the pursuit of very definite objectives. And although their motives are by definition as irrational as love is supposed to be, the language of the deceptions themselves is pointedly the language of reason.

Valentine begins by presenting himself as now enthralled by the 'mighty lord' (II.iv.136) he once had scorned, yet he depicts Silvia as a commodity that enriches and empowers him:

> Why, man, she is mine own,

And I as rich in having such a jewel
As twenty seas, if all their sand were pearl,
The water nectar, and the rocks pure gold.

(168–71)

Clearly, his love is less the point than his extravagant self-satisfaction, as Proteus recognizes when he objects to his 'braggardism' (164) after Valentine has disparaged Julia. The new lover goes on to boast of the completeness of his plan – 'our marriage hour,/With all the cunning manner of our flight,/Determin'd of' (179–81) – and even speaks of something indeterminable indeed as securely contained within his design: 'all the means/Plotted and 'greed on for my happiness' (182–3). The romantic metonymy – 'happiness' for 'consummation' – is a familiar enough formula, but it is deconstructed here by the lexis of calculation and the exclusivity of 'my'. In pretending a control not only over time but over human situations and feelings, Valentine's confident plot reveals its own instability. More pragmatically, it completely fails to reckon with the Duke's authority or, for that matter, to take his legitimate interests into account.

It is only a few lines later that Proteus in effect imitates Valentine, echoing in soliloquy his disclosure of passion for Silvia. In Proteus' speech, too, the emotional premise – that he is the slave of love – is set off against the language of rational control: 'Is it mine eye, or Valentinus' praise,/Her true perfection, or my false transgression,/That makes me reasonless, to reason thus?' (196–8). By the end of the soliloquy – 'If I can check my erring love, I will;/If not, to compass her I'll use my skill' (213–14) – the triumph of the discourse of policy signals that the outcome of the self-struggle is a foregone conclusion. And it is equally clear that the 'erring' quality of this love has nothing in it of the creative disruption associated with wandering in Ephesus or in the Athenian wood, where painful bewilderment and apparent loss are the devious means to joyous gain.

More accurately, the soliloquy does not end here but merely pauses – on a note of suspension as false as the sentiments themselves. The parodic reunion of Launce and Speed, full of verbal mistaking, truth-in-folly, and mocking good fellowship, only provides a suggestive interruption of Proteus' dialogue with himself. When it resumes in Act II, Scene vi, so does the

rationalization, in terms that turn inside-out the positive implications of error. In weighing the allure of folly against the
cautions of reason, Proteus is not reckless of self, like Antipholus
of Syracuse when confronted by Luciana, but narrowly self-
protective:

> Julia I lose, and Valentine I lose:
> If I keep them, I needs must lose myself;
> If I lose them, thus find I by their loss –
> For Valentine, myself; for Julia, Silvia.
> I to myself am dearer than a friend,
> For love is still most precious in itself.
>
> (II.vi.19–24)

The key to the contradictory subtext, clearly, is that the perceived
threat to his constituted ego proceeds not from Silvia, but from
the true imaginative focus of these speeches: 'I cannot now prove
constant to myself,/Without some treachery us'd to Valentine'
(31–2). His disparagement of Julia ('a swarthy Ethiope' (26)) is
merely another echo of Valentine's judgement. And he never
more closely resembles his rival than when citing his
subservience to passion to justify his calculating manipulation of
events: 'Love, lend me wings to make my purpose swift,/As thou
hast lent me wit to plot this drift' (42–3). If there is delight here, it
is the same chilling enthusiasm displayed by Hamlet in scheming to outmanoeuvre his own former friends: 'I will delve one
yard below their mines,/And blow them at the moon' (III.iv.208–
9).

Thus the language of trickery appropriated by Valentine and
Proteus – from the former's 'cunning' to the latter's 'sly trick'
(II.vi.41) – paradoxically serves to mark their distance from the
amorous folly each of them loudly proclaims, while establishing
their rivalry as the crucial focus of self-interest for each.[17] This is
also backhandedly to anticipate the conclusion, with its sudden
exaltation of 'friendship' over 'love', by portraying the
submerged competition between the men as already prevailing
over their love affairs. Silvia is relegated early on to the position
of silent pawn that she will come to occupy quite literally. In this
light, the much-maligned ending of the play need not be seen as
either botched or 'magically denying conflict' (Adelman 1985a:
79); rather, it brings to the surface the subtext of the previous
action, and in a way that subjects the professed values to a potent

irony. I shall be arguing that, like Proteus himself, the element of conflict changes its shape but, even in the context of a self-consciously artificial closural harmony, retains and actually extends its problematizing function, as in the case of Katherina.

That function is introduced in the first scene of the play, where Valentine scorns the love-stricken Proteus for neglecting, not the claims of his own affection, but the duties of young manhood. Good-natured though the banter seems, and conventional as the sentiments are, the exchange hardly evokes the often-invoked Elizabethan model of ideal friendship. Valentine revels smugly in his superiority, and, as he soon reveals in soliloquy, Proteus is keenly sensible of his shame, which, ominously, he projects upon the object of his passion:

> Thou, Julia, thou hast metamorphis'd me,
> Made me neglect my studies, lose my time,
> War with good counsel, set the world at nought;
> Made wit with musing weak, heart sick with thought.
>
> (I.i.66–9)

It is the standard role of the courtly lover to deplore his enslavement to desire, but the specific echo of Valentine's contempt helps reveal Proteus as divided against himself in a way that makes his subsequent behaviour less arbitrary. He is not simply devastated but of two minds when his father orders him off to Milan, thus severing him from Julia: 'my heart accords thereto,/And yet a thousand times it answers "no" ' (I.iii.90–1). The part of him that already rejects his relation with Julia as degrading will shortly come into its own.

It is at the beginning, then, that Proteus genuinely struggles with himself, not when he posturingly agonizes over Silvia. And his self-struggle is presented as a contest between worldly wisdom and subversive folly. The main target of Valentine's attack, and of Proteus' subsequent echo, is the damage done by love to 'future hopes' (I.i.50) – that is, ultimately, to a self constructed in opposition to the destructive effects of time. As he hastens to embark, Valentine actually chides himself in these terms: 'But wherefore waste I time to counsel thee/That art a votary to fond desire?' (51–2). Later, too, when Antonio follows advice to end his son's 'loss of time' (I.iii.19) by committing him to the 'world' (21) and time's 'swift course' (23), his self-confessed 'peremptory' (71) haste has meaning beyond the arbitrary wilfulness belonging to the stereotype. Ignorant though he is of his son's love, he implicitly raises Valentine's opinion to the level of conventional wisdom. Yet before we assume the Elizabethan audience's monolithic endorsement, we do well to remember that the contrary view – that love alone offers an antidote to time – is the insistent burden of Shakespeare's own sonnets.

The part of Proteus that dotes on Julia, his 'metamorphis'd' self, is in the trickster's grasp and capable of the trickster's voice. In his only defence of the value of love he moves towards an acceptance of subversive process: 'eating love/Inhabits in the finest wits of all' (I.i.43–4). There is at least a passing glimpse here of a wisdom within the folly Valentine so aggressively dismisses as destructive. Even in Proteus' own troubled enumeration of the branches of that folly, there is an underlying sense of an alternative identity. To 'neglect [his] studies, lose [his] time,/ War with good counsel, set the world at nought' is in fact to be the perfect subversive fool, and to be a fool is not to be nothing, as Lear's Fool reminds his master. But then we have just seen three of these four forms of subversion – assaults on 'time', 'good counsel', and 'the world' – figure as precisely the mechanisms of comic transformation. (In order to add the fourth – 'neglect' of 'studies' – to the list, we only need to consider *Love's Labor's Lost*.)

As if picking up the buried suggestion in the soliloquy, the text immediately associates Proteus with a conventional figure of subversion. The dialogue with Speed concerning his master's departure and his delivery of the letter to Julia is full of the typical clown's verbal tricks, including the mistakings that insinuate hidden truths. What stands out here is Proteus' ready and natural participation in this dynamic. In a suggestive departure from the aloof frustration usual for the master in such situations, he matches wits with Speed in a way that places them, if never quite on the same level, at least on the same wave-length. It is a style of interaction that figures between Antipholus and Dromio (both of Ephesus) at moments when the master's openness to foolery is also suggested, and between the mechanicals of *A Midsummer Night's Dream* and their oblivious courtly audience. In *Two Gentlemen*, there is a pointed contrast between this exchange and the subsequent encounters between both young masters and their own subversive servants. It is as if the scene must be staged between a mismatched master–servant pair in order to show it as anomalous – with a suggestion, perhaps, of the chiastic processes of suspended identity. More typical is the dialogue between Speed and Valentine at the beginning of Act II, where the servant displays a superior knowledge of the semiotics of love.[18] Similarly, in a rough anticipation of Ariel's non-human humanity, Launce's sensitivities and loyalties, ironically focused on his dog, first comment on Proteus' machinations, then bring master and servant into direct conflict, forcing Proteus to speak truer than he knows: 'A slave, that still an end turns me to shame!' (IV.iv.62). (Prospero, by contrast, will turn his potential shame to good account.)

This is, of course, the mode of parodic subversion popularly considered Shakespearean, although it has a rich dramatic heritage. The prevalence of this dynamic in Shakespeare's work from about 1595 until the late romances makes it all the more suggestive that such conflict is the exception rather than the rule in the early comedies. Certainly, there are prominent subversive clowns – the Dromios, Bottom and his companions. However, the disruptive antics of these figures more often serve to echo and reinforce the frustrating but ultimately productive confusions in which the principal characters are also involved – processes which make the latter equally 'foolish' in their own right. A notable exception is Grumio in *Taming*, a vocal authority on his master's problematic temperament who foresees the outcome of the struggle with Katherina. Grumio's verbal mistaking provokes Petruchio into beating him when they first appear before Hortensio's house, and it is suggestive that, far from accepting this conduct as normal, Hortensio rebukes Petruchio for the breakdown in harmony: 'Why, this' a heavy chance 'twixt him and you,/Your ancient, trusty, pleasant servant Grumio' (*Shr.*, I.ii.46–7). All in all, such subversion – literally, in the social sense, an overturning from beneath – generates friction only when the higher characters are engaged in some comic version of Cain's destructive self-delusion and evasion of responsibility. The servant's anarchic folly then serves to undercut the master's pretences to wisdom and control. It is the master, then, who ultimately generates the servant's function as 'foil' or 'parody', and this is the key to the contingency of that distinction. Proteus' move into an antagonistic relation with his servant marks a shift from one sort of folly, in which the possibility of fulfilment is latent, to another which fosters false claims to self-realization.

Subversive clowns may slow their masters down from time to time, but they are essentially instruments for exposing contradictions to the audience, not for influencing the action. What ultimately unravels the attempted duplicities of the Gentlemen is the comic process itself, with its commitment to poetic justice. Valentine does achieve Silvia in the end, but only after the requisite painful loss and displacement from identity. Proteus finally gets not only Julia but first refusal on Silvia, although he must suffer humiliation in the most thorough possible form – degradation in the eyes of Valentine. The extent to which the intrinsic mechanisms of the play produce these changes is shown by the parts successively played by each of the Gentlemen in the other's downfall. Yet those mechanisms are also abetted by a shadowy agent of change who hovers on the verge of a trickster's role and whose power must be reckoned with by the lovers.

It is easy to write the Duke off as the stereotypical *senex* and certainly imprudent to place too great a burden on him. After all, the character is so doubtfully presented in the First Folio text, our only version of the play, that at times he seems intended to be an emperor. Yet his function in the dynamics of exposure is well developed – so much so, perhaps, as to remind us of that much later Duke of Milan who also uses devious means to test his daughter's suitor. What is most obviously devious about this Duke is his method of exposing Valentine's scheme to elope with Silvia – a scene that stands out as a comic set-piece. His preposterous pretence to be a wooer asking for advice draws the overconfident Valentine step by step into his trap but also into increasing 'braggardism': 'That man that hath a tongue, I say is no man,/If with his tongue he cannot win a woman' (III.i.104–5). Even as the self-assured lover exposes his own plot, he unfolds the signs of his unworthiness. Yet this is merely the climax of a long-term trick: the Duke has deliberately allowed Valentine, whose love for Silvia he had perceived for some time, to continue in his course, whether to justify or to condemn himself.

If the Duke is so shrewd about Valentine, it is hard to believe that he is so naïve as he seems about Proteus, whose own 'fawning smiles' accompany his betrayal of his friend. His elaborately unctuous protestations of concern for the Duke's welfare culminate in a lie that brings a buried motive closer to the surface than even his soliloquies have done: 'For love of you, not hate unto my friend,/Hath made me publisher of this pretense' (46-7). The rhetorical excess, by contrast with the Duke's terse responses – 'Proteus, I thank thee for thine honest care,/Which to requite, command me while I live' (22-3) – virtually topples of its own weight. Certainly, the Duke appears to have been thoroughly taken in, to the point of seeking Proteus' aid several scenes later in turning Silvia's affections towards the doltish Thurio. Yet this subsequent exchange is strikingly reminiscent of the Duke's ensnaring of Valentine. Proteus might as well have a ladder and a cloak to conceal it, and he is every bit as secure as his predecessor, blithely supplying self-revealingly self-serving advice in response to the Duke's promptings:

> *Duke*: What might we do to make the girl forget
> The love of Valentine, and love Sir Thurio?
> *Pro.*: The best way is to slander Valentine
> With falsehood, cowardice, and poor descent,
> Three things that women highly hold in hate.
> *Duke*: Ay, but she'll think that it is spoke in hate.
> *Pro.*: Ay, if his enemy deliver it;
> Therefore it must with circumstance be spoken
> By one whom she esteemeth as his friend.
>
> (III.ii.29-37)

Evidently, it is Proteus who supposes himself in control here; when he accedes to the Duke's spuriously reasoned request to take on the job himself, there is a smug triumph behind his, 'You have prevail'd, my lord' (46). In fact, the pointed recapitulation of the exposure of Valentine suggests that the extreme irony of the Duke's concluding declaration of confidence, which corresponds to his 'discovery' of Valentine's bad faith, is not at his own expense: 'You are already Love's firm votary,/And cannot soon revolt and change your mind' (58-9).

Whether Proteus has more than met his match in trickery or simply overbalanced himself is impossible to determine – and beside the point. There is little to the Duke outside of these two scenes that is not purely conventional, and his desire to have Thurio as a son-in-law hardly endows him with either wisdom or regard for his daughter. The fact remains that Thurio's favoured presence provides the occasion for the testing of suitors, including Thurio himself. And it is remarkable how ready the Duke later is to reject Thurio for his display of cowardice, when his multiple unsuitability had previously counted for nothing.

However, the Duke by no means contains the creative energies he helps to set in motion. He creates opportunities – banishing Valentine, giving Proteus the proverbial sufficiency of rope. But he does not bring Valentine amongst the outlaws, or put him in a position to stop the attempted rape, or introduce the disguised Julia. So if, in the suggestion of creative purpose attached to his structural role as obstacle, there is some anticipation of Prospero's management of Ferdinand, when this Duke steps from the margins of the text into the foreground, he does so as the vehicle of the text's larger mechanisms of trickery, not as their originator. Despite his position of social authority, then, he is formally in contrast with Prospero and Vincentio in *Measure for Measure* – fabricators of dénouement – and more closely allied with Theseus and the Duke of Ephesus, who merely rubber-stamp, however heartily, ready-made resolutions presented to them.

This is to refocus attention on the most problematic feature of the play – its 'absurd' and 'contrived' ending. The objectionable sense of artifice here for most critics arises out of the text's silencing of disturbing contradictions to meet the requirement for an idealizing closure. Yet surely the events in the forest, archetypally the locus of creative folly, are self-referentially about artifice, contrivance, and silence. In fact, the previous uneasy tension between creative trickery and counter-trickery fittingly issues in a resolution that resolves only the plot, separating it from its own transforming energies. The ultimate index of this process is the change in the Duke's position, which makes his ratification of the restored harmony less than voluntary. For if Proteus has finally had stability imposed upon him, by way of the bonds of shame applied by Valentine, the Duke's power, too, is finally confined and compromised.

When the Duke delivers his encomium of Valentine's 'spirit' (V.iv.140) in defying Thurio and decrees him 'a gentleman and well deriv'd' (146) – no longer 'that peasant Valentine' (V.ii.35) of only two scenes before – he speaks the language of the testing father who rejoices at discovering the truly 'worthy' (V.iv.141) suitor. When he welcomes the exile home to matrimony and honour, then extends the pardon to the other outlaws, he puts in practice the final harmony. Yet he does so, unlike Theseus or the Duke of Ephesus, after having been displaced as the source of real authority in the situation. He enters, not as the customary

disposer of destinies, freeing those who have been bound, but as
the outlaws' 'prize' (121), and in yielding, with an echo of
Proteus' previous submission to himself, to Valentine's
persuasions – 'Thou hast prevail'd; I pardon them and thee' (158)
– he also yields his power to pass judgement on the processes of
transformation. Valentine, as he has made himself the judge of
Proteus' reformation – 'once again I do receive thee honest' (78) –
moves into place as the authority on the outlaws' deserts:

> Forgive them what they have committed here,
> And let them be recall'd from their exile;
> They are reformed, civil, full of good,
> And fit for great employment, worthy lord.

> (154-7)

'Civil' ironically harks back to the beginning of the scene,
where Valentine complains that he has 'much to do/To keep
them from uncivil outrages' (16-17). This is hardly surprising,
given that the outlaws' pasts include murder and 'such like petty
crimes' (IV.i.50). Despite the reference to Robin Hood (36), this
'wild faction' (37) has little in common with the genteel political
refugees of Arden. They are more like Oberon's instinct-driven
company of fairies, with a more fully developed sinister side –
thanks, no doubt, to their humanity. And as part of the typical
romance world of exile in nature, they would seem similarly to
embody a subversive energy with creative potential. In accord-
ance with the transformational paradigm, the passionately loving Valentine is brought in contact with that energy as part of a
symbolic self-fragmentation and reconstitution – a process into
which Proteus and the Duke (as embodiment of the social order)
are later integrated. Yet by instantly making Valentine their
sovereign – and inhibitor – rather than subjecting him to some
version of transforming magic, the outlaws problematize this
process. The work initiated by the Duke's exercise of trickery is
curtailed. Valentine manages, again, to take control of the
dynamic of deception, to appropriate subversive energies in
service to his manipulative ego.

Thus the final scene, despite his claim to have come under the
forest's influence – 'How use doth breed a habit in a man!'
(V.iv.1) – shows Valentine turning familiar emotional habits to
familiar account. His sighing for the absent Silvia in the most
artificial vein of courtly love ('Thou gentle nymph, cherish thy

forlorn swain' (12)) signals that imaginatively he does not live in the forest at all – or does so, at least, in the anomalous way of the ethereally pastoral Sylvius in the (relatively) flesh-and-blood world of Arden. And shortly afterwards, when he encounters Silvia in the flesh, with Proteus attempting to engage her on that level, his earlier attitudes to both friend and lover are wholly renewed. Proteus' drive to displace Valentine as possessor of Silvia is no longer enacted figuratively, through his desire for her portrait, but literally – and it is countered in its own terms. The exposure of Proteus comprises only the first stage of his defeat. It is when Valentine offers him 'all that was mine in Silvia' (83) that the triumph is complete, and not only because Valentine's prodigious generosity shames him further. The ultimate manifestation of possession, after all, is the power to dispose of what one owns.

That Julia becomes the instrument of resolving the plot at this point should not produce an exaggerated sense of her influence, even her moral influence. She and Silvia both have taken serious risks, most notably the risk of 'shame' (106), for passion's sake, with results that appear to confirm the revelatory power of folly. But what Julia actually offers Proteus here is the fool's cap as refuge from his own quite involuntary shame. As he originally rationalized his infidelity, he hastens to rationalize his renewed preference for Julia. He has, on the surface, returned, like Demetrius, to his original, truly instinctive, choice. But, in contrast with the continued openness to their 'dream' shown by the lovers in *A Midsummer Night's Dream*, his 'right mind' entails a Theseus-like dismissal of the vagaries of imagination:

> O heaven, were man
> But constant, he were perfect; that one error
> Fills him with faults; makes him run through all th' sins:
> . . .
> What is in Silvia's face, but I may spy
> More fresh in Julia's with a constant eye?
>
> (110–15)

The mention of 'error', the motif of the inconstant eye, bring to mind the creative confusions of the other two comedies, but in such a way as to define Proteus' distance from the broader understanding of Hippolyta:

all the story of the night told over,
And all their minds transfigur'd so together,
More witnesseth than fancy's images,
And grows to something of great constancy;
But howsoever, strange and admirable.

(*MND*, V.i.23-7)

In asking his rhetorical question here, 'What is in Silvia's face
. . .?', Proteus helps to ensure that the audience will take the full
impact of her powerful silence - a precursor of Isabella's
notorious failure to reply to Vincentio's proposal.[19] His words
also bring to bear the earlier song, 'Who is Silvia? what is she
. . .?' (IV.ii.39ff.). The answer, it is amply clear by now, is not
within the grasp of any of her lovers. Yet we possess, thanks
largely to her conversations with Julia, a secure image of Silvia's
ethical sensitivity and strength of feeling, and this we project
upon her in lieu of speech. The effect makes an ironic supplement to the earlier praise of Julia by Proteus, who is himself
never at a loss for words: 'What, gone without a word?/Ay, so
true love should do: it cannot speak,/For truth had better deeds
than words to grace it' (II.ii.16-18).

Specifically, Silvia's silence refuses to endorse the final harmony proclaimed by her lover and father, each of whom affirms
his right to dispose of her - a right, in romantic comedy, more
usually associated with initial discord. So, parodically, does
Thurio, whose crudity - 'Yonder is Silvia; and Silvia's mine'
(V.iv.125) - begets Valentine's equally crude re-appropriation of
the woman he has just offered to give away. His words, too,
impose silence on her by reifying her and pre-empting response:
'Here she stands,/Take but possession of her with a touch:/I dare
thee but to breathe upon my love' (129-31). Such silence exposes
the possessive bluster of the others as itself a form of silence. Not
only do the men fail to address her; they fail to address the issues
that she so eloquently poses.

There is a backhanded anticipation here of the final scene of
The Winter's Tale, where Hermione alters from statue to moving
flesh to living eloquence in response to the capacity of Leontes
and Polixenes to resolve the problematic of an analogous
triangular relation. Leontes' attempt to silence Hermione in the
trial scene enacts his psychological casting of her as the destructive subversive, a witch to be '[g]iven to the fire' (II.iii.8); he

must then answer the silence of her supposed death. As with Silvia, the test of 'faith' imposed by Hermione involves coming to terms with tough emotional realities. When that test is passed, reality at large is infused with magic, stone with speech. Ultimately, in *Two Gentlemen* the faithless evasions expressed in the failure to speak to Silvia ensure that she speaks, if only to us, with the trickster's voice.[20]

To this extent, the courtly Silvia – who is, in the several Renaissance meanings of the term, gentleness itself – aligns herself with the shrewish Katherina, whose final docility amounts to a silent register of the price paid for social order. In co-opting the trickster's creative energies, Valentine has played a version of Petruchio's part. The large differences between the plays owe much to the conventions of romantic comedy as Shakespeare practised it in his early works, where the triumph of young love is essentially identified with the triumph of those energies. They have at last been contained, perhaps, by Valentine's manoeuvres, but they have still transformed the play-world by way of those structural disruptions that fall under the standard rubric of 'obstacles to love'. This study will soon be dealing with plays where such forces are more narrowly focused and marginalized, as in *Taming* – confined, like Milan's Duke, but from the start – while the specious mechanisms of romantic narrative go on without and despite them.

IV

First, however, there remains a work in which an attempt to lay claim to comic closure by invoking the structures of transformation is successfully challenged. In terms, at least, of the thwarting of repressively manipulative intentions, *Love's Labor's Lost* is straightforward. Commentators have had no more trouble than some of the characters themselves in recognizing the plan of the would-be Academicians as an effort to govern aspects of the human animal that prove – first through Costard's lapse with Jaquenetta, then first-hand – quite ungovernable. Instinct and appetite, supposed enemies to intellectual improvement, are initially associated with death by the King and his nobles: they aim the Academy squarely at 'cormorant devouring Time' (I.i.4) and aspire to a fame that will 'make us heirs of all eternity' (7). By the end of the play, they are forced by the Princess and her ladies to acknowledge precisely what they have denied – essentially, the realm of the body – as the basis of life and to confront mortality as a condition of existence within the eternal round of seasons depicted in the final songs. This is the 'harsh' burden of the 'words of Mercury' (V.ii.930), the Olympian trickster. The message is brought home largely through an opposition between male illusion-making and female realism,[21] structurally reinforced by parodies of courtly-love and morality-play sieges: the self-appointed castle of virtue yields to seductive forces of folly that turn out to be the *avant-garde* of an uncompromising wisdom; the self-declared besieged reveal their true identities when they disguise themselves to mount their own futile assault.

So much, then, may be taken for granted, and readily understood in terms of creative folly, revelatory disruption. Once again, the repudiation of the ambiguous irrational guarantees its return in subversive form: insisting on acknowledgement, the spirit of the trickster transforms the universe to accommodate himself. Yet despite the clarity of the broad pattern, here, even more than in *Two Gentlemen*, he appears in a multiplicity of interactive forms. Obviously, Costard and, in a much narrower fashion, Moth embody the subversive principle. But the Princess and her ladies, realists though they are, are also its vehicles, while they in turn are seconded by its expression in the notorious twist of plot – the message of the French King's death – that frustrates the lovers' (and to some extent the audience's) expectation of an ending 'like an old play'. [22] As a result, uniquely in the canon until the late romances, a *new* kind of play emerges, marked by the trickster-principle's triumph, not merely over naïve or helpless mortals, but over at least one self-conscious appropriator of trickery's own language. It is as if Silvia and Julia were free enough of both generic and social constraints to reject both of their men, or as if Katherina were allowed, not only to get the better of Petruchio, but to set him on a course of rigorous self-analysis. Such an outcome would require suspending the conditions of power in gender relations, as is done here by superimposing the mechanisms of diplomacy. From this angle, the 'realistic' outcome of the love-plot appears fantastic indeed.

In the face of the compounding forces of disruption, the efforts of the lords to sustain their vain self-images do not stand a chance. Their defeat is quite predictable from the absurdity of their initial position. And because verbal wit is the primary weapon of both sides, the shifting relation between true subversiveness, functioning on behalf of the 'reality principle', and a mere mocking cleverness, ultimately defensive, is thrown into relief. This is a neglected dimension of the proliferating language-tricks and linguistic self-reflexiveness that much criticism has dwelt on. The play's anatomies of wit and folly are best appreciated when we recognize with Ralph Berry that, in their sallies of wit, the women and the men 'are only superficially sharing the same idiom' (R. Berry 1972: 80).

It is the distinctive role of the Academy's intellectual leader and spokesman that chiefly complicates the play's treatment of subversion. At the outset, Berowne proclaims himself a subversive and displays his subversiveness in linguistic terms, cleverly turning the Academicians' words against them. Yet, unlike Costard's on-going attack, as spontaneous and instinct-driven as the rest of him, on the unitary signification of language itself, Berowne's splitting of words from their ostensible meanings reflects a Petruchian arrogation of creative authority: 'How well he's read, to reason against reading!' (I.i.94). He steps into the very gap he opens, as he first exposes the contradictions in the Academy's founding charter, then casually subscribes his name. That he takes names so lightly ('Every godfather can give a name' (I.i.93)) will rebound upon him when he suffers for mistaking one lady for another.[23] Such mistaking, as a means of breaking down artificial structures, is standard in early Shakespearean romantic comedy. Yet it is here produced, neither by the dynamics of the text itself, nor by self-deceptive male inconstancy, but by the women, whose clear-sightedness coexists with – and so is not subverted by – their capacity for passion. In its most radical departure from romantic convention, from which the ending follows as the night the day, the play dares to expose constancy itself as inconstant because of its foundation on a broader hypocrisy.

In Berowne's case, this hypocrisy is established by his eloquence on behalf of the aspects of human nature that he agrees to repudiate – and whose part will be taken so effectively by the play's subversive mechanisms. He even anticipates the concluding songs by professing an acceptance of seasonal processes: 'At Christmas I no more desire a rose/Than wish a snow in May's new-fangled shows;/But like of each thing that in season grows' (I.i.105–7). The wisdom of the play's conclusion, it would seem, is his already. Such possession, however, excludes the folly contained within that wisdom, in keeping with Berowne's rational distance from his supposed subversiveness. His relentless wit – 'Not a word with him but a jest' (II.i.216), in Boyet's phrase – is never a sign of openness to paradox and contradiction but a strategy for blunting the impact of the very truths he articulates. And the surest gauge of this 'gibing spirit' (V.ii.858), as Rosaline calls it, is his decision to provide himself with intellectual cannon-fodder and a position of detached superiority by joining the Academy, just as the Academicians plan to keep Don Armado on hand as a source of ego-flattering entertainment.

Berowne's aloofness is enacted physically through his 'overview' (173) in Act IV, Scene iii, when he witnesses the other lords successively revealing their love. As when the Academy was first set up, it takes Costard to undermine the entire structure, this time by means of the 'treasonous' letter exposing Berowne's previous capitulation to passion and forcing him to acknowledge his status as one 'fool' among four (IV.iii.203). Berowne hits the nail on the head when, in a manner resembling Proteus' rebuke of Launce, he curses Costard for, in effect, his structural function – 'Ah, you whoreson loggerhead, you were born to do me shame!' (200). Yet the Clown, as he squires Jaquenetta off stage, coolly turns the curse right-side-out: 'Walk aside the true folk, and let the traitors stay' (209). For even Berowne's self-proclaimed status of 'fool' is false – a mere rationalizing posture.[24] Rather than allow his fellows to reconstruct and read his letter, after all, he regains control over the situation by developing, at their urgent request, a strategy for at once enjoying the fruits of their subversion and evading its subversive nature: 'now prove/Our loving lawful, and our faith not torn' (280–1). It is explicitly a call for counter-subversive measures – 'Some tricks, some quillets, how to cheat the devil' (284) – yet he wittily fabricates a case for subversion, a Neoplatonic encomium of love reminiscent of his earlier repudiation of the rational. His conclusion is a calculated invocation of the paradox that carries transformational significance elsewhere. It is one thing for Antipholus of Syracuse naïvely to describe the process, blind to its positive implications: 'So I, to find a mother and a brother,/In quest of them (unhappy), ah, lose myself' (Err., I.ii.39–40); it is quite another for Berowne to appropriate it as his rallying cry, 'Let us once lose our oaths to find ourselves,/Or else we lose ourselves to keep our oaths' (358-9).

In fact, the rationale has been pre-prepared. The audience has already seen him reaching his private accommodation with love, also in terms of the value of subversion and with a shrewd analysis of the mechanism as it operates in the play: 'It is a plague/That Cupid will impose for my neglect/Of his almightly dreadful little might' (III.i.201-3). In soliloquy, too, he has just acknowledged himself as 'fool' (IV.iii.16). His attitude is engaging – not only perceptive, but winningly self-mocking ('Some men must love my lady, and some Joan' (III.i.205)). Until the Ladies give their lovers a taste of their own manipulative medicine, there is no reason to suppose that such an expert in the processes of comic transformation through subversion will not get his Joan as surely as, according to Puck's promise, 'Jack shall have Jill' (*MND*, III.ii.461).

The possibility of such a resolution hovers throughout the courtship scenes. It is obvious that the women are predisposed, while the momentum of the comic pattern, the magnetism of the amatory symmetry, suggest that the 'lesson' of humiliation in the masquing scene will be sufficient to earn the men their reward. On the other hand, the desire to teach them such a lesson has measurably grown as the women have got to know their wooers. The Princess recognized from the start the naïve romantic projection in the recollected first impressions of her ladies: 'God bless my ladies! are they all in love,/That every one her own hath garnished/With such bedecking ornaments of praise?' (II.i.77-9). The salient quality in all three descriptions, after all, is precisely the superficial charm and mocking wit, those tokens of insular self-satisfaction, that the men will finally be enjoined to reform before they may woo again. The play's subversion of comic form begins with its portrayal of the women as outgrowing, or at least growing beyond, the helpless passion that elsewhere – from one Helena (in *A Midsummer Night's Dream*) to another (in *All's Well*) – appears to scatter its female victims like straws. Here, perhaps uniquely in the canon, those smitten by love at first sight are granted the benefit of sober second thought. Thus Rosaline moves from a Titania-like rapture over Berowne's jests ('younger hearings are quite ravished,/So sweet and voluble is his discourse' (75-6)), to the impulse to impose seasonal decorum on his verbal aggression ('How I would make him fawn, and beg, and seek,/And wait the season, and observe the times,/And spend his prodigal wits in bootless rhymes' (V.ii.62–4)), to the repudiation at once of his 'wormwood' (847) and of her own former susceptibility:

> Oft have I heard of you, my Lord Berowne,
> Before I saw you; and the world's large tongue
> Proclaims you for a man replete with mocks,
> Full of comparisons and wounding flouts,
> Which you on all estates will execute
> That lie within the mercy of your wit.
>
> (841–6)

Rosaline's language here points unmistakably to the behaviour of the men during the abortive Pageant of the Nine Worthies, and so confirms the climactic role of that episode in the play's counter-comic movement – the progressive disillusionment of the women at their lovers' failure to respond to their disruptive tactics. The Pageant serves to test the impact that ought to have been made by the humiliation of the Muscovites, but at this crucial point Berowne's ability to keep one step ahead of subversive forces finally lets him down. The King yet again fears being shamed – an indication that the point has been missed and little distance travelled since his initial congratulating of Berowne: 'How well this yielding rescues thee from shame!' (I.i.118). Now Berowne reveals his acceptance of these terms in undertaking their collective rescue from foolishness by exploiting the foolishness of others: 'We are shame-proof, my lord; and 'tis some policy/To have one show worse than the King's and his company' (V.ii.512–13). In insisting on hearing the Pageant, the Princess furnishes a double echo of Theseus at reconciliatory moments in *A Midsummer Night's Dream*, most obviously his decision to hear the play of Pyramus and Thisby ('Our sport shall be to take what they mistake' (V.i.90ff.)), but also his countering of Egeus' spoilsportism ('I will overbear your will' (IV.i.179)):

> Nay, my good lord, let me o'errule you now;
> That sport best pleases that doth least know how:
> Where zeal strives to content, and the contents
> Dies in the zeal of that which it presents.
> Their form confounded makes most form in mirth,

When great things laboring perish in their birth.

(515-20)

Berowne is quick enough to spot the allusion to their recent debacle – 'A right description of our sport, my lord' (521) – but not the trap. He reads into the words an invitation to get their own back, vicariously; that is, he hears the Princess according to his own narrow and negative understanding of 'sport' and 'mirth'. It is true that, unlike Theseus, who still supposes (not to say, *imagines*) that he has a dignity to stand on, the Princess argues for subjecting inept zeal to subversion, but the sequel proves that she and Berowne – more largely, the women and the men – have very different ideas as to what this means. The Princess addresses the performers by their stage names, as Leggatt remarks (1974: 81), and with consideration. She joins in the merriment but attempts to mitigate the mockery of the lords, who this time, in contrast with their Muscovite exploit, make their assault, not only on defenceless victims, but on the principle of imaginative play itself. Notoriously, their jibes reach a cruel frenzy capable of investing even Don Armado, their resident emblem of folly in captivity, with wisdom and dignity by contrast. Thus a creature who 'speaks not like a man of God his making' (526) rises to an eloquent defence of experience lived within the context of mortality – a context soon to be made pressing: 'The sweet war-man is dead and rotten, sweet chucks, beat not the bones of the buried. When he breathed, he was a man' (660-1). And so the image of the very event that in *A Midsummer Night's Dream* marks the breaking-down of barriers by drawing the courtiers, despite themselves, into communion with the clowns, here confirms the division of the on-stage audience between those for whom the barriers do not exist and those for whom they are impenetrable.

The basic sympathy of the women's world with the ethos of Costard is established with his original quest for the 'head lady' (IV.i.43).[25] Not only does his misdelivery of the letter anticipate the misdelivered declarations engineered by the Princess, but his bantering discourse fits in, to the point of outdoing Boyet in *double entendre*, with the ambience of raillery. Certainly, he feels at home – in contrast to his adversarial relations with his patrons: 'O' my troth, most sweet jests, most incony vulgar wit!/When it comes so smoothly off, so obscenely as it were, so fit' (142-3).

It is not surprising, therefore, that his part in the Pageant, which he plays with a mischievous lightness alien to his fellows and which culminates in his exposure of Armado's cowardice by way of his sexual false-dealing, should establish a 'chance'-rooted communion, across the theatrical boundary, with the Princess herself:

> 'I here am come by chance,
> And lay my arms before the legs of this sweet lass of France.'
> If your ladyship would say, 'Thanks, Pompey,' I had done.
>
> *Prin.:* Great thanks, great Pompey.
>
> (V.ii.554–7)

His fictional identity sets the seal on his resemblance to that later instrument by which abstemious figures of authority will be confronted with sexual truths, Pompey Bum, whose arresting officer, Constable Elbow, is descended from Dull.

It is one of the provocative features of this play that all subversive roads – including the final disruption by which, as Berowne puts it, 'the scene begins to cloud' (721) – lead to the Princess. As the elusive figure presiding over the operations of the trickster-spirit, she has something in common with *Two Gentlemen*'s Duke, even more with the Abbess of *The Comedy of Errors*. The message of death comes from outside, as a product of 'pure' plot, as if to set the seal on the men's continuing unfitness. Yet it must be applied, its impact mediated, by the character to whom it 'belongs'. She must reject, first, the shallow Claudius-and-Gertrude rhetoric of the King ('to wail friends lost/Is not by much so wholesome-profitable/As to rejoice at friends but newly found' (749–51)), then the infinitely subtler 'honest plain words' (753) of Berowne. That subtlety may be gauged, not only by his recovered mastery of the language of self-transformation through error, but by the uncanny resemblance to the argument by which Richard III woos the Lady Anne in the presence of the corpse of her royal father-in-law:

> For your fair sakes have we neglected time,
> Play'd foul play with our oaths. Your beauty, ladies,
> Hath much deformed us . . .
> . . . Therefore, ladies,

Our love being yours, the error that love makes
Is likewise yours. We to ourselves prove false,
By being once false for ever to be true
To those that make us both - fair ladies, you;
And even that falsehood, in itself a sin,
Thus purifies itself and turns to grace.

(755-76)

Viewed in the light of his sophisticated and persistent appropriation of the linguistic mechanisms of creative folly, the
penance and trial imposed on Berowne themselves take on new
subtlety. 'To move wild laughter in the throat of death' (855), for
'mirth' to 'move a soul in agony' (857), seems to him merely
'impossible' (856), but he misses the crucial distinction.[26] By
appearing in his primeval form, the trickster has finally stolen a
march. When Rosaline insists, in this context, that 'A jest's
prosperity lies in the ear/Of him that hears it, never in the
tongue/Of him that makes it' (861-3), she leaves plenty of room
for the Fool in *Lear*, who 'labors to outjest' his master's 'heart-
strook injuries' (III.i.16-17). Far from making an absolute con-
demnation of jesting - a stance that would contradict the very
subversive principle that the women have exemplified - she is
demanding that Berowne measure his self-indulgent foolery, the
assumption that life is *his* comedy, against the redemptive role of
folly in the *new* play that has just unfolded to include them all.

97

5

THE DEATH OF MERCUTIO

Amongst the plays of Shakespeare's mid-career – overwhelm-ingly histories and comedies – *Romeo and Juliet* fits as uneasily in this study's terms as it does generically. It does not obviously participate in the patterns I shall be tracing – various forms of conflict, opposition, and ambiguous interplay between agents of subversion, on the one hand, and, on the other, forces endowed with a Petruchio-like mission of civilization and socialization. Shakespeare's romantic tragedy does, however, comment on those patterns. My title is intended to cast a shadow over this chapter's main business by marking a major distinction between the earlier plays, including *Taming*, and those that follow.

The textual impact of the trickster has not necessarily been measurable, to this point, by his personal fate: silenced though they are, in different ways, Katherina, the Bastard, Aaron, and Richard III transform their dramatic universes as thoroughly as do the fairies of *A Midsummer Night's Dream* or the ladies of *Love's Labor's Lost*. If the instrument of subversive energy is finally expendable, this signifies that the energy itself has done its job for the play, even if our sense of that accomplishment remains in tension with a sceptical appraisal of the outcome in social and political terms. *Romeo and Juliet* stands out as the first play in which a character identified with such energy is simply disposed of in mid-career, his potential creative contribution suddenly cut off. And the emblematic quality of Mercutio's death is powerfully enhanced by its circumstances and consequences.

With the bawdy but sinister banter of the Capulet servants in its first lines, *Romeo and Juliet* announces that the self-serving instinctual drive and wit typically associated with the truth-telling indecorum of parodic servants have been assimilated into

98

an institutionalized and socially sanctioned (if illegal) form of irrationality. Sampson and Gregory, like their Montague counterparts, do their exposing of destructive hidden folly, here in the guise of honour rather than wisdom, by sincerely 'backing', not by challenging, their betters: 'The quarrel is between our masters, and us their men' (I.i.19–20). This is a sign of the closed structure of social madness that the lovers will have to face. Even Juliet's nurse, despite her bawdy energy, will declare her allegiance to that structure: 'I think it best you married with the County' (III.v.217). By default Mercutio assumes the whole burden of subversive energy in the play.

In a relatively mimetic work, Mercutio stands out by embodying a Vice-like spirit with insistent symbolic and supernatural overtones. His name is that of the trickster-god and the alchemical spirit of transformation;[1] his identity is shifting and elusive: 'A visor for a visor!' (I.iv.30). He acts and speaks for openness, for confrontation, for the breaking-down of barriers – between the families (in 'crashing' the Capulet party), between spiritual and sexual love, between dream and waking. By the familiar paradox, he also applies the reality principle, even to his own death:

> Rom.: Courage, man, the hurt cannot be much.
> Mer.: No, 'tis not so deep as a well, nor so wide as a
> church-door, but 'tis enough, 'twill serve.
>
> (III.i.95–7)

And so he offers hope, not by playing the peace-maker, like the ineffectual Benvolio, but by mocking, questioning, and stirring up trouble for its own sake – creatively, but non-teleologically. For while he picks his fight with Tybalt on Romeo's behalf, the disruptive impulse comes first, and he has no stake in the feud itself. As the indirect, unacknowledged instrument of social transformation, he is indeed the Prince's kinsman, much as Oberon is the unseen subversive shadow of Theseus. The Queen Mab speech, his nearly manic excursion into the realm of the unfettered imagination, confirms his link with that shadow world.

It is this catalytic potential that makes the generic impact of Mercutio's death most richly significant. As has been observed (Snyder 1979: 57–63), that event writes finished to the possibility that comedy will prevail over tragedy. Until this point, we have had a behind-the-scenes version of the conflict between Comedy and Envy in *Mucedorus*. The comic tendencies latent in the theme (romantic young love meets parental opposition) and encouraged by the prevailing lightness of tone have remained suspended in tension with the sinister overtones, as well as with the formal direction announced by the Prologue. With Mercutio dies, one might say, the comic spirit itself, extinguished by this oppressively violent milieu. Yet the death is also, as Mercutio insists, Romeo's fault – 'Why the dev'l came you between us? I was hurt under your arm' (III.i.102–3) – and to recognize the particular nature of *this* comic spirit is to appreciate that such a result is not merely the unhappy accident of 'fortune's fool' (136).

Romeo's morally impeccable impulse to placate Tybalt, then to keep Mercutio from confronting him, is bound to do more harm than good because it stands in the way of revelatory disruption – Mercutio's way. Moreover, it belongs to the self-consciously conspiratorial and mysterious quality of his love, which has been obvious from the first, when the love-object was Rosaline. In pointed contrast to Juliet's father, whom Romeo never dreams of approaching, Tybalt 'deaf to peace' (158) incarnates the irrational but tendentious violence of the feud – precisely the fact that makes him Mercutio's natural enemy, playing Envy to his Comedy. Self-indulgent 'riddling' here will gain no 'shrift' at all: 'I do protest I never injuried thee,/But love thee better than thou canst devise,/Till thou shalt know the reason of my love' (68–70). Romeo volunteers as 'fortune's fool' by attempting to impose his romantic vision, in the same spirit that he has vowed to be 'new baptiz'd' (II.ii.50) and claimed, 'Alack, there lies more peril in thine eye/Than twenty of their swords!' (71–2).

Friar Lawrence, whose fond indulgence, disguised as sober counsel, has encouraged Romeo's adolescent idealism, takes up the attempted manipulation of fortune where his protégé leaves off. In a similar way, he effectively invokes the 'greater power than we can contradict' (V.iii.153). No further explanation is needed for the disappearance of the formal choric prologues after Act II: the picture of an all-governing external destiny has given way to a deterministic momentum generated by human actions – less the feud itself than the attempts to circumvent it. Lawrence adopts the mechanisms of trickery to conceal and evade – that is, in opposition to the mode of Mercutio. His desperate scheme is guaranteed to go wrong simply because it depends on so many

things going right. The disastrous interventions of time flow
from the assumption that time can be shaped and controlled.

Thus the generic destiny of the text is logically related to the
elimination of a genuine agent of disruption and the assumption
of responsibility for the plot by a would-be engineer of comic
closure. For Lawrence's scheme to succeed would require the
playwright's own conspicuous indulgence. An argument can be
made that, in this most insistently fatalistic of all Shakespearean
tragedies, the dice are not loaded after all. *Romeo and Juliet*
helps expose the extent to which, by allying the triumph of
comic closure or social order with the outwitting of a figure of
subversion, certain comedies and histories of the subsequent
years are cutting across their own generic grain.

I

This effect is disguised, though it is far from obliterated, by the
displacement of the attractively amoral energy of Mercutio into
various immoral – that is, socially threatening – forms. Unlike
Aaron and Richard III, the villains of the middle plays are not
blatantly emblematic of their milieux. Their villainy is set off as
anomolous and perverse – until we allow it to deconstruct the
dominant counter-subversive discourses. Moreover, in several
plays the stigmatizing of trickster-figures is supported by relegat-
ing them to subordinate plots that enact their defeat, humiliation, and (in some form) banishment – to the point where
overtones of ritual scapegoating have been widely perceived.
Such a process comprises the main action of Shakespeare's only
'citizen comedy'. In a work that, after all, contains the outline of
a conventional romantic plot, Falstaff becomes the dramatic
centre of attention despite himself; in effect, this trickster's desire
to confine himself to a subplot, to conduct his subversions in
private, is thwarted by the forces of communal morality: their
counter-machinations, redolent of an impulse not merely to
banish but to exorcise, force him, whale-like, to the surface,[2]
while the eventual love-match of Fenton and Anne Page becomes
all but redundant. This structural inversion proves the rule: the
development of the subplot in the middle plays is closely tied to
the splitting-off of subversive elements from the primary
dramatic business, as it carries forward to an ostensibly self-
sufficient resolution.

At the same time, the sheer dramatic power of Shylock and of the Henriad's Falstaff, a power inextricable from their subversiveness, threatens to tip the structural balance in their favour – that is, given the course of events, in the direction of tragedy. The result is a radical generic instability. But then no comedy in this group achieves a formal closure that is not problematized by darker elements disjoined from the final harmony. Puck's final reminder of the terrors of the night confirms the integration of the shadow-world into the fertile power of nature celebrated by the lovers. This is a far cry from Malvolio's 'I'll be reveng'd on the whole pack of you' (*TN*, V.i.378) or Jaques's 'I am for other than dancing measures' (*AYL*, V.iv.193) or Benedick's promise of 'brave punishments' (*Ado*, V.iv.128) for Don John. Such nagging declarations of exclusion and alienation reflect a new friction between order and disorder, which are no longer allowed to demonstrate complementarity and mutual dependence. On the contrary, the middle plays are all preoccupied with internal threats to social stability. Rebellion is a constant motif, whether in the political or the domestic sphere, or, as in *Henry IV*, in both at once – a transgeneric link that opens the way, I believe, to an extension and re-application of Greenblatt's (1985) paradigm of subversion and containment, as defined with respect to the Henriad. The sense of residual doubt about the very forms of order they are concerned to protect reveals these works as not only setting limits to the disruptive principle but seeking uneasily to justify those limits. Perhaps oddly, *Julius Caesar* most succinctly illustrates, through the dilemma of Brutus, the ambivalence of the texts themselves.

Separating the principles of order and disorder entails, among other things, the specialization and marginalization of fool-figures. The spontaneous clown of the early comedies, often in harmony with the creative folly of his masters and always with the *telos* of his text, is now giving way to the professional wise fool,[3] who exists in the same paradoxical relation to his text as to his master or mistress. He can be 'all-licens'd' because his subversiveness is safely contained by his formal role, which is visually marked by his regalia. He is, in short, no trickster. Even as he asserts that '[f]oolery . . . shines every where' (*TN*, III.i.38–9), Feste redefines foolery in terms of limitation and dependence:

Vio.: Art thou not the Lady Olivia's fool?

102

Clo.: No, indeed, sir, the Lady Olivia has no
folly. She will keep no fool, sir, till she
be married. . . . I am indeed not her fool,
but her corrupter of words.

(32-6)

Olivia confidently assures Malvolio, 'There's no slander in an
allow'd fool, though he do nothing but rail' (I.v.94-5). The
linguistic subversion that has always been the province of clown
and fool is now largely divorced from the subversive effects – the
productive mistakings of Costard or the Dromios – that manifest
textual power. *Keeping* a fool comes to mean confining and
denying folly – in oneself and in the dramatic world at large:
Viola merely proves Feste's point by admiring his mastery of 'a
practice/As full of labor as a wise man's art' (III.i.65-6).

II

A number of elements make Portia's eventual domination of the
world and the text of *Merchant* seem an unlikely outcome, even
apart from the imaginative appeal of Shylock, which threatens
the primacy of the romantic action itself. She is introduced
indirectly, through a conspiracy of males for whom she is the
object of a mercenary wooing; her first appearance shows her
obediently confined by her father's will, albeit chafing under its
constraint. Subsequently, her love for Bassanio displays a dreamy
self-abasement akin to the longing of Helena in *A Midsummer
Night's Dream*, while her submission to him as 'her lord, her
governor, her king' (III.ii.165) exceeds even Katherina's final
declaration as an abdication of independence – an abdication
made more pointed by her use of the patriarchal terms 'lord' and
'master' for her former role:

But now I was the lord
Of this fair mansion, master of my servants,
Queen o'er myself; and even now, but now,
This house, these servants, and this same myself
Are yours – my lord's! – I give them with this ring.

(167-71)

Yet by the end of the play, Portia has acquired such pervasive
control and taken on such dynamic vibrations that some com-

mentators endow her with more-than-human status. And it is undeniably tempting, given the background of Renaissance anti-semitism, to allegorize her resoundingly Christian triumph over the Jewish 'devil', followed as it is by affirmations of harmony in Belmont and the miraculous refloating of Antonio's sunken ships.

The case of Petruchio has shown, however, how readily a supernatural aura can be appropriated in decidedly natural causes. Prospero, I shall be suggesting, fits this pattern. So does Vincentio, who, for a number of critics, as well as more under-standably for Angelo, gives the impression of 'pow'r divine' (*MM*, V.i.369). More immediately to the point is the self-managed apotheosis of Prince Hal.[4] He contrives to 'imitate the sun' (*1H4*, I.ii.197) so successfully – and surely the standard pun on 'Son' comes into play – that he gets away, not only with versions of murder (after all, this goes with the political territory), but with much the same relationship to his divine father as elsewhere epitomizes hypocrisy: 'I thank my God for my humility' (*R3*, II.i.73).

The structural parallels with the case of Hal should not be obscured by the large differences related to genre and gender. Like Portia, the Prince begins as a background figure who must free himself from a father's confining legacy. Like the Prince, Portia moves towards the eventual acquisition and consolidation of power in her realm and beyond it: 'second world' though it technically is, Belmont ethically and textually prevails over the milieu of Venice. Both characters achieve their gains through role-playing; both set the seal on the process in a highly theatrical public confrontation with a character defined as the embodiment of dangerous subversion. Perhaps most fundamentally, in both instances a distinctive premise functions, though generally behind the scenes, as a source of power: Portia's equivalent of Hal's royal birth, the 'given' of identity that, from his self-disclosing soliloquy in *1 Henry IV*, is felt to underlie all his actions, is her seemingly boundless wealth.

The play-world of *Merchant*, as has often been observed, revolves around money, and Portia has infinitely more of it than anyone else. Even before his downfall, Antonio's fortune has its bounds, as does Shylock's. Despite Shylock's parable of Laban's sheep (which defends not usury but *trickery* as creatively natural), and Antonio's expectation of receiving 'thrice three times' (I.iii.159) the sum he owes, both men must in reality deal with their wealth as limited and vulnerably divided into parts – witness Antonio's scattered argosies, Shylock's need to resort to Tubal, his lost ducats, his final forced division of assets. By contrast, Portia's financial power remains a transcendental absolute, supported by motifs of multiplication:[5] 'Pay him six thousand, and deface the bond;/Double six thousand, and then treble that' (III.ii.299-300); 'You shall have gold/To pay the petty debt twenty times over' (306-7). Even when she depreciates her worth, there are strong connotations of cornucopia in her language:

> Though for myself alone
> I would not be ambitious in my wish
> To wish myself much better, yet for you,
> I would be trebled twenty times myself,
> A thousand times more fair, ten thousand times more rich,
> That only to stand high in your account,
> I might in virtues, beauties, livings, friends,
> Exceed account.
>
> (III.ii.150-7)

The effect is to endorse the mythical status of 'golden fleece' (I.i.170) that Portia possesses for Bassanio (and Gratiano at III.ii.241) – a reflection, initially, of his impoverished perspective. For as Portia is endlessly fruitful, Bassanio is endlessly needful, with a chain of dependencies trailing after him:

> when I told you
> My state was nothing, I should then have told you
> That I was worse than nothing; for indeed
> I have engag'd myself to a dear friend,
> Engag'd my friend to his mere enemy,
> To feed my means.
>
> (III.ii.258-63)

In a play that presents human relations in terms of debt and payment, with the double meaning of 'bond' resonating throughout, it is clear that Portia, superficially the victim of designing suitors, actually holds all the cards. The magnetic appeal of her fortune draws in rivals 'from every coast' (I.i.168), prepared to sacrifice their happiness for a chance at the jackpot. And when it draws Bassanio, encouraged by the 'fair speechless messages' (164) he once received from her, it brings her exactly what she has desired.[6] Yet to take such power as flowing naturally from her carnivalesque superabundance is to ignore the text's interrogations of the relation, not only between the spiritual and the material, but between the 'foolish' and the calculating.

Portia's attitude is first displayed through conversations in which Nerissa functions as a sort of *alter ego*, supportive but mildly corrective. When Portia sighs with world-weariness, her companion points out the 'abundance' of her 'good fortunes' (I.ii.4–5); when the heiress protests against the conditions of the will, Nerissa affirms that she 'will no doubt never be chosen by any rightly but one who you shall rightly love' (31–3) – a confidence repeated after the failure of the second suitor: 'The ancient saying is no heresy,/Hanging and wiving goes by destiny' (II.ix.82–3). Moreover, it is Nerissa who brings into the open the idea of Bassanio as the perfect suitor (I.ii.112ff.), then later intuits his arrival: 'Bassanio, Lord Love, if thy will it be!' (II.ix.101). In short, she combines clear-sighted realism with faith in the processes of time. To this extent, she is aligned with the subversive principle, and it is structurally appropriate that she should make her match with Gratiano, whose trickster credentials are at the service of Bassanio.

Nerissa's endorsement supports the mystical overtones of the casket-business. To risk self-loss in this way is, by definition, to play the fool. On the other hand, success depends on applying highly conventional Renaissance precepts – something at which Bassanio proves adept despite the value he otherwise places on gold and silver, as opposed to lead. In using his wits, in effect, to circumvent the challenge posed by the leaden casket, he anticipates Portia's mastery of the Saturnine (hence leaden) Shylock. However heady the ambience of romantic fulfilment, the outcome hardly proves either his moral superiority or the power of his love. It is Bassanio's very detachment that enables him to see so clearly. By contrast, to reason badly earns the 'deliberate fools', in Portia's contemptuous phrase (II.ix.80), contemptuous images of Death and the Fool – that traditional subversive pair, here safely contained within their caskets and despatched with their victims. Apparently, there is little room in the exercise for the trickster after all.

The dream-like atmosphere provided by Portia's song plays a

significant role in concealing this fact, whether or not its lyrics
are taken as revealing the secret (through the reiterated rhymes
with 'lead' or the theme of deceiving appearances). To demand
'hard evidence' on this question, as does Ralph Berry (1972: 142),
is beside the point: the lack of reaction on Bassanio's part suits
the sense of the mercenary and calculating as *naturally* infiltrat-
ing Belmont's glistering spirituality – its pretence, in effect, to be
a projection of creative folly. In suggesting a manipulative
purpose cloaked by the apparatus of inspiration, the musical
'clues' anticipate the ambiguous function of music in the last act.

Certainly, Portia furnishes no background music for the earlier
suitors. She also shows herself less than straightforward in
dealing with them. Despite comments before and after rejecting
Morocco precisely for his colour, she professes attraction; if only
it were not for her father's will, she claims, 'Yourself, renowned
Prince, then stood as fair/As any comer I have look'd on yet/For
my affection (II.i.20-2). If he, with his heroic history, is a
prototype of Othello, this dissembling is the exact inverse of
Desdemona's, who seeks to evade a living father's will, for 'when
she seem'd to shake and fear your [Othello's] looks,/She lov'd
them most' (*Oth.*, III.iii.207-8).[7] Portia may not technically be a
Venetian, but she dwells hard by, and subsequent events come
closer than anything in the tragedy to justifying Iago's comment
(though in a more innocent sense): 'In Venice they do let God see
the pranks/They dare not show their husbands' (202-3). Moreover, Morocco's failure, like Othello's, springs from naïve
idealization: 'this shrine, this mortal breathing saint' (II.vii.40).
His (unanswered) prayer for inspiration (13) picks up his earlier
poignant acknowledgement of fortune's power, his acceptance of
the irrational: 'And so may I, blind fortune leading me,/Miss that
which one unworthier may attain,/And die with grieving'
(II.i.36-8). In contrast with the caricatured conceit of Arragon,
Morocco's fate has dignity because he authentically lives what
Bassanio merely contrives to understand – he really does 'give
and hazard all he hath' (II.vii.9). 'Let all of his complexion
choose me so' (79) hardly makes 'a gentle riddance' (78).

What is perhaps most significant about Nerissa is the silencing
of her distinctive voice from the point where the matches are
made. She becomes a mere 'yes-man', even a 'straight-man' –
'Why, shall we turn to men?' (III.iv.78) – as if to give Portia
occasions for witty expatiation. From her marriage to the ring-

trick, her actions blandly shadow those of her mistress, with no effect of interrogation. A superficially contrary change takes place in Gratiano. Always vociferous, he becomes more so during the trial scene, mocking the defeated Shylock with the shouted offer, in lieu of mercy, of 'A halter gratis – nothing else, for God's sake' (IV.i.379). Yet he, too, is being made to redeploy his subversiveness in a conformist direction. In so far as he calls into question the values of the textual establishment, he does so, like the Capulet servants, by excessive reinforcement.

Gratiano is initially marked as a sceptical outsider-commentator, speaking on behalf of open folly ('Let me play the fool (I.i.79ff.)) and against the affected wisdom that is folly in disguise. This he detects in Antonio's self-conscious melancholy, and Bassanio is forced to the rescue of his friend's feelings in a way that confirms the subversive casting: 'Gratiano speaks an infinite deal of nothing' (114). Still, Gratiano is always a tame subversive. There is nothing 'infinite' about him, and his per-spective, like Nerissa's, is only obliquely challenging. Neverthe-less, in a remarkable passage, Bassanio later insists that he tone himself down further:

> Pray thee take pain
> To allay with some cold drops of modesty
> Thy skipping spirit, lest through thy wild behavior
> I be misconst'red in the place I go to,
> And lose my hopes.

> (II.ii.185–9)

Such a linking of romantic fulfilment with the suppression of disruptive energy marks a new direction in Shakespearean com-edy.

Gratiano's last fling, warmly endorsed by Bassanio ('put on/ Your boldest suit of mirth' (201-2)), is the masquing revel that effects Jessica's elopement with Lorenzo. Unlike Mercutio's attending of Capulet's feast, this is hardly festivity for its own sake. As elsewhere in the play, an overlay of the irrational covers a calculating design. Indeed, to the extent that the scheme is aimed at Shylock, it has overtones of a ritual punishment of offenders against community standards such as figures more explicitly in *Merry Wives*. Such an application of the carnivalesque must be recognized as profoundly counter-subversive.

The elopement proves part of a major movement of characters into Portia's sphere of influence, with Jessica's theft of her father's treasure unsettlingly anticipating Portia's favours to Bassanio: 'Here, catch this casket, it is worth the pains' (II.vi.33).[8] The corollary is the increasing isolation of Shylock, which begins, significantly, with the desertion of that 'merry devil' (II.iii.2), Launcelot. This figure of 'pure' subversive energy, another deceiver of his father, acts against his conscience in joining Bassanio's entourage. Having pretended to be dead, he takes on a new identity in Belmont. There he becomes a tame household fool of the type common in the middle plays, with his trickery pointedly relegated to the linguistic sphere and made an occasion for Lorenzo's self-satisfied moralizing:

> The fool hath planted in his memory
> An army of good words, and I do know
> A many fools, that stand in better place,
> Garnish'd like him, that for a tricksy word
> Defy the matter.

(III.v.66–70)

If 'every fool can play upon the word' (43), not only words but foolery threatens to lose substance and meaning. Launcelot's dismissive attitude to the Moor he gets with child confirms his link with the exploitive Touchstone rather than the ingenuous Costard – besides recalling Portia's contempt for Morocco.

As other forces of disruption are co-opted by the magnetism of Portia's ordered universe, with its convenient fusion of moral (coded as Christian) virtues and enormous wealth, Shylock takes on a darker colouration: his 'otherness' forfeits its trickster-potential – present even in the malicious impulse to 'catch [Antonio] once upon the hip' (I.iii.46) with the 'merry sport' (145) of the bond – and becomes simply and actively evil. This is not, however, a mere matter of filling a textual vacuum. As has often been observed, Shylock is collectively constructed as villain and scapegoat for the sake of Belmont's harmony; he bears, in effect, the burden of the golden world's sordid material foundation.[9] Given this functional parallel with Richard III and Aaron, the differences are telling. Shylock neither seeks his disruptive role nor revels in it. While he displays, until the loss of daughter and ducats, an active wit and flair for argument, the temperament established in his self-introductory soliloquy (I.iii.41–52) is glum and grudging. Even on the verge of his revenge, he is desperately earnest, never self-delighting.

In effect, the comprehensive principle of subversion becomes split between idle merriment, on the one hand, and, on the other, a deadly serious assault on shared values. Comedy, one might say, is differentiating itself from tragedy, producing tragicomedy according to the definition of Shakespeare's contemporary John Fletcher – namely, that 'it wants deaths, which is inough to make it no tragedie, yet brings some neere it, which is inough to make it no comedie' ('To the Reader', 497). But this differentiation is generated anxiously, self-consciously, and on the basis of a far narrower concept of the comic than informs Shakespeare's previous work. The adherent of the Old Law is made to stand, ultimately, for a threat not only to Christianity, Venetian-style, but to a New Law of genre. This lends metadramatic significance to the role of law as the medium for both his challenge and his defeat. In, effectively, rewriting that law in order to counter subversion on its own terms, Portia is also going, perhaps, about her creator-father's business – fulfilling *his* 'will'. In the manner of Barabas, Shylock's notable predecessor, the trickster, not only as villain but as rival dramatist, needs to be both out-tricked and upstaged.

What lays this process open to view is the notorious ambiguity of Shylock's presentation, which can be denied only by presupposing a sudden monolithic indifference to nuance on the part of an Elizabethan audience simply because Shylock is a Jew. Shylock is allowed to call into question the very basis of Belmont. Yet his very problematizing power is conferred by textual forces – the cruder forms of Christian aggression, manipulation, and self-deception – which are themselves purportedly transcended in the final harmony. This is what makes Shylock's scapegoating transformative, not just a stop *en route* to a happy ending. The self-doubting malaise of this society is emblematized by the world-weariness of both Antonio and Portia, as well as the sexual-political tensions that, as many commentators have observed, complicate the Antonio–Bassanio–Portia triangle.[10] That malaise can be exorcised only by conjuring the spirit of its destructive 'shadow', the 'power and danger' of the marginal. Still, the challenge is kept external, the self-doubt projected rather than integrated. Like the shrews of the early plays, then, Shylock is catalytic, but because he is artificial as an incarnation of subversion, so is the purgation achieved at his expense.

Given his construction as scapegoat over the course of the play, Shylock is structurally analogous to Falstaff. By contrast, his character-type puts him in the family of those melancholic outsiders in the middle plays, Jaques, Don John, and especially Malvolio, who himself, thanks to his link with the Puritan 'Jews of England', carries a trace of religious anomaly. In Shylock's case, however, the stereotype of anti-carnivalism,[11] like that of Jewish evil, is ambivalently fleshed out. Before Jessica's Christian-instigated flight and robbery, Shylock is governed merely by a sombre, resentful, and contemptuous attitude to what he sees as a libertine society. His board is too abstemious for Launcelot, but then Launcelot, like any descendant of the Vice and Parasite, lives to serve his appetite, and Shylock tolerates him, if grudgingly. His house is 'hell' (II.iii.2) – but only for a high-spirited, self-indulgent young woman. Moreover, his fear of festivity is reasonable, to the extent that he (rightly) trusts neither her nor the false-faced Christians:

> What, are there masques? Hear you me, Jessica:
> Lock up my doors, and when you hear the drum
> And the vile squealing of the wry-neck'd fife,
> Clamber not you up to the casements then,
> Nor thrust your head into the public street
> To gaze on Christian fools with varnish'd faces;
> But stop my house's ears, I mean my casements;
> Let not the sound of shallow foppr'y enter
> My sober house.
>
> (II.v.28–36)

Paradoxically, the very element of caricature has a softening effect. The images of noise as corruptingly invasive make Shylock the prototype of Jonson's Morose; the anticipation of Corvino's confinement of his wife is also strong. Closer to home, one is reminded of Malvolio's wet-blanketism: 'Do ye make an alehouse of my lady's house, that ye squeak out your coziers' catches without any mitigation or remorse of voice?' (*TN*, II.iii.88–91). All three instances support a more conventionally comic, more humorous (in both senses), reading of Shylock's role than seems consistent with his subsequent demonization. But then Malvolio's opposition to agents of revelry even more

obviously results in his construction and punishment as a form
of dangerous subversive. He, too, is 'notoriously abus'd' (*TN*,
V.i.379) where he is vulnerable and driven into a desire for
revenge. In both cases, as in *Merchant*, such a 'casting', then outcasting, suits the interests, not of 'authority' in the New Historicist sense, but, more provocatively, of a festively sanctioned,
comically coded social renewal (even if, in *Twelfth Night*, Sir
Toby and his crew are also chastised).

The transformed world of Belmont offers as its premise the
realization of human love and the intuition of divine harmony.
The atmosphere, as evoked by the amorous banter of Lorenzo
and Jessica, self-consciously contains a proto-Chekhovian
admixture of sadness, but also some unacknowledged darker
undertones. It has often been noted that the famous love-stories
invoked are tales of betrayal, tragic death, and desertion, which
contribute to a sustained motif of human imperfection.[12] The
knowledge and acceptance of that imperfection may be seen as
part of Shylock's legacy, suitably appropriated to Christian use.
From the height of their transcendent bliss, the lovers seem to
look down at the mortal world of mutability, while wistfully
realizing that their place is in that world, rather than with the
stars above them:

> There's not the smallest orb which thou behold'st
> But in his motion like an angel sings,
> Still quiring to the young-ey'd cherubins;
> Such harmony is in immortal souls,
> But whilst this muddy vesture of decay
> Doth grossly close it in, we cannot hear it.
>
> (V.i.60–5)

Their first allusion, which is to the sighing of Troilus, points
up the parallel with the final stanzas of Chaucer's *Troilus and
Criseyde*, in which the spirit of the slain lover rises through the
spheres, hears their immortal music, and gazes down upon the
vanity of earthly endeavours, including love:

> And ther he saugh with ful avysement
> The erratik sterres, herkenyng armonye
> With sownes ful of hevenyssh melodie.
>
> And down from thennes faste he gan avyse
> This litel spot of erthe that with the se

Embraced is, and fully gan despise
This wretched world, and held al vanite
To respect of the pleyn felicite
That is in hevene above.

(5.1811-19)

But while Troilus' perspective leads him to condemn 'al oure werk that foloweth so/The blynde lust, the which that may nat laste' (5.1823-4), Lorenzo and Jessica go on to celebrate, in effect, the power of earthly causes to produce divine effects. Despite lip-service to the vicissitudes proper to 'this muddy vesture of decay', their own happiness claims an absolute quality, refusing to recognize that souls are still at stake. In the absence of the music of the spheres (unheard till *Pericles*), Lorenzo calls for human music to sustain the mood, then invests it with magical proper-ties – a recapitulation of the scene of Bassanio's choice. The magic is welcomed by the returning Portia, too, and when Nerissa points out, 'It is your music, madam, of the house' (98), she enables her mistress to incorporate the supernatural over-tones into a 'realistic' relativism – kept safely distant from the issues focused in the Venetian courtroom: 'Nothing is good, I see, without respect;/Methinks it sounds much sweeter than by day' (99-100).

The conclusion of Lorenzo's disquisition on music, combin-ing the sense of a world purged of discord with a further acknowledgement of human limitations, points directly to Shylock:[13] 'The man that hath no music in himself,/Nor is not moved with concord of sweet sounds,/Is fit for treasons, stratagems, and spoils' (83-5). By way of the last line, however, the reminder recoils upon the lovers themselves, especially given the previous intrusions of a materialist perspective into the love-banter. The mention of Medea (12-14) again brings to bear the legend of the Golden Fleece, with its double message. And when the pair turn to their own past made legend, they expose the doubtful purity of their contribution to the pastoral idyll:

> In such a night
> Did Jessica steal from the wealthy Jew,
> And with an unthrift love did run from Venice,
> As far as Belmont.

(14-17)

The pun on 'steal' – and Jessica ripostes by accusing Lorenzo of '[s]tealing her soul' (19) – works with 'unthrift' to echo one of Shylock's most resonant statements of self-defence: 'thrift is blessing, if men steal it not' (I.iii.90). But then in reducing him to 'the wealthy Jew', they rob Shylock again – this time of identity and fatherhood. Belmont has not merely failed to exclude the values it has chosen to represent in Shylock; it has failed in its attempt to excuse itself by allowing him to recall, from a safe distance, its own fallenness. As *The Tempest* will confirm, to 'acknowledge' a 'thing of darkness' as one's own is not necessarily an act of openness or humility.

The fragile beauty of this magical night, with its contradictions in uneasy suspension, is inauspiciously converted to 'daylight sick' (124) by Bassanio's arrival, which triggers the conclusion. It has been observed that, in revealing her role as saviour, which is reinforced by the ring-trick and her news of Antonio's ships, Portia puts her husband and Antonio deeper in debt than ever they were.[14] Antonio now pledges his soul instead of his body on behalf of his friend's good faith – a 'merry bond' that Portia will hold fast: 'Then you shall be his surety' (254). As Shylock's forced conversion confirms, souls are the ultimate medium of exchange here. Antonio aims at regaining some of his lost ground in Bassanio's hierarchy of emotional obligations – the ground earlier secured by his pledge of his life. Portia's restoration of his wealth, which is deliberately made, like the revival of *Measure for Measure*'s Claudio, a matter of marvel – 'You shall not know by what strange accident/I chanced on this letter' (278-9) – deprives him of his stock-in-trade, the claim to pity. This completes his indebtedness to her for 'life and living' (286) – a phrase indirectly supporting Shylock's recent declaration, 'you take my life/When you do take the means whereby I live' (IV.i.376-7).[15] As Harry Berger puts it, her 'negative usury' thoroughly 'mercifies' him (1981: 161-2).

It is important to many feminist critics that Portia must take on a man's role in order to function in a men's world. In fact, Portia's disguise has been the means also of resolving the contradiction present in her situation from the start between wealth as a source of power and women's wealth as subject to male control. A sense of this contradiction informs her ostentatious undoing of herself as 'lord' and 'master'. On the one hand, she is manipulating a 'foolish' posture so as to impose a sense of obligation on Bassanio.[16] Yet, like Richard II in his analogous renunciation of his kingly status (*R2*, IV.i.203ff.), she simultaneously betrays an awareness that self-dramatization does not alter the actual balance of power: Bassanio, like Bullingbrook, can afford to be indulgent. Given that the most realistic form of power she can retain is emotional, Portia's final dramatic exercise amounts to a regaining of the upper hand. The world she had given away is palpably her own again when she returns. The magnetic attraction of her wealth has modulated into a magnetic moral and spiritual authority. Yet this aura has been produced, not only in male garments, but by using that supposedly masculine faculty – the reason – to vanquish the incarnation of irrational evil. When she discloses her imposture through the ring-trick, she unites a masculine potency with that traditional female source of power – the ability to make cuckolds.[17] And since that power also affirms sexual energy, with its overtones of festive renewal, the revelation signals her assimilation, in sterilized form, of Shylock's subversive 'soul'. This use of the highly rational ring-trick to engage the mechanisms of comic energy anticipates the bed-tricks of the Problem Plays. Here, at least, the ghost of Shylock soul-less hovers to decry the partial and political nature of a resolution premised on such appropriation.

III

Although the destiny of Falstaff as Hal's and England's scapegoat has been familiar since the seminal work of Barber (1959: 206–9), it still requires a wrenching of our usual perspective to think of Falstaff's very subversiveness as imposed upon him rather than somehow 'his own'. Thus Blanpied insists, 'Falstaff is not only alive, but powerfully alive, and certainly no figment of Hal's fantasy' – a fact that 'spares Hal the need of inventing him' (Blanpied 1983: 167–8).[18] For critics with a socioanthropological bent, moreover, Falstaff is 'alive' as the trickster *par excellence* in one or more of the traditional guises – Battenhouse's Biblically derived Holy Fool (1975), Barber's buffoon and Lord of Misrule (1959: 195–7), Bakhtin's grotesque body (1968).[19] The last model, dominant in recent commentary, best allows for the trickster's paradoxical incorporation of extremes of life and death. It does not, however, show him in the process of production. Rather, the invocation of such a vast and vague psycho-cultural archetype threatens to overdetermine Shakespeare's fiction. But then even Holderness (1985: 79–130), who aims to de-essentialize Falstaff into a 'site of contradictions' where Bakhtinian carnival meets the Puritan tendencies of the Oldcastle heritage, contributes in the end to the character's overstuffing with significance, so that he threatens to take on, no longer life, perhaps, but lives, outside the text. By contrast, Greenblatt's resolutely materialist application of the subversion-containment paradigm, whose general relevance I hasten to endorse, flattens Falstaff into an instrument of parody and 'cynical wisdom' (Greenblatt 1985: 41), who is merely a more articulate opponent of order than his companions.[20] My argument is that the thorough success of Hal's machinations depends on his appreciation and appropriation of the spiritual potency of the trickster-archetype as Falstaff is made to incarnate it.

It is unnecessary to add here to the 'meaning' or meanings of Falstaff's subversive energy. Still adequate is the model of a disruption that endlessly problematizes fixed structures and so creates the possibility of renewal, although Falstaff's relentlessly physical incarnation of such disruption stresses the most basic level of this process: the organic cycle of creation and destruction. More pressing is the paradox that this monumental manifestation – in effect a 'present-absence' throughout Shakespeare's work – should appear now, in a set of texts and contexts calculated to contain and destroy him. He is, in the final analysis, a spirit conjured – by Hal, in part, but with the abettance of the text at large – precisely in order to be laid, and, if the spirit is made flesh with improbable excess, the fatter the scapegoat, presumably, the more efficacious his ritual slaughter. From this perspective the Hal-less *Merry Wives*, otherwise radically dislocated from the dramatic sequence, fits quite comfortably into place.

It may be argued that the much-touted multidimensionality of Falstaff's comic presence actually serves to restrict its impact. After all, the double-functioning of his humour – he is both subject and object of mirth – amounts to a granting of constructive power to those who mock him, since to 'invent' jests upon him involves, in a sense, inventing the man himself. Such power not only keeps his subversive energy at a safe distance but comes at the expense of his independence, as he appears to acknowledge:

Men of all sorts take a pride to gird at me. The brain of this foolish-compounded clay, man, is not able to invent any thing that intends to laughter more than I invent or is invented on me: I am not only witty in myself, but the cause that wit is in other men.

(2H4, I.ii.6-10)

Falstaff enjoys the spotlight, but visual interpretation is linked with confinement, beginning with the urinalysis – Falstaff in a jar, as it were, a precursor of the buck-basket of *Merry Wives* – and continuing as he calls attention, in a metadramatic gesture, to the absurd tableau coupling him with his tiny Page. This effect is, literally, the Prince's design: 'If the Prince put thee into my service for any other reason than to set me off, why then I have no judgment' (12-14).

As for his self-consciousness itself, it similarly enlarges Falstaff's comic girth only while setting a limit to it. For Kaiser (1963: 167-8), amongst others, Falstaff's ability to see himself as others see him, his status as at once *eiron* and *alazon*, is what decisively places him in the tradition of the folly that is wisdom. But this is to neglect folly's transmutation into the 'allow'd' variety, as illustrated by the career of Launcelot. To function within a social structure as an essentially powerless semi-official teller of truth-in-folly is a far cry from provoking that structure's transformation by shaking it at the roots. Nor is such transformation the business of *Henry IV*, though Hal might like the world to think so. Falstaff, then, looks not only backward – perhaps with a certain nostalgia – to Moria, Pantagruel, and Montaigne, but forward less gloriously to Touchstone, the first formal 'wise fool', who follows soon after (probably in 1599).

Still, Falstaff's self-consciousness is not a constant; it evolves together with other aspects of his role. His famous analysis of his comic function, by which he (re-)introduces himself in the second Henry-play, marks, according to Barber (1959: 214-15), a new stage in the process of isolating and diminishing the character preparatory to disposing of him. This veritable de-carnivalization in the direction of the 'isolated bourgeois ego' (Holderness 1985: 95), as Holderness applies Bakhtin, is helped along by Falstaff's growing moral stigmatization, developed through the disease-motif; by his flouting of textually sanctioned principles (and representatives) of justice; by the increased

117

sordidness of the tavern-life; and, above all, by the physical separation from Hal (they meet, before the final encounter, only in Act II, Scene iv, where the familiar exposure-and-excuse game is played quite mechanically).

As the attenuation of the low-life scenes mirrors the suspension of political process in the play, pending the succession, so the new sense of moral degeneracy comments on the ethos of the power structure.[21] With the death of Hotspur on Shrewsbury field has finally died, in effect, an at least nominally honour-driven politics, on the wane since the rudely interrupted trial by combat in *Richard II*. In its place evolves, as Greenblatt has pointed out (1985: 39), an image of the modern corporate state, in which policies are coolly executed by surrogates (the Chief Justice, Prince John) and 'dishonourable' actions are legitimized in the service of law and order. The betrayal of Hotspur by his fellow-conspirators, when they withhold the King's offer of pardon, is presented as part and parcel of the discord associated with rebellion – the proverbial falling-out among thieves illustrated by the aftermath of Gadshill. Yet John's sleight-of-hand with the apparent offer of pardon in Part 2 issues in an anticipation of Henry V's theme-music, the *Non Nobis*: 'God, and not we, hath safely fought to-day' (IV.ii.121). It will be Hal's (as it seems to have been Elizabeth's) triumph to institutionalize such tricks of state under cover of a revival of the age of chivalry, emblematized by Edward the Black Prince[22] – hardly a fiction with room in it for a 'dry, round, old, wither'd [knight]' (II.iv.7–8). In the meanwhile, Hal's impatience shows (in the crown-stealing scene, despite his fast talking), and he matches Falstaff's *ennui* with an echo of Portia's opening complaint, similarly countered by a loyal minion:

> Prince: Before God, I am exceeding weary.
> Poins: Is't come to that? I had thought weariness
>   durst not have attach'd one of so high blood.
>
> (II.ii.1–3)

The sequel to that heiress's impatience bodes ill for the figure constituted as the ultimate threat to Hal's secure inheritance.

The challenge presented by Portia's first suitors to her realization of power resembles that posed by Hotspur: it is external and superficial, susceptible to direct confrontation. The casket-business is Portia's Shrewsbury field. Such conquest, however, cannot reconstruct a dramatic world or invest a new monarch-playwright with creative hegemony. Consolidation of the paternal legacy – psychic, political, and textual – depends on defeating, by counter-subversion, an emblem of subversiveness itself whose energy can be appropriated. (Hamlet's difficulty, I shall be suggesting, involves trying to defuse subversiveness from beyond the grave – and within the psyche – by constructing a series of Hotspurs.)

Such a perspective sheds light on the political – and stylistic – evolution of the Second Tetralogy. As *Richard II*, alone in the canon, never descends to prose or low comedy, so it uniquely lacks agents of subversive energy. It is full of strife and rebellion, of course, but the dour and thoroughly teleological Bullingbrook hardly qualifies as a trickster; in fact, his first act of power is to 'weed and pluck away' those 'caterpillars of the commonwealth' (II.iii.166–7), Bushy and Green, who come closest in function (if not very close in spirit) to the Vice-like misleaders of royalty in the late morality plays. Overall, the play enacts a rigorous denial of the carnivalesque and festive, a denial related to the successive vulnerability of Richard and Bullingbrook to political subversion. This is an early version of a dynamic crucial in the late tragedies, where protagonists project subversiveness outward in the form of opposition.

In his possession of a tragic psychology, Richard anticipates those protagonists: his refusal to acknowledge his humanity – the subversive within – both provokes and leaves him open to his enemies. On the other hand, once Bullingbrook strips away the 'cares' of Richard's kingship (IV.i.194ff.), the human 'cares' that Richard retains themselves become a threat to the new régime, as he gains pity and new rebellions arise in his name. Bullingbrook's ritualistic attempt to impose historical closure at the end of *Richard II*, after putting down the first rebels, is thwarted by the entrance of Richard's coffin – the royal actor's last upstaging of his antagonist, but also the objectification of the futility of eliminating the trickster-principle. Carlyle's apocalyptic prophecy resonates in the background, and the bloody cycle seems doomed to continue, on the model of the First Tetralogy, until the very spirit of subversion should violently intrude from the margins to usurp the text. Hal's dextrous management of that spirit breaks the cycle. His defeat of Hotspur and battlefield rescue of the king begin the transfer of paternal authority; but it is only the end of Part 1. As Hal has foreseen, the key to the transcendent moral authority acknowledged by the churchmen at the opening of *Henry V* lies in Eastcheap. By opening up the textual world of *Richard II* to low comedy and affiliating himself with it, Hal produces the repressed trickster in the accommodating form of Falstaff rather than Richard of Gloucester.

Paradoxically, it is the increasingly realistic portrayal of Falstaff as a moral and political threat to the realm that, by tending to demythologize him, diminishes the energies of the underlying trickster-archetype. In this, too, he is like Shylock, who loses the power of his mystery as his menace becomes exactly defined, and so susceptible to being confined. Part 2's depiction of Falstaff's corrupt recruiting practices is standard comic business, with a satirical edge. His more sinister exploitation of the recruits in Part 1, though presented indirectly, is far more potent imaginatively. There, in a soliloquy inviting the audience's complicity (IV.ii.11ff.), Falstaff displays a Vice-like satisfaction at his mischief, while one of his most genuinely subversive moments is his later graphic dismissal: 'I have led my ragamuffins where they are pepper'd; there's not three of my hundred and fifty left alive, and they are for the town's end, to beg during life' (V.iii.35-8). This renews the genuinely chaotic dimension of Falstaff's role at a point where its sympathetic aspects might otherwise unbalance the picture. Even when he resurrects himself to claim, so persuasively, that 'to counterfeit dying, when a man thereby liveth, is to be no counterfeit, but the true and perfect image of life indeed' (V.iv.117-19), his subversiveness is enriched by a blasphemous parody of Christ, as well as by an allusion to 'atheistic' denigrations of religious miracles as fakery.[23] Such larger-than-life identification with life incorporates the trickster's darker side, his link with death.

Another pointed contrast is between Falstaff's catechism on honour in Part 1 (V.i.130ff.) and Part 2's battlefield soliloquy (in so far as there is a battle) in praise of sherris-sack (IV.iii.87ff.). The first speech is profoundly and revealingly disruptive. Even if Hotspur has proved the vanity of honour when pursued as an absolute, that chivalric value retains its imaginative currency, as is clear not only from Hal himself but from the willing services of Sir Walter Blunt for honour's sake - services mocked, in Falstaff's reading, by his death-grin. By the time of the false climax in Gaultree Forest, Falstaff is reduced to a pale praise of physical folly – a parodic rhetorical exercise, which, incidentally, over-estimates the transformation of Hal's 'cold blood' (118).

There is no mystery to the mechanisms by which Hal fosters and shapes Falstaff's subversive role. It has often been observed that he 'scripts' virtually all the action involving his friend – and much besides – and that the pattern involves setting Falstaff up in order to knock him down. Falstaff is put into successive positions where his subversive energy, particularly his talent for lying, is stimulated and encouraged – at least until the battle of Shrewsbury. The parting of the ways may be dated from the moment when the alcoholic contents of Falstaff's pistol-case – a veritable dagger of lath – offend, in genuine subversive fashion, against Hal's new-found commitment to temporal decorum: 'What, is it a time to jest and dally now?' (*1H4*, V.iii.55). This harks all the way back to the resistance to confusion expressed by Antipholus of Syracuse: 'learn to jest in good time – there's a time for all things' (*Err.*, II.ii.64–5). As the princely sun begins to break through the 'base contagious clouds' (*1H4*, I.ii.198), '[r]edeeming time' (217), the suspended time of the tavern world, in which 'hours [are] cups of sack' (7), changes from the more neutral 'idleness' of his first soliloquy (196) to acquire the actively dangerous quality of a sort of anti-time. From now on, this concept of folly will be paramount, as Hal makes clear later in adapting the imagery of elevation: 'Well, thus we play the fools with the time, and the spirits of the wise sit in the clouds and mock us' (*2H4*, II.ii.142–3).[24]

Hal goes on to affirm, as he plans his 'heavy descension' (173) in order to get a view – his last one – of Falstaff 'in his true colors' (170), that 'in every thing the purpose must weigh with the folly' (175–6), and when we try to go beyond mechanisms to purposes, the picture clouds. How to take Hal's self-disclosing soliloquy in Act I, Scene ii, of Part 1 ranks easily as the most vexed question bearing on his character. Notoriously, the difficulty lies in reconciling the cold calculation evident there with his seemingly warm participation in the tavern-world. Theatrically speaking, the plays have it both ways, and criticism should take its cue from this effect, giving full weight to Hal's engagement in the process of constructing the subversion he later repudiates. When Hal proposes to 'uphold/The unyok'd humor of your idleness' (I.ii.195–6), his choice of verb bespeaks far more than observation and toleration. Yet as with any 'allow'd fool', only in the safe forms of jest and role-playing can this truth be spoken – 'God send the companion a better prince! I cannot rid my hands of him' (2H4, I.ii.201–2) – and the intrusions of authorized reality, the sheriff at the door, ensure that challenges to the official version of the relationship, which casts Falstaff as the active partner, cannot go too far: 'Out, ye rogue, play out the play, I have much to say in the behalf of that Falstaff' (1H4, II.iv.484–5). That would be too long for *this* play.

Even Warwick's defence of the Prince as a mere student of morals contradicts the posture of passivity. Like a language, the subversive must be thoroughly assimilated in order to achieve contemptuous detachment with 'the perfectness of time' (2H4, IV.iv.74):

> The Prince but studies his companions
> Like a strange tongue, wherein, to gain the language,
> 'Tis needful that the most immodest word
> Be look'd upon and learnt, which once attain'd,
> Your Highness knows, comes to no further use
> But to be known and hated.
>
> (68–73)[25]

In the immediately preceding scene, Falstaff had, in effect, defined his trickster-identity in the same terms: 'I have a whole school of tongues in this belly, and not a tongue of them all speaks any other word but my name' (IV.iii.18–20). It is precisely by refusing to acknowledge that name – 'I know thee not, old man' (V.v.47) – that Hal, the master-rhetorician, will silence those tongues. The motif also links Falstaff with the subversive Rumor[26] – 'Upon my tongues continual slanders ride,/The which in every language I pronounce' (Induction 6–7) – who is himself made to lend his voice to the new King's harmony: 'I heard a bird so sing,/Whose music, to my thinking, pleas'd the King' (V.v.107–8). In much the same way does Portia, by mastering the legal language that is Shylock's weapon, make way for the concluding music of Belmont. Hal's triumph completes the project that began with his silencing and appropriating, in another publicly staged encounter, of the voice openly raised against his political legitimacy. The *alter ego* who owned that voice was a thief on a grander scale, who also raised the question of who is stealing what from whom:

Hot.:   O Harry, thou hast robb'd me of my youth!
       I better brook the loss of brittle life
       Than those proud titles thou hast won of me.
       . . .
              O, I could prophesy,
       But that the earthy and cold hand of death
       Lies on my tongue. No, Percy, thou art dust,
       And food for –
Prince: For worms, brave Percy.

                                     (*1H4*, V.iv.77-87)[27]

Increasingly dangerous as he is made from a rational point of view, Falstaff never wholly loses his appeal for an audience. The rejection scene, in which Hal 'kill[s] his heart' (*H5*, II.i.88) – note the slippery pronoun reference in the Hostess's phrase – is prepared for and structured so as to encourage a qualified tragic response. But whereas the conclusion of *Merchant* must live with the ambivalence caused by the crushing of Shylock, the tetralogy has the leisure and the cast of characters to capitalize on sympathy for Falstaff precisely by limiting it to him. Even before the end of Part 2, the *demi-monde* of which Falstaff has been the linchpin is pointedly stripped of 'redeeming' qualities; the arrest of Hostess Quickly and Doll Tearsheet has been recognized (Rhodes 1980: 117; Holderness 1985: 129) as adapting the grotesque mode to the sordidness that comes with Pistol: 'the man is dead that you and Pistol beat amongst you' (*2H4*, V.iv.16-17).

In *Henry V*, the debased heirs of Falstaff are successively eliminated as further sacrifices to the purity of the new régime. Detached as the milieu already is from the King himself, who keeps his old acquaintances at double arm's-length throughout, its severing from the catalytic potential of comic energy is recapitulated through the off-stage death of Falstaff. That potential – momentarily revived by the Hostess's poignantly comic narrative, with even Pistol responding ('for Falstaff he is dead,/And we must ern therefore' (II.iii.5-6)) – goes into the grave with him. There follows an abrupt descent into the merely vicious, making unmistakable the threat to the national purpose: 'Let us to France, like horse-leeches, my boys,/To suck, to suck, the very blood to suck!' (55-6). Once in France, the last remaining thread linking this crew to Falstaff (and beyond him to

Prince Hal) is cut when the Boy rejects them as cowards and villains; significantly, the rhetoric of his soliloquy appropriates the subversive word-play of the Vice in a highly moral cause:

> They would have me as familiar with men's pockets as their gloves or their handkerchers; which makes much against my manhood, if I should take from another's pocket to put into mine; for it is plain pocketing up of wrongs. . . . Their villainy goes against my weak stomach, and therefore I must cast it up.
>
> (III.ii.47–53)

Fluellen, together with the other comic ethnic characters, inherits the mantle of Falstaff in his creative capacity. Thus the subversive forces are clearly divided along moral lines, according to the adage that Henry more obviously implements in politics – divide and rule. That Fluellen gets the dramatic job of putting paid to Pistol and what he represents fulfils the link with Henry that begins with their common Welshness, includes their mutual admiration, and extends to Fluellen's forgetting of Falstaff's name (IV.vii.48ff.). The changing of the low-comic guard[28] is formalized on the eve of Agincourt, when Pistol's cowardly bluster, which fails to recognize Harry Le Roy, gives way to the 'care and valor', only 'a little out of fashion', which Henry deduces from Fluellen's lecture on discipline. Fluellen takes on overtones of an Oberon-like shadow-self – except that his visibility is the point and that the balance of power has been reversed. When he becomes Henry's champion as simultaneously agent and butt of the practical joke on Williams, we get an emblem of the King, not as trickster (*pace* Mallett 1979), but as the trickster's would-be puppeteer. What remains constant about Henry is his detachment from the games he plays, even when he plays them in person (as in exposing the English traitors).

As a group, the ethnic characters, lively as they are, make tame bearers indeed of the comic burden. Their status as sober courageous officers marks them as mutations of the *miles gloriosus*, directly contradicting Falstaff's drunken and cowardly knighthood from their position in the middle-class – the solid core of the new state, despite the idyllically aristocratic inset death-scene of York and Suffolk (IV.vi.7ff.) perceptively singled out by Erickson (1985: 54–5). And, needless to say, by representing those nations of the British Isles whose factiousness runs from Richard II's Irish Wars to Owen Glendower to the Douglas, they promote a unity that hardly squares with their disruptive literary heritage. They willingly lend their festive sanction to Henry's struggle to make the play-world safe, hardly for democracy, but for romance.[29]

In Henry's manly but tender wooing of Katherine, a scene intensely engaging on the theatrical level, lies a parallel with the concluding romantic celebration of *Merchant*. Here, too, a manipulative and materialist context qualifies the ending's claim to transcendental closure. On the one hand, in professing his love Henry emblematically opens up his masculinist vision to the feminine – a suitable accompaniment to his restoration of Peace, gendered as female in Burgundy's plea ('Dear nurse of arts, plenties, and joyful births' (V.ii.35)). On the other hand, he conspicuously appropriates rather than integrates this dimension, thus doubly refuting the Salique law's prohibition against 'claiming from the female' (I.ii.92). Those who want peace 'must buy' it (V.ii.70), and Katherine is his 'capital demand' (96). This is her only role – one she has been preparing since the English lesson of Act III, Scene iv; by contrast, Henry is extending his repertoire of political postures and his mastery of languages. The same blunt eloquence that signals his sincerity denies emotional vulnerability: 'to say to thee that I shall die, is true; but for thy love, by the Lord, no; yet I love thee too' (150–2). The 'witchcraft in [her] lips' (275–6) will be put to work in making her 'a good soldier-breeder' (206).

Notoriously, Henry's accomplishments, like those of many other dramatic power-brokers in Shakespeare, remain morally reversible, depending on point of view. It is through the dynamic of subversion and counter-subversion that his final position most clearly reveals its false premises. For his success in imposing his script is frankly based upon the conscription of comic surfaces and the exclusion, justified by stigmatization, of the disruptive power associated with the potential for real transformation. Henry has worked to make himself master of that power, and the text has ostentatiously – one might say, overprotestingly – acted as his accomplice, producing a Pistol, a Fluellen, and a Katherine when required, to say nothing of effusive choric celebration. In the end, however, the Chorus itself hints that the 'spirits of the wise' are still in a position to mock him from the clouds. His romance world, premised on his 'redeeming' of 'time', his refusal to 'play the fools with the time', is overshadowed by the bloody future, '[w]hich oft our stage hath shown' (Epilogue 13). He is, like his father before him, a puppet of the past after all. Time reasserts itself as the ultimate subversive, irresistibly reproducing the human comedy in tragic guises.

IV

The Chorus's final subversion of temporal process by *preposterously* putting the future before the present roughly matches the pointedly anomalous relation of *Merry Wives* to the three Henry-plays. That relation is not substantially affected by the much-debated issues of dating or circumstances of first production. Fenton's mysterious past association with Hal and Poins makes for a gap that can never be filled, while the fact that Mistress Quickly and Falstaff are not acquainted suggests a calculated absurdity. Whatever the sequence of composition, Falstaff and his cronies existed, within a span of a few years, in two quite incompatible versions. By actively defying chronological placement *vis-à-vis* the tetralogy, *Merry Wives* becomes commentary upon it.

The burden of such commentary, no doubt, is the danger posed by the likes of Falstaff to the upright values of English community life. To this extent, the action reiterates (retrospectively or not) Falstaff's banishment in *2 Henry IV* and the later defeat of Pistol by Fluellen, with an explicit emphasis this time on the middle-class citizenry as the backbone of the nation. This much is amply acknowledged by the large body of criticism – amounting now to the dominant school – that deals with Falstaff's public punishment as a ritual scapegoating.[30] What remains to be recognized, however, is the central role of the dynamic of subversion and counter-subversion – a role that goes well beyond a pervasive 'delight in trickery' (Leggatt 1973: 146). The 'merry wives', though secure in their own virtue, respond to Falstaff as the threatening incarnation of disruptive energies and, like Hal, employ plots as a weapon against him. 'Trick' is the term of choice on both sides (see III.iii.191 and III.v.7), and both victors and victims point the moral in the lexis of festivity: the women set out to prove that 'Wives may be merry, and yet honest too' (IV.ii.105); Falstaff concludes, 'See now how wit may be made a Jack-a-lent, when 'tis upon ill employment!' (V.v.126–8).

But this is where the much diminished nature of this Falstaff comes in, when we compare him (as we are invited to do) with his counterpart in at least Part 1 of *Henry IV*. Disappointed as critics have generally been by the difference – to the point, in some cases, of scorning the character's lack of sexual prowess – it is highly functional. For Falstaff is pointedly punished for subversive energies that he does not possess:

> Fie on sinful fantasy!
> Fie on lust and luxury!
> Lust is but a bloody fire,
> Kindled with unchaste desire,
> Fed in heart, whose flames aspire,
> As thoughts do blow them, higher and higher.
>
> (V.v.93–8)

In fact, Falstaff's motives have been merely mercenary, while his crude schemes have notably lacked the witty invention, bordering on 'fantasy', of his opponents. He is consistently more duped than duping, beginning with his betrayal by Pistol and Nym (the isolation of the scapegoat is carried to the improbable extreme of having Pistol join his righteous tormentors). While Falstaff may well be 'given to fornications, and to taverns, and sack, and wine, and metheglins, and to drinkings and swearings and starings, pribbles and prabbles' (158–60), Sir Hugh's rhetoric exposes itself as inflationary. This scapegoating, then, involves an even more obvious construction of Falstaff as emblem of threatening disruption than is the case in the Henry-plays. When he puts on witch's clothing, he does so quite unwillingly.

At the same time, the self-consciously triumphant outcome of the multiple practices celebrates trickery's production of comic resolution. Apart from the exposure of Falstaff, the Host's deceptions make peace between Evans and Caius; Ford's jealousy is cured by the recoil of his own scheme; a three-layered plot, by which 'deceit loses the name of craft' (V.v.226), effects the romantic union of Fenton and Anne, prompting Ford to proclaim the defeat of rational plans by higher powers: 'Stand not amaz'd; here is no remedy./In love, the heavens themselves do guide the state' (231–2). The irony is that, apart from the motive, there has been nothing irrational or even impulsive about the lovers' actions – it is hardly an encounter with the unknown, a venturing of self – or for that matter about any of the other plots

and counterplots. In contrast with the comedies of transformation, there is no room for true trickery in this world, whose
interest is in preserving itself and its values intact.

The real trick, then, lies in creating the illusion of transformation: Ford comes to self-knowledge; Anne's parents are reconciled
to her match; even Falstaff is folded willy-nilly into the harmonious mixture: 'let us every one go home,/And laugh this sport
o'er by a country fire – /Sir John and all' (241–3). Yet Ford's
'madness' never possesses the diseased menace of, say, Jonson's
Kitely or Corvino, not to mention Shakespeare's later jealous
figures (despite striking anticipations of *Othello* in the exchange
with Pistol (II.i.109ff.)). Similarly, the parental opposition to
young love is unparalleled for its mild reasonableness, while the
dice are further loaded by having mother and father favour
different but equally absurd suitors. They are perfectly susceptible to Fenton's concluding speech, which both romantically
affirms the union as 'holy' (V.v.225) and, by condemning forced
marriage, claims further support in terms of social realism. In
sum, there is no need for the profound re-creation of the play-
world produced by the chaotic energies of Puck.[31]

This brings us to the ersatz fairies by whom Falstaff is 'made an
ass' (119) – though he can never be made a Bottom. They furnish
abundant echoes of the earlier play – certainly enough to bring
out the differences – but also anticipate *The Alchemist*, where the
Fairy Queen is played by the namesake of Mistress Quickly's
companion elsewhere (with a character to match). The show that
Dol Common, Subtle, and Face put on is similarly in aid of a
fraudulent process of transformation.[32] There, too, the reality is
the outwitting of the gull who fancies himself clever. But
Jonson's text, far from harnessing its tricks to a resolution
borrowed from romantic comedy, merely exposes them; it
embraces its cynicism by having the principal thief get away with
his loot. In *Merry Wives*, there is only one such unresolved
duping – a highly suggestive one, however. In a conspicuously
extraneous incident, three Germans steal the Host's horses.
According to Bardolph, they 'set spurs and away, like three
German devils, three Doctor Faustuses' (IV.v.68–70). It is as close
as the play comes to genuine subversive magic, to the 'cozenage'
of Ephesis, and there is a contrast both with Falstaff's failed
swindling and, as the gloating Sir Hugh realizes, with the Host's
smug cleverness:

there is three cozen-germans that has cozen'd all the hosts of
Readins, of Maidenhead, of Colebrook, of horses and
money. . . . You are wise and full of gibes and vlouting-
stocks, and 'tis not convenient you should be cozen'd.

(77–82)

Like the allusions to less-than-idyllic futures with which both
Pistol and the Chorus take their leave in *Henry V*, this points to a
world beyond the play where subversiveness is not so easily
appropriated and exorcized. Windsor may not be the universe
after all.

V

When Falstaff, moving, in the guise of self-expansion, towards
the powerless role of 'allow'd fool', defines himself as 'not only
witty in myself, but the cause that wit is in other men', he
detaches 'wit' from his own subversiveness; in effect, he gives it
away to be used against him, just as Hal is currently doing
through the Page and as he will continue to do in more serious
ways. It is clear even from *Taming* that linguistic subversiveness,
the natural ally of catalytic disruption in the early plays, can be
appropriated for the specific purpose of resisting such disruption. In *Love's Labor's Lost*, 'wit' emerges as a specialized and
self-conscious language-game, playable – and potentially win-
nable – by both the allies and the opponents of transformation. If
the self-protectively mocking lords are finally sent off to reform
their wits, the witty subversives conspicuously owe their triumph
less to their superiority in that department than to death as *deus
ex machina*.

The intensely witty romantic comedies of the middle period –
Much Ado about Nothing, *As You Like It*, and *Twelfth Night* –
uniformly presume an opposition between wit, even when
ostensibly linked with folly, and elements presented as authentically disruptive. Thus in the mock-prayer of Feste, transparently
'the witty rationalist who assumes the motley of the fool' (Lyons
1971: 58), technical skill takes the place of inspiration: 'Wit, and't
be thy will, put me into good fooling!' (I.v.32–3). He is telling a
truth foolishly even when he denies the outward signs of his
profession and identifies himself as merely a 'corrupter of words'.

A paradox lurks in the conspicuous support that wit lends to

129

the pursuit and fulfilment of love. That emotion, moreover, presents itself as more deeply subversive for most of these romantic principals than it is for Portia and Bassanio, whose 'course of true love', but for Shylock, would run altogether too smoothly. Love, for the later figures, tends to involve the overturning of a mode of being, a displacement from identity, a posture of conflict and struggle. The amorous Rosalind and Viola are trapped by their disguises, as are Beatrice and Benedick by their public personae. Yet, as has often been observed, such calculated alternative identities also confer liberation by supplying a distance and perspective on feelings – an effect consistent with a defensive application of wit.

Certainly, perspective on their situations is widely recognized as a source of strength for these characters; their self-possession has inspired much critical admiration. At the same time, Shakespeare's development of the witty heroine in particular has been credited with producing a new order of comedy based on disruptive–creative playing. Nevo speaks of a virtual feminizing of subversive elements, 'the transmission to the woman of a masculine comic energy, of racy wit and high spirits, of irony and improvization, of the uninhibited zest for mockery which were the prerogatives of maverick and adventurous males' (Nevo 1980: 160). Yet, as with Falstaff, such engaging self-consciousness may mask a textual strategy for blunting subversion. After all, one of the basic principles of the early plays is the value, for the sake of personal and textual transformation, of a reduction to utter helplessness such as Hermia articulates: 'I can no further crawl, no further go' (*MND*, III.ii.444).

Despite the successful romantic consummations in the later plays, that part of love's potential to transform which works through chaos and destruction is resisted by their central characters – literally, outwitted. It may be argued that the 'loose ends' notoriously present in the resulting comic closures, in comparison with *The Comedy of Errors* and *A Midsummer Night's Dream*, reflect a corresponding incompleteness in the experience. At the same time, the characters left out of the final harmonies – Don John, Jaques, Malvolio – hardly pose challenges or provoke reservations on the scale of Shylock. There is a similar symbolic splitting of the subversive between positive and negative: wise folly in various forms is harnessed to comic closure; opposition to such closure is stigmatized as villainous, melancholy, or both.

But so successful is the former operation that lesser scapegoats can effect the second.

VI

Much critical ado has been occasioned by the tendency of Beatrice and Benedick to eclipse Hero and Claudio. The parallel with Falstaff and Shylock, who similarly threaten to take over their texts (but are punished for it), points to the imaginative appeal of subversive energy, but it is easy to mistake the reciprocal jibing of the two rivals in wit, highly energetic as it is, for the essence of their dynamism. What lends them their compelling interest is the interplay between hostility and attraction – the coexistence of war and love, in contrast to Claudio's cold-blooded decision to interest himself in one after the other. In this interplay, wit is employed to keep subversive feelings at bay by projecting them outwards in rationalized form. It is a tactic familiar from Berowne, who has much in common with Benedick in particular, including a penchant for eavesdropping.

But whereas Berowne uses his fortuitously acquired knowledge in aid of his counter-subversive manipulations, Benedick is duped into love, or the realization of love – hence the parallel with Malvolio in his subsequent 'reading' of Beatrice's superficially hostile words: 'Ha! "Against my will I am sent to bid you come in to dinner" – there's a double meaning in that' (*Ado*, II.iii.257-9). On the other hand, Sir Toby and company, with their strong subversive affinities, redirect their victim's self-love in order to expose it, while Benedick and Beatrice are merely manipulated into dropping barriers of 'will' self-protectively erected against their feelings for each other. The presence of such feelings may be inferred from their obsessive antagonism, but the text provides more pointed hints – Beatrice's initial enquiry about Benedick's safety, her veiled allusions to love as having once been an issue between them.

The first of these allusions introduces the equivocation regarding folly that runs throughout the play:

> He set up his bills here in Messina, and challeng'd Cupid at the flight, and my uncle's fool, reading the challenge, subscrib'd for Cupid, and challeng'd him at the burbolt.
>
> (I.i.39–42)

To engage oneself for love is to become a fool. The idea is a commonplace of the dynamics of comic subversion, and it figures equally in Benedick's resistance (revealingly, before it would seem to be needed) to the threat he reads into Claudio's example:

> I do much wonder that one man, seeing how much another man is a fool when he dedicates his behaviors to love, will, after he hath laughed at such shallow follies in others, become the argument of his own scorn by falling in love – and such a man is Claudio. . . . [Love] shall never make me such a fool.
>
> (II.iii.7–26)

Yet it is precisely Beatrice's compulsive exercise of scornful wit, keeping such folly at a distance, that makes her her 'uncle's fool' in a narrower, less flattering sense, as in the verbal sparring that begins Act II, Scene ii. The same goes for her counterpart. Her description of him (to his vizored face) as 'the Prince's jester, a very dull fool' (II.i.137–8), hits home, even if her further accusation of a taste for 'slanders' (138) and 'villainy' (140) gives him credit for a deeper, darker subversiveness, which in fact the text locates elsewhere.[33] In effect, both characters are taking refuge from the disruptive energy of passion in the role of 'corrupter of words', and it is especially apparent how hard Beatrice must struggle to keep her heart, 'poor fool . . . on the windy side of care' (314–15).

The actual tricking of Beatrice and Benedick, then, merely releases, rather than imparts, subversive energy. In this respect, at least, the gullers are less powerful than they imagine. Nor is their trickery in itself an exercise of such energy – it could not be, given their *sang froid*. In contrast with the duping of Malvolio, which is boisterously conceived in terms of gulling, fooling, and sport (see *TN*, II.iii.133ff. and II.v, *passim*), Don Pedro employs the language of calculation, setting himself to 'practice' (II.i.382) against Benedick's 'quick wit and his queasy stomach' (383–4). When he echoes Beatrice's image of the archery contest in expressing his plan to displace Cupid as 'the only love-gods' (II.i.386), he aims the project at control not merely over Benedick, whose cleverness and independence are clearly threatening, but over love itself.[34] He has already hastened to assume such a power in wooing on behalf of Claudio. Certainly, he and his protégé will later appear god-like – super- and so in-human – when they hurl their thunderbolt at Hero. It is obviously ironic that these manipulators of false appearances in order to produce love prove so vulnerable to a fabricated scenario (also involving the malleable Margaret) intended to destroy it. Yet in both cases their attitude is characterized by coldness, distance, and a preoccupation with gaining the upper hand:

> Claud.: If I see any thing to-night why I
> should not marry her, to-morrow in the
> congregation, where I should wed, there will
> I shame her.
> D. Pedro: And as I woo'd for thee to obtain
> her, I will join with thee to disgrace her.
>
> (III.ii.123–7)

The laugh that Benedick invariably provokes when he emerges from his hiding place is ultimately on the audience itself, for, in a basic sense, he is right: 'This can be no trick' (II.iii.220).

When we return, from this vantage point, to the relation between plot and subplot, it is easy to recognize Don Pedro as an internal playwright along the lines of Prince Hal.[35] Beatrice and Benedick effectively enact, for his benefit, a play-within-the-play *containing* those subversive elements which apparently have no place, despite the much-invoked name of love, in the sound arrangements and ordered patterns of his world. Claudio makes a natural accomplice, a young egotist whose tie with his patron, revealed as shallow by a readiness to believe him treacherous, still appears far more important than the love he professes. Don Pedro is, in effect, as much a plotter as his melancholy brother, except that he seeks to control and sanitize, rather than to overturn. In the absence of political considerations, moreover, his motives become equally mysterious – that is, they recede into his structural function. The effect is to throw into relief Don John's emergence as his disruptive opposite.[36]

Don John has nothing tangible to gain, apparently, but he takes the conventional trickster-villain's delight in thwarting the plans of Don Pedro and his favourite, who 'hath all the glory of my overthrow' (I.iii.67). Such a triangular power-struggle anticipates Iago's relation to Cassio and Othello, but the ultimate model is Satan's use of mankind as a vehicle for revenge against God. In this light, Don John appears all the more clearly as a stigmatized emblem of the subversive principle, ready

equipped, like the 'devil' Shylock, to serve as eventual scapegoat. Yet the obvious implication of the splitting of good and
evil between brothers – a motif doubled (through a change in
the source) in *As You Like It* – is that both belong to the same
family.

Don John's trick makes a revealing mirror-image of his
brother's conspiracy. While Don Pedro and his minion put off
the emotional potency of love upon Beatrice and Benedick, they
retain intact its courtly façade, the self-aggrandizing idealization
and trappings of honour. In the guise of an assault on their
friend's misogyny, they project a far deeper fear and distrust of
women. Don John ensures that these manoeuvres become visible
– at least to those who can read the signs. Sign-reading is
precisely the issue, as the well-known pun in the title signals, and
it is especially notable that the Friar embraces the imputation of
folly for the sake of the innocence written in Hero's face: 'Call me
a fool,/Trust not my reading, nor my observations' (IV.i.164–5).
The career of the slandered Hero has often been compared to that
of Hermione; a more telling parallel is between the impact of
Margaret's performance and Leontes' grotesquely faithless response to the scenes that he observes between his wife and friend.

Beatrice instantly reads correctly, in the light of her faith in her
cousin, the subtext of the would-be wedding that Don Pedro and
Claudio turn into the equivalent of Hermione's trial. The
chillingly self-congratulatory apostrophe of Claudius ('O Hero!
what a Hero hadst thou been' (IV.i.100ff.)) deploys sensitivity
and disillusion as a transparent screen for gratification at being
able now to 'turn all beauty into thoughts of harm' (107) – the
very credo of Don John. Yet Leonato is merely overwhelmed,
reacting first with one of Shakespeare's single most powerful
tragic lines – 'Hath no man's dagger here a point for me?' (109) –
then with desperate rage. Beatrice takes on Paulina's role,
defiantly rejecting the notion that Hero has reason to swoon:
'Why, how now, cousin, wherefore sink you down?' (110). What
is more, she is seconded by Benedick, who decisively separates
himself from his friends by staying behind, solicitous for both
daughter ('How doth the lady?' (113)) and father ('Sir, sir, be
patient' (143)).

Benedick remains, of course, for Beatrice's sake. In a *de facto*
alliance of subversive energies, the emotional chaos stirred up by
Don John provides the real meeting ground for their mutual

feelings, although it takes some pressure before Benedick accepts her injunction – a shocking contrast with her earlier witty poses – to '[k]ill Claudio' (289). Her challenges to his manhood, which signal a frustration at female victimization, are mingled with perfectly accurate depictions of Claudio's conduct: 'What, bear her in hand until they come to take hands, and then with public accusation, uncover'd slander, unmitigated rancor-' (303-6). Benedick's response should not be dismissed as a shallow chivalrous posture; his sense of injustice is foregrounded, and shown to be bound up with faith in Beatrice:

> *Bene.:* Think you in your soul the Count
> Claudio hath wrong'd Hero?
> *Beat.:* Yea, as sure as I have a thought or a
> soul.
> *Bene.:* Enough, I am engag'd, I will challenge
> him.
>
> (328-32)

The stressful and destructive quality of the disaster, then, has a productive, as well as a revelatory, aspect. Nor is this limited to Beatrice and Benedick. In his grief and anger, even Leonato – almost universally the victim of bad critical press – develops unsuspected depths, including a renewed trust in his child ('My soul doth tell me Hero is belied' (V.i.42)). His rhetoric of pain in this scene is certainly inflated, but in a way that carries a distinctly tragic coding. A cognate dramatic situation is Hieronimo's response to the death of his son in Thomas Kyd's *The Spanish Tragedy*, and I suggest that the encounter of the two pathetic old men with Claudio and Don Pedro swells the generic counter-current by intertextually engaging that perennially popular play. Despite its knowledge of Hero's survival, a contemporary audience would surely have been put in mind of the notorious tragic precedent for a callous refusal, also on the part of a Spanish nobleman and his protégé, to hear a father's plea for justice – a refusal that pointedly generates the fulfilment of 'revenging threats' (Kyd, *Spanish Tragedy*, III.vii.73):

> *Leon.:* My lord, my lord –
> *D. Pedro:* I will not hear you.
> *Leon.:* No? Come, brother, away! I will be heard.
> *Ant.:* And shall, or some of us will smart for it.
>
> (106-9)

The self-righteous brutality of Claudio and Don Pedro is nowhere more grotesque than in their mockery of these brothers, in which they expect Benedick to join: 'We had lik'd to have had our two noses snapp'd off with two old men without teeth' (115–16). The bitter effect gains an edge from the reminiscence of Leonato's praise, in the first scene, of Claudio's own uncle for emotionally greeting the news of his safety: 'How much better is it to weep at joy than to joy at weeping!' (I.i.27–9). The Friar's main rationale for his ruse – 'Th' idea of [Hero's] life shall sweetly creep/Into his study of imagination' (IV.i.224–5), filling Claudio with remorse – has been shattered. But then the openness to such subversion explicitly depends on emotional commitment ('If ever love had interest in his liver' (231)).

The conflict between Benedick's passionate sincerity and his former friends' immunity to feeling directly focuses on the role of wit. Benedick not only refuses to employ his wit to amuse them ('It is in my scabbard, shall I draw it?' (V.i.125)) but recognizes their use of wit to parry urgent emotional reality as essentially aggressive: 'Sir, I shall meet your wit in the career, and you charge it against me' (135–6). Yet, ominously, their witty banter frustrates Benedick's attempt to press home his challenge; the two sides are simply speaking different languages, and the encounter ends with an absence of resolution that makes the gap obvious. Benedick's statement of unfinished business again hints at a tragic outcome – 'You have among you kill'd a sweet and innocent lady. For my Lord Lack-beard there, he and I shall meet, and till then peace be with him' (192–3) – but the last word goes, in effect, to the comic framework, as Don Pedro comments, 'What a pretty thing man is when he goes in his doublet and hose and leaves off his wit!' (199–200). This is the cue for the 'corrupter[s] of words' who bear legal authority in the world of this text to enter, bringing as prisoners – one recalls the bound Duke in *Two Gentlemen* – the instruments of comic resolution. The generic reversion is focused by a reprise of *The Spanish Tragedy*, particularly recalling the moment when Hieronimo learns the murderers' identities by way of the intercepted letter of Pedringano to his master, the King's nephew:

Holp he to murder mine Horatio?
And actors in th' accursed tragedy

Wast thou, Lorenzo, Balthazar and thou,
Of whom my son, my son, deserv'd so well?
(Kyd, Spanish Tragedy, III.vii.40–3)

<table>
<tr><td>Leon.:</td><td>Art thou the slave that with thy breath hast kill'd
Mine innocent child?</td></tr>
<tr><td>Bor.:</td><td align="right">Yea, even I alone.</td></tr>
<tr><td>Leon.:</td><td>No, not so, villain, thou beliest thyself.
Here stand a pair of honorable men.</td></tr>
</table>

(V.i.263–6)

In making Dogberry and his crew the means of exposing the slander, Shakespeare superficially places a value on 'wise folly' at the expense of the aristocrats' foolish wisdom. Yet the privilege of stating this moral – 'What your wisdoms could not discover, these shallow fools have brought to light' (V.i.232–4) – goes to Borachio, that prototype of the slandering Jachimo, and while his momentary centring as truly repentant comes at the expense of Don Pedro and Claudio, he also offers them a way out of responsibility. In a way that anticipates the villains of *As You Like It*, he not only assumes the burden of guilt, repudiating his subversive affiliation, but makes good and evil black and white, the truth a matter of factual discovery. Such 'wise' – and here explicitly legal – folly as Dogberry's is analogously 'shallow': the mistaking of words cancels out the mistaking of appearances. 'Noting' actually becomes 'Nothing'. To be written down an ass is a far cry from becoming one.

Given the revelatory impact of Don John's subversions, to vindicate the play as comedy by reviving Hero requires his defeat by a plausible representative of the genre itself. It is precisely Dogberry's flagrant clownishness that enables him to reimpose the law of genre so genially, coming to the rescue of the truly destructive textual manipulators while draining the potential of the disruptive emotional forces that have been unleashed.[37] A more than superficial transformation in the play's characters and relationships would require pursuing the chaos and confrontations set in motion by Don John and sustained by the love-driven Benedick. Instead, Don Pedro's (literal) construction of Don John as outlaw – 'He is compos'd and fram'd of treachery,/ And fled he is upon this villainy' (249–50) – enables Claudio to fulfil the Friar's expectation, in a highly ironic way, by recovering faith in his own former projection – a process to which death, apparently, poses no obstacle: 'Sweet Hero, now thy image doth appear / In the rare semblance that I lov'd it first' (251–2). Since it is the 'semblance' that has counted all along, he has no trouble accepting as a substitute '[a]lmost the copy of my child that's dead' (289), especially given her status as prospective double-heiress.

More remarkable is Leonato's immediate turnabout, not only in attitude, but in style – his willingness, despite the unapologetic insistence of Claudio and Don Pedro that they 'sinn'd . . . not, / But in mistaking' (274–5), to settle for a gesture of penitence. In effect, he offers them another occasion for egotistical self-display and assures them that responsibility can be kept at a safe distance. But then the next scene strangely shows Benedick and Beatrice, too, returning to something very like their earlier witty sparring even before they hear of Don John's exposure. Certainly, the new premise is their acknowledged love, but the supposed opposition between 'wisdom' and love has clearly been re-established in Benedick's mind: the only rhymes he can devise to express love are 'baby', 'horn', and 'fool' (V.ii.37–9), so he gives up on poetry. He soon tells Beatrice, 'Thou and I are too wise to woo peaceably' (72). Even the recent focuses of painful emotion, the challenge of Claudio and the suffering of Hero, are incorporated into the lighter tone, given the distance of a remembered dream. Yet far less has changed – indeed, *nothing* – than in the post-Puckian dispensation of *A Midsummer Night's Dream*. It is as if the tragic cloud has simply passed over, or, more precisely, as if those characters susceptible to subversive energy, having stretched their comic tethers nearly to the breaking point, have been snapped back sharply into place. Dogberry's revelation and the casting out of Don John serve above all to emblematize the text's generic dynamic.

In so far as that dynamic is self-protective, keeping subversive elements at bay, it is inevitable that the outlook of Don Pedro and Claudio triumphs at the conclusion. Wit is securely installed as the sign of comic energy under control, while Beatrice and Benedick retreat from their mutual commitment. They are at once driven back together by a brief reprise of the original conspiracy, as evidence of their affection is produced – an artificial 'miracle' ('our own hands against our hearts' (V.iv.91–

2)) that puts them at the mercy of the dominant characters. The subplot is effectively re-integrated on the main plot's terms. Benedick is meekly reconciled to Claudio. He stops Beatrice's potentially subversive mouth with a kiss[38] – an emblem of the silencing of women in the cause of romantic closure (and an anticipation of Troilus (*Tro.*, III.ii.133ff.)). He not only accepts again the role of jester, wittily making light of love, but extends it, in the decisive breaking of the subversive alliance, to include the witty punishing of the scapegoat: 'I'll devise thee brave punishments for him' (127–8). There is just a hint of deeper anxieties in Leonato's wish to delay the dance until after the wedding, but it is Benedick who addresses the element most profoundly qualifying this festivity: 'Prince, thou art sad, get thee a wife, get thee a wife' (122). Don Pedro's sadness goes well beyond any sense of loneliness one might sentimentally wish to project upon him. In terms of his textual status, his is the sadness, less of Antonio, about to lose Bassanio to Portia, than of Prospero. He is left in the position of the manipulator–dramatist who has succeeded so thoroughly that he no longer has a part to play: he is, in a double sense, written out.

VII

The tribute conventionally paid to *As You Like It* and *Twelfth Night* as the supreme examples of Shakespeare's art of romantic comedy is also a tribute to the sophistication of these texts in suppressing the very comic energies they appear to celebrate. I do not wish to suggest that there is something 'dishonest' about this achievement or that to be conscious of it should spoil an audience's enjoyment of Arden or Illyria, Rosalind or Viola. But the titles of both plays, even as they link that enjoyment with wish-fulfilment, also point to the gifts offered the heroes and heroines themselves: they are surely comprehended in the 'you' of *As You Like It* and *What You Will*. And perhaps foremost amongst those gifts is the fragmentation, displacement, and assimilation of subversive forces to the extent that no character *need* take on the cunning of Portia or the coldness of Hal or the smugness of Claudio in order to avoid subversive challenges. These are, in fact, the two plays in which the text most willingly takes upon itself, for the sake of its characters' smooth sailing, the responsibility for withholding confrontation with the darker sides of life and love. The extent of the evasion, nevertheless, may be read as a measure of underlying textual anxiety.

In these last two plays of the middle series, the prismatic splitting of disruptive energy into more-or-less marginal forms is carried farther than ever before – one of the reasons, ironically, that they are so often perceived as pervasively festive.[39] We get a professional 'wise fool' in both, and each is further labelled with a traditional subversive sign – Touchstone's sexual drive, Feste's parasitical scavenging. However, their reassuring tameness is quickly established: Touchstone would 'go along o'er the wide world' (*AYL*, I.iii.132) with his mistress; Feste's fecklessness and world-weariness take the sting out of his cynicism – except with regard to Malvolio.

In *Twelfth Night*, the pointed lack of the *festive* spirit in its eponymous representative is superficially more than balanced by its ostentatious abundance in and around Sir Toby. In fact, that emblem of licence remains firmly under his niece's thumb, as well as being stigmatized by his dependence on drink (as opposed to Falstaff's identification with it) for subversive inspiration.[40] At the same time, the figure formally defined as anti-festive is made more potent than his counterpart in *As You Like It*, so that his defeat through the 'midsummer madness' (III.iv.56) thrust upon him carries stronger overtones of festive affirmation, even as these are kept at a safe distance from the lady of the house, whose rules, after all, he has been enforcing ('My lady bade me tell you, that though she harbors you as her kinsman, she's nothing allied to your disorders' (II.iii.95–7)). Malvolio's scapegoating thus helps make up for the absence of the killjoy villains Frederick and Oliver, whose conversions can more positively authorize the pastoral vision. In contrast with Malvolio, Touchstone's puritanical 'opponent' gladly functions as court-entertainer, takes the world as grist to his mill ('I can suck melancholy out of a song, as a weasel sucks eggs' (*AYL*, II.v.12–13)), and has the source of his hypocrisy located more abstractly in the off-stage past: 'For thou thyself hast been a libertine,/As sensual as the brutish sting itself' (II.vii.65–6). Discreetly marginal throughout, he can be allowed to exempt himself from the comic closure without impinging on its validity. He need not be run out of town.

Touchstone would range over the world – but only in order to remain with Celia; his influence is personal and local. Feste is not even bound by steady employment, and he does in fact have the run of Illyria, as if he embodies an aspect of its atmosphere: 'Foolery, sir, does walk about the orb like the sun, it shines every where' (III.i.38–9). He even gets the last word on that world in his concluding song. The contrast suggests much about Illyria as opposed to Arden. So does *As You Like It*'s assignment of the initiatory disruption – the ticket to Arden – to human agents, while *Twelfth Night* supplies a shipwreck whose finesse in separating but preserving brother and sister would do credit to Ariel. Frederick and Oliver, wicked brothers both, are graduates of the Don John academy of comic villainy; *Twelfth Night* does without villains at all. All in all, despite their obvious links, including a similar diffusion of subversive elements, the two plays operate on sharply divergent premises.

Just as Illyria encompasses the entire action of *Twelfth Night*, so it comprises a spectrum of positive and negative forces, which, although sometimes associated with particular characters, certainly do not depend on human agency. It is a universe with its own deterministic dynamic, anticipating, in this respect, the worlds of the late romances. The initiatives of its inhabitants are circumscribed; the broader pattern is always understood to be out of their hands, and Viola's acknowledgement of this fact, in terms of time itself as the governing principle, is linked to her success: 'O time, thou must untangle this, not I,/It is too hard a knot for me t'untie' (II.ii.40–1).[41] Feste is not just mitigating his own responsibility but recognizing the wider context of his actions when he moralizes the humiliation of Malvolio: 'And thus the whirligig of time brings in his revenges' (V.i.376–7).

The looming shadow of textual destiny reinforces the entropic quality of Illyria, the fantasy-ridden self-indulgence of its inhabitants. In contrast with *The Comedy of Errors*, where the Abbess suddenly intervenes as *dea ex machina*, equally surprising the audience and the characters themselves, this play sets reassuring limits throughout to its productive 'errors'; a heavy hand is palpable in the convenient provision of substitute partners – Sebastian for Cesario, Viola for Olivia. Yet the supply of substitutes, by supporting the premise of inclusiveness, helps to obscure the fact that challenging elements are repressed and excluded, not integrated. Neither Orsino nor Olivia need come to terms with the futility of impossible longings, while Sebastian's openness to the impossible in the form of Olivia's offered love recalls *The Comedy of Errors* only so as to reveal major differences: 'Or I am mad, or else this is a dream./Let fancy still my sense in Lethe steep;/If it be thus to dream, still let me sleep!' (IV.i.61–3). Superficially, he resembles Antipholus when confronted by Adriana, as is noted by Leggatt (1974: 245), but there is no context of spiritual quest – he is on a sight-seeing tour – and the present handed him is no 'tangled chain' to draw him into confusion, but the nearest road to romantic closure. He shortly learns on his own to distinguish 'wonder' and 'error' from 'madness' (IV.iii.1ff.). His sibling, meanwhile, in a blatant reversal of the effects of mistaking in the early play, is able to deduce his existence when she is approached by Antonio; far from tricking her into chaos, her imagination points her towards the dénouement two acts away: 'Prove true, imagination, O, prove true,/That I, dear brother, be now ta'en for you! (III.iv.375–6).

As You Like It, on the other hand, purports to give its characters both the duty and the power of shaping their world, at least to a point. What Arden chiefly offers them, with its pointedly *natural* mixture of good and bad, wisdom and folly, realism and fantasy, is the freedom to do so ('Are not these woods/More free from peril than the envious court?' (II.i.3–4)). There is indeed, as Orlando points out, 'no clock in the forest' (III.ii.301) – no time in Viola's sense. Rather, Rosalind, Touchstone, and Jaques all, in their diverse ways, establish time as the medium and measure of human existence. In the final matching-up, the only amatory substitution – Silvius for Ganymed – is Rosalind's own contrivance. Apart from the benediction of Hymen, it is only to deal with the threats posed to Arden itself that a supernatural helping hand is needed, and it comes in the conventional form of sudden susceptibilities to conversion; significantly, too, the villains first weaken themselves – divide the force they represent – by turning against each other:

Oli.:   O that your Highness knew my heart in this!
          I never lov'd my brother in my life.
Duke F.: More villain thou.

                                                        (III.i.13–15)

The basic difference between the dramatic universes has an obvious bearing on the two central heroines, who, in their attitudes towards the world around them, are virtual opposites.

Viola's passivity is signalled by an attraction to servitude and self-concealment suggestive of a retreat to the womb:

> O that I serv'd that lady,
> And might not be delivered to the world
> Till I had made mine own occasion mellow
> What my estate is!
>
> (I.ii.41–4)

In the absence of a clear rationale, her disguise simply externalizes her sense of lost identity, and even this is mitigated by the fact that, as she later discloses, she is imitating her brother. Her posture of resignation makes a convincing imitation of openness to disruption. Yet she is never called upon to undergo the radically disorienting and disheartening experiences of her counterparts in *The Comedy of Errors* or *A Midsummer Night's Dream*. Her encounters with disruptive characters hardly intrude on her sensibility: she admires Feste's professionalism; the challenge instigated by Sir Toby literally recoils (thanks to a highly artificial coincidence) on his own head. And as for love, that internal source of subversion which elsewhere enables transformation, Viola shields herself from its impact, chiefly through a well-founded teleological faith in the dramatic medium she calls 'time'. Her self-protective bent is clearly displayed when, through narrative, she projects the fatal effects of unrequited love upon an imaginary sister (II.iv.107ff.).

Rosalind, by contrast, has won critical hearts for generations by her strength, initiative, and, especially, wit. Her disguise, assumed for perfectly rational purposes, is maintained for the opportunities it offers her. Even if she sometimes expresses a sense of entrapment, it increasingly indicates power, not impotence. Recently, she has renewed her attractiveness as a positive model of androgyny, a successful mediator/mediatrix between 'feminine' and 'masculine' qualities (Rackin 1987: 36–7). Such praise understandably comes at the expense of the egregiously sappy Orlando, although it may also undervalue the heroine's (shorter) side-kick, who chooses exile with her friend in a more decisive way than in the source[42] and who achieves the rare feat of spending most of the play unequivocally female, unfailingly supportive, and *not* in love. Paradoxically, Rosalind's sceptical undercutting of the excessively romantic seduces so thoroughly because her driving motive is always understood to be romantic fulfilment. So it has generally escaped notice that her genial domination of her milieu, pointedly extended to the audience in her Epilogue,[43] is also an evasion of love's disruptive influence. Disruption in this play, after all, is more obviously located externally and dealt with accordingly.

Such is not the case with the crudely conventional model of inner conflict that Shakespeare found in Thomas Lodge's narrative romance. Particularly striking, given the association of chaos elsewhere with potentially creative disorder, is Lodge's account of his Rosalynde's debate with herself 'betwéene a *Chaos* of confused thoughtes', as she struggles with 'passions . . . greater than [her] patience' (Lodge, *Rosalynde*, 174). The obstacle to her love is a highly rational one – the low estate of Rosader (Orlando's counterpart) – and when it is overcome, a song celebrates (in delectably infelicitous verse) the delectable infelicity of love itself:

> *Love in my bosome like a Bee*
> *doth sucke his sweete:*
> *Now with his wings he playes with me,*
> *now with his feete.*

(175)[44]

In Lodge's version, Rosalynde does no 'educating' of her lover; their courtship games in the forest are simply (not just partly) her device to keep him close to her. Though less detached (joining him in a love-duet), she is more passive, and when she effects the climactic revelation, she does not take credit for the 'magic': in a way familiar to psychiatrists, the responsibility is assigned to a (male) 'friend' (246). But in a sense, she really does not transform herself: transformation is the text's prerogative, as much beyond her control as the helpless folly of love itself. Shakespeare's development of this one-dimensional figure into an instrument for gentle and sophisticated parody of romantic love involves at once a repression and an appropriation of the transformational dynamic. Rosalind's 'magic' is her own, but it is not magic, any more than Sir Hugh Evans and Pistol and Mistress Quickly are true fairies.

Apart from the distance on her love-stricken self that Rosalind maintains through her wit and her disguise, the dice are further loaded by the treatment of Orlando. He is not merely subject to a genteel 'amorous melancholie' (Lodge, *Rosalynde*, 210), like Rosader, but tainted (albeit charmingly) with a generalized emotional excess more reminiscent of his name-sake in Ariosto. The ambivalence attached to this quality begins with his initial rebellion against his brother. Just though his case is, his hostility and potential for violence – there is an anticipatory trace of Edmund ('The courtesy of nations allows you my better, in that you are the first born, but the same tradition takes not away my blood' (*AYL*, I.i.46–8)) – signal a wildness in need of love's civilizing influence. Obviously, the key to harmony in Arden is to '[find] tongues in trees' (II.i.16), not to impose one's own language on them, and Orlando's folly is pointedly shown to be out of step even with the authorized version of Touchstone, who finds his poetry deficient, interestingly, in the rational quality of craftsmanship: 'This is the very false gallop of verses' (III.ii.113). Overall, Orlando's experience within the 'free' world of Arden, beginning with the Duke's rebuke of his brash (but selfless) demand for food, is aimed at teaching him emotional self-control. Unimpeachable as that virtue may be, earlier comic transformations have depended precisely on a loss of control. Here, through its benign interventions, the text presents such a state of chaos as an obstacle to romantic fulfilment, even while pretending to value it, as when Rosalind – wittily – finds Orlando deficient in signs of 'careless desolation' (381).

Thus the deflation of Orlando's romantic fantasies, in the face of his desire not to be 'cur'd' (425), is both more and less than the education in reality it pretends to be: 'But these are all lies: men have died from time to time, and worms have eaten them, but not for love' (IV.i.106–8). The sentiment is worthy of the ladies in *Love's Labor's Lost*, with its implicit insistence on mortality as the context for all human passion and relationships. And it is expressed with a similar wit. But conspicuously absent here is the praxis that backs up the idea in the earlier play and signals the need for its integration into the romantic self. Arden makes an easier training ground than a hospital; the death of deer is easier to accommodate, as the Princess herself makes clear (*LLL*, IV.i.24ff.), than the death of human beings. We should equally allow ourselves to be reminded of the hard-headed 'realism' of Benedick, whose wit, like Berowne's, is counter-subversive:

D. Pedro: I shall see thee, ere I die, look pale with love.

Bene.: With anger, with sickness, or with hunger, my lord,
not with love.

(Ado, I.i.247–50)

In this context, the educational programme that Rosalind
administers appears notably superficial. Yet thanks to the miracles that rally to the aid of her project, nothing further is needed.
Jaques's repudiation of the dance, his plan to seek out the
convertite, and his retreat to the Duke's 'abandon'd cave'
(V.iv.196) – an emblematic rebuke, it seems, of the unfulfilled
'uses of adversity' (II.i.12) – do no more than gesture, from a
discredited stance, towards the incompleteness of the learning
that has taken place: they situate the dark side of subversion far
more innocuously than does the unresolved hostility of Malvolio.
Still, his choice of 'other than dancing measures' (193) comments
sharply on the Duke's triple use of the word 'measure' to link the
dance, the lovers' joy, and the restored social structure. After
declaring that all shall partake in the new order 'according to the
measure of their states' (175), he has urged, 'you brides and
bridegrooms all,/With measure heap'd in joy, to th' measures
fall' (178–9). The term signals that the dancing which ends *Much
Ado* and *Twelfth Night* (but not the earlier comedies) with a
metatheatrical illustration of festivity provides a Renaissance
image of energy firmly harnessed in the service of social and
cosmic order. The pointed insinuation of measurement into
comic resolution suggests a qualitative difference from the
measureless joy and wonder that conclude *The Comedy of Errors*
and *A Midsummer Night's Dream.* It also looks forward to the
retributive ethic and more severely circumscribed fulfilments of
Measure for Measure.

VIII

Finally, a brief return to the dilemma of Brutus, mentioned
earlier as epitomizing the problematic attitude of the middle
plays towards the disruptive energies within them. He is no
Richard III, no scourge of the times produced by the times
themselves, but a 'realistically' drawn character in whom a
conflict between the impulse to transform the state and the
ethical obstacles to this desire enacts, on a political level, the
standard opposition between principles of disorder and order.

His decision to act releases a bloody chaos which devours thousands and from which no obvious benefit to the commonwealth results. The murderous fury of the mob that refuses to distinguish between Cinna the conspirator and Cinna the poet (III.iii) is Shakespeare's most unequivocally damning representation of irrational destructive energy. In the broadest sense, the spirit of the murdered Caesar returns for vengeance. Open as we may initially be to Brutus' idealism, the outcome would seem to resolve any doubt as to the reading expected of us, and it is a reading consistent with the anti-subversive bias of the middle plays generally. It would be hard to imagine a more thorough stigmatization of disruptive energy. Yet in light of the dynamic of subversion, including its suppression and its appropriation, that has been traced in this chapter, a new and complicating element is revealed, one that looks forward rather than backward.

Brutus, whose perfect mixture of elements and honourable – essentially, rational – motives Antony can generously praise once he is safely dead (V.v.68ff.), first experiences the idea of moving against Caesar in Macbeth-like fashion. The temptation of Cassius powerfully arouses the subversive impulse within him: 'the state of a man,/Like to a little kingdom, suffers then/The nature of an insurrection' (II.i.67-9). Yet Antony is obviously right to differentiate Brutus from the other conspirators, whose 'envy' (V.v.70) produces subversiveness in its pure form – the impulse to overturn for overturning's sake. In effect, they translate into terms of the political macrocosm the trickster's hostility towards any blindly secure and exclusive structure, a structure in this case called Caesar. Brutus' unique and fatal talent is the ability to rationalize the subversive impulse, to disguise it in his own sight, while allowing himself to be impelled by it. In effect, he is controlled by his more primitive collaborators. He is left wholly without manipulative authority over the energies he is the means of unleashing, in contrast with Prince Hal, Portia, and Rosalind. The illusion that he has no enemy, including Caesar, proves an enemy indeed.

It is Antony, the manipulator *extraordinaire*, who steps in to direct and exploit these energies, which his oration in effect transfers from the revolutionary to the counter-revolutionary cause, as the Plebeians rush off-stage with, 'Go fetch fire. . . . Pluck down benches. . . . Pluck down forms, windows, any thing' (III.ii.257-9). His comment on the anarchy he has provoked – 'Now let it work. Mischief, thou art afoot,/Take thou what course thou wilt!' (260–1) – displays the trickster's delight in service to the politician's cold satisfaction. Thus the restless but comic mechanicals of the first scene, the locus of latent subversive energy, are metamorphosed into indiscriminate killers. Thus naïve concerns with distinctions of identity are roughly overruled – concerns that, while they are epitomized by Brutus' misguided insistence on different treatment for Antony and Caesar, are first conveyed, ironically, in the night-scene introducing Cinna the conspirator:

> Casca: Stand close a while, for here comes one in
> haste.
> Cas.: 'Tis Cinna, I do know him by his gait.
> He is a friend. Cinna, where haste you so?
> Cin.: To find out you. Who's that, Metellus Cimber?
> Cas.: No, it is Casca, one incorporate
> To our attempts. Am I not stay'd for, Cinna?
> Cin.: I am glad on't. What a fearful night is this!
> There's two or three of us have seen strange sights.
>
> (I.iii.131–8)

The strong resemblance to the initial atmosphere of Elsinore makes the background especially suitable for Brutus, who has often been compared to the nearly contemporaneous Hamlet. The resemblance extends to their treatment of the subversive impulse, which for Hamlet arrives in the more succinct form of his father's ghost. (Note, however, Cassius' appeal to Brutus' supposed ancestor: 'O! you and I have heard our fathers say/ There was a Brutus once that would have brook'd/Th' eternal devil to keep his state in Rome/As easily as a king' (I.ii.158–61)). However one reads Hamlet's response, it is clear that his own difficulties in reading the message of the ghost produce unanticipated casualties – some of them virtually indiscriminate (Polonius, Ophelia) – as well as Claudius' redirection of his own subversiveness against him.

I shall be returning to Hamlet in a subsequent chapter. Of interest here is the anticipation of his pattern in Brutus' failure to recognize subversion for what it is, to accept and integrate it. In the absence of the comic safety net, to deny or evade the trickster is to put oneself into his hands, and to guarantee that those hands will be bloody. Beginning with *Julius Caesar*, we get a succession of tragic protagonists who, little worlds in themselves, enact the processes of history presented impersonally in the early political plays – processes that *deform* disruptive human energies and forms of knowledge into various equivalents of Richard III.

6

LOVE'S TYRANNY INSIDE-OUT IN THE PROBLEM PLAYS: YOURS, MINE, AND COUNTER-MINE

It suggests an intuitive grasp of psychic paradox that Christian mythology came to attach the name of Lucifer, the light-bringer, to the guileful Prince of Darkness. In *Measure for Measure* an analogous attachment is at once vigorously promoted – by Lucio, the self-proclaimed 'bur' who will 'stick' (IV.iii.179) to the 'Duke of dark corners' (157) – and indignantly resisted.[1] In the end, of course, it is the Duke, self-invested with 'pow'r divine' (V.i.369), who tricks Lucio into bringing to light the very circumstance that will force him back into the shadows. For Lucio, the consigning of sexual and linguistic freedom to the care of the doubly aptly named Kate Keepdown looms as 'pressing to death, whipping, and hanging' (522–3). By pulling off the Friar's hood to make him 'show [his] knave's visage' (353), Lucio is made to 'change persons' (336) with him and take this term of abuse, as he must acknowledge his child and the slanders spoken 'according to the trick' (504–5) as his own: 'Thou art the first knave that e'er mad'st a Duke' (356). A residual sense of the unmasking as a more creative act than the masking – for indeed, '*Cucullus non facit monachum*' (262) – shows in Lucio's plea for mercy: 'Your Highness said even now I made you a Duke' (515–16). But the Duke's re-created world cannot tolerate, any more than God's heaven, a rival claimant to the creator's prerogative.[2] Lucio's very defence of his slander contains a *de facto* recantation of numinosity; to use 'trick', as he clearly does, in the sense of 'custom' or 'fashion' (*OED*, II.7,8) is to strip the word of the subversive potency (realized or not) that it typically carries in connection with Shakespearean clowns, fools, and deceptive practices. From this perspective, 'according to the trick' signals, in the guise of disruptive assertion, a fundamental acquiescence in the discourse

150

of counter-subversiveness. His is a 'mystery' (like Abhorson's (IV.
ii. 28ff.)) in the service of radical de-mystification.

In a play otherwise about conflicting claims less to hegemony
than to separateness, in which a source of friction between the
comic form and several principal characters is their drive for
barricaded self-sufficiency, the silencing of Lucio presses to death
the hitherto irrepressible voice of relatedness and contingency.
And it does so on behalf of a comic resolution that cannot
persuasively speak for itself because its beneficiaries, too, are
largely silent. Isabella's is the notoriously problematic example –
the more so because it recalls the pivotal moment when Lucio's
call at the convent gate led Francisca to inform her further about
the 'restraint' (I.iv.4) she was so eager for:

> When you have vow'd, you must not speak with men
> But in the presence of the prioress;
> Then if you speak, you must not show your face,
> Or if you show your face, you must not speak.
>
> (10–13)

Isabella's first encounter with Angelo showed her '[a]t war 'twixt
will and will not' (II.ii.33), trying to withhold speech. Now,
confronted by the prospect of withholding from a man nothing
of herself, should her face show her similarly at war? The
momentum of the Duke's disclosures, culminating in the revelation (withheld precisely for its impact) that he has saved her
brother's life, has co-opted even her silence. It has been
transformed from a correlative of self-'restraint' to an index of
powerlessness and sexual vulnerability, with the subtextual
support of another proverb – 'silence gives consent'. But if it is
hers that resonates most strongly, it also joins the successive
silences of others. Lucio's is the only voice apart from the Duke's
for the last forty-five lines of the play. Even the relief of Angelo is
the Duke's creation: 'Methinks I see a quick'ning in his eye'
(V.i.495). What Angelo last articulated was a longing for death.[3]

I

The manifold discrediting, outmanoeuvring, scapegoating, and
evasion of subversive forces in Shakespeare's middle plays testify
to a deep textual anxiety – not something the text concerns, but

something that concerns it – centring on the competing claims of order and disorder. One source of such anxiety may be the continuing formal allegiance of comedies and histories alike to the principle of renewal through the very subversion that calls their values and goals into question. In order to maintain their claim on this process, the power of disruptive energy must be conjured and experienced even as it is resisted. Folly, too, must be enlisted in the cause, however marginalized and confined. Rebirth continues to require symbolic death, a return to chaos. There is more to this than a reductively materialist approach allows: one is put in mind of the religious impulse to renew the sense of salvation by confronting, and even temporarily succumbing to, the devil.

This brings us back to *Measure for Measure*. Lucio's subversive tendencies may be illuminating for the audience – he is, after all, *there*, a presence unthinkable in Illyria, where there is 'no slander' and the corruption only 'of words'; they may appear, in one of many ironic applications of the title, a highly fitting recompense for Vincentio's explicit concern with avoiding slander. Yet they scarcely constitute a substantial threat to the latter's control of events: unlike Don John's, Lucio's slanders are, one might say, like water rolling off a Duke's back, even before the final silencing. Nor, apparently, is there any need for the Duke to rally emblems of folly to his purpose: no 'wise fool' is attached to the court of Vienna. As for subversive impulses, even apart from Angelo, instinct and appetite are as thoroughly stigmatized as could be, thanks to Lucio, Pompey, and Bernardine. Claudio and Juliet do little to redeem passion in the cause of romance, while the Duke's interest in Isabella stands at a discreet, if not chilling, distance from the standard irrationality of love; it does not more than superficially contradict his early declaration of immunity: 'Believe not that the dribbling dart of love/Can pierce a complete bosom' (I.iii.2–3).

The fundamental changes in tone and balance of power amount to far more than the cynicism or sexual revulsion widely perceived in the 'problem comedies' and sometimes projected upon their 'disillusioned' author.[4] I propose that in *Measure for Measure* and *All's Well That Ends Well* we have to do with texts that reflect, in their depiction of subversion, a resolution – however partial, unstable, and open to question – of the ambiguity of the middle plays concerning disruptive energy.

152

This resolution is, in turn, reflected in the very susceptibility of the play-worlds to manipulative experts in public (and private) relations. Quite simply, despite Helena's 'love' for Bertram and the sexual trappings of her role as social renewer, the operative (if hardly avowed) assumption of both shapers of narrative – an assumption, moreover, that *works* – is that disruptive energy has no legitimacy and therefore no contribution to make to comic closure. In so far as romantic consummation is necessary to the genre, it can be mechanically produced and perfunctorily gilded: these are the plays of the bed-trick, which is, in this study's sense, no trick at all. It is the radical disjunction between this new attitude and the continuing transformational connotations of comic form that produces the unsettling anti-comic overtones and the radically 'unsatisfying' endings. These are the contradictions of successful repression (in both the political and psychological senses) and overconfidence – contradictions naturally focused in the manipulations of the dominant characters and the vulnerable deformities of their victims.

Troilus and Cressida, too, may usefully be considered in these terms, despite its problematic genre (comitragedy, perhaps?), the seeming absence of a central manipulator, and, above all, the abundant lip-service paid to amorous folly as the source of both spiritual elevation and despair. In fact, these variations help to expose the new dynamic buried (albeit shallowly) beneath the comic form of the other two plays: not the struggle between principles of order and disorder – that is now a 'dead issue' – but the drive on the part of certain characters for a domination extending to the psyches and self-images of others. Difference itself is constituted as subversive. For Ulysses, the reimposition of Degree blatantly involves psychological warfare; the love-agonies of Troilus, I shall be suggesting, amount to a more subtle but more profound hegemonism.

II

An objective glance at the realities of power in the Viennese state suffices to prove the point, promoted by Dollimore (1985) and others, that the fictional universe of *Measure for Measure* is hardly endangered by disruptive impulses. Eloquent as he is on behalf of such impulses, Pompey is Costard's *deformed* descendant, and part of his deforming involves stripping him of any real capacity to make trouble – there are no misdelivered letters here. The respectfully sceptical Friar ('doubting'?) Thomas gets no quarrel from the Duke when he credits him with an absolute power to have dealt with the Pompeys and Overdones at will (I.iii.31–4). Angelo's abuse of power is tracked step-by-step by an irresistible force *in potentia*. Only Barnardine's refusal to be executed puts Vincentio in a tight spot, and the Provost and Ragozine – that is, the text itself – immediately step in to extract him. The Duke's disguise – a parody of symbolic losses of identity elsewhere – merely refocuses his withholding of correction, while endowing him with a temporary (but potent) marginality.

Such continuity tends to confirm that, for the Duke, the goal of social reform lags well behind the desire to 'see/If power change purpose: what our seemers be' (I.iii.53–4). Vincentio's project impresses many commentators as essentially a duel between him and Angelo,[5] and since the latter '[s]tands at a guard with envy' (51), his opponent is betraying motives considerably more questionable than the 'fault' (35) of lax government to which he willingly admits. The political situation speaks for itself, and perhaps with an echo of Puritan-generated tensions in Jacobean society: given the moral negligence of the Duke's rule, Angelo's ostentatious uprightness constitutes an implicit critique, hence a prospective danger. No further revelations come by way of the Duke's words; even in soliloquy, no feelings obtrude on his impersonal, platitudinous cadences, which claim for his discourse the authority of a transcendent wisdom: 'He who the sword of heaven will bear/Should be as holy as severe' (III.ii.261–2). His actions, notoriously, are another story, riddled as they are with dubious manipulations, as he prepares Angelo for the subversive villain's role in the final scene's ritual of public humiliation. There, putting his proverbial/Biblical discourse multiply into practice – beginning with 'Like doth quit like, and *Measure* still *for Measure*' (V.i.411) – he triumphantly re-integrates moral with political power.

This virtual play-within-the-play makes quite a production, as has often been observed, for one who supposedly does 'not like to stage' (I.i.68) himself to the public eye: the Duke is not only playwright and director, but the busy actor of two of the main roles.[6] In contrast with the fifth-Act festivity of that earlier pageant of love gone wrong, the tragedy of Pyramus and Thisby, this performance is calculated to re-establish boundaries more strongly, and on Vincentio's own terms. And when the part he has written for Isabella is taken into account, it is clear how thoroughly and variously the play's strange versions of love serve the interests of his political theatre. First, the Duke coolly appropriates the results (whatever we may think of them) of Angelo's crackdown on sexual licence. Then, he exposes the deputy's lapse, together with his own duping of Angelo's desire: Angelo has been tricked into giving his sexuality into the custody of a woman he had repudiated – essentially the fate of Lucio. Finally, Vincentio puts himself in the way of taking Isabella's virginity. His multiple hegemony on the sexual level makes an ironic answer to Pompey's rhetorical question: 'Does your worship mean to geld and splay all the youth of the city?' (II.i.230–1).

No longer, it would seem, is the counterfeit trickster concerned to outmanoeuvre disruptive energies while laying claim to their benefits; rather, he seeks to redefine the very terms on which characters form bonds with one another. In so far as the Duke is not merely purging but re-creating his world, in pseudo-divine fashion, it is not subversive forces as such that threaten (and so enable) this activity: it is the very existence of 'free' wills, the concept of separateness. Thus the thrust of his project is to re-incorporate characters who would have preferred life on the margins. Angelo does not ask for the post of deputy; Isabella has sought formal withdrawal from the world and sexuality in order to serve another deity; and Mariana surely would have been better off musically enjoying her sorrow in her moated grange, Orsino-like, than she is in getting what she thinks she wants. Through Angelo, 'th' ambush of [his] name' (I.iii.41) functions like a dragnet, not only catching up Claudio and Juliet, who merely want to be left alone, but sweeping the suburbs into the prison; in the broadest sense, the likes of Froth are indeed 'drawn in' (II.i.210). Even Lucio's offensive interventions are rooted in a role thereby imposed upon him – that of Claudio's advocate – and, once centred in the Duke's angry gaze ('here's one in place I cannot pardon' (V.i.499)), he is prevented from retreating to the marginal position of 'allow'd fool', by definition slanderless.

Such absolute domination as the Duke practises unapologetically denies the legitimacy of error, instinct, and desire in shaping existence. It also necessitates the breaking and reforging of self-images – a substitute, in effect, for the transformational processes enacted in the early comedies. Vincentio's power (or potency) substantially exceeds Hal's: its emblem is not exclusion, banishment, or even execution – Pompey and Barnardine can be neither reformed nor eliminated – but imprisonment. It is a deeply fascistic vision – perhaps even more so than has been recognized by commentators, such as Dollimore (1985), who are concerned with Renaissance representations of authority,[7] for authority in this play reaches into the most intimate areas of personal experience, the 'dark corners' of the psyche. State affairs and social issues are pervasively intertwined with appetite. This, of course, is the very tainting of which Angelo stands as an *exemplum*, duly punished, in a way that obscures the subtextual presentation of the drive for power as itself a destructive appetite. That concept is more openly (albeit conditionally) expressed by a politician in a neighbouring text:

> Force should be right, or rather, right and wrong
> (Between whose endless jar justice resides)
> Should lose their names, and so should justice too!
> Then every thing include itself in power,
> Power into will, will into appetite,
> And appetite, an universal wolf
> (So doubly seconded with will and power),
> Must make perforce an universal prey,
> And last eat up himself.
>
> (*Tro.*, I.iii.116–24)

It is precisely this nightmare that will burst through the containment walls of ritualized statecraft into the world and the mind of Lear.

As for the 'appetite' formally exposed and condemned in *Measure for Measure*, the ruthless isolation of sexuality from a more general subversiveness, and from the love-impulse in particular, functions less to stigmatize it, despite critical perceptions of 'the generalized degradation of sexuality' (Wheeler 1981: 116) or the political construction of 'deviance' (Dollimore 1985: 73–5), than to make it a mechanical substitute for deeper bonds. The Duke hardly denies (Wheeler 1981: 149) or, except for form's sake, 'demonis[es]' (Dollimore 1985: 73–4) sexuality; it is rather, as with Pandarus, his stock-in-trade. The sordidness of libertinism functions to taint 'liberty' itself, as Claudio's first speech makes clear (I.ii.125ff.), while the role of 'bawd' serves to demean union that is not on the Duke's terms. (After all, the only sexual congress actually effected within the play involves Vincentio and Isabella as go-betweens.) Sex itself emerges as intrinsically neutral, recuperable in the service of the larger design – a sort of glue that, once applied in a bed-trick, sticks fast and applies, however crookedly, the label of romantic fulfilment. Separating love from sex is a job largely done before the play begins, but the punishment and severing of Juliet and Claudio neatly recapitulate the process. In this, too, Angelo is 'doing the Duke's dirty work'.[8]

So he is even in pitting himself against Isabella's saintly self-image. Isabella, it is often said, learns humanity at the Duke's hands;[9] certainly, he puts her through the motions of comic transformation, with a plausible culmination in her plea for Angelo's life. Even if one ignores the backhanded self-congratulation in this final speech, however – 'I partly think/A due sincerity governed his deeds,/Till he did look on me' (V.i.445-7) – and allows that her earlier lack of charity towards her brother is behind her, it remains obvious that the Duke's handy solution, which she embraced with unsettling haste, has got her off the subversive hook. The cost is that the counter-trickster can then supply a hook of his own: his script takes her well beyond the part she anticipated playing. Ironically, only Angelo undergoes significant inner conflict, confronting his conscience in a way strongly reminiscent of *Hamlet*'s Claudius and experiencing a profound despair when exposed: 'I crave death more willingly than mercy:/'Tis my deserving, and I do entreat it' (476-7). Yet this response, as I suggested earlier, is not allowed to lead anywhere. The benignly despotic master of ceremonies applies Portia's tactics in sparing Angelo's body but, in effect, taking his soul: 'By this Lord Angelo perceives he's safe' (494).

III

What chiefly complicates the picture in *All's Well* is the status and purpose of the chief manipulator: while Helena has often been recognized as an analogous internal dramatist,[10] her gender, her social dependency, and her emotional obsession all situate her well down from Vincentio on the scale of power. Moreover, her love-longing automatically invokes the powerful mechanisms of romantic comedy on her behalf. The Duke may gain, at most, our approval; Helena at least begins with an abundant supply of sympathy. Undoubtedly, the acquisition of social and political power figures in Helena's case as well – so strongly as to invalidate, for some commentators, her susceptibility to love. Yet to reduce her to a rank hypocrite and fortune-hunter is both to distort the text and to miss the point. A love-relation, for Vincentio, can be an adjunct to and demonstration of other forms of power; for Helena, power can come only through love. As he also does with Portia – whose problem is too much wealth and status, not too little – Shakespeare presents manipulation in the romantic sphere not as calculation, but as a natural response to female powerlessness. He thus exposes the tendency of repressive social structures to foster resistance to disruptive folly even on the part of their victims.

From the first, Helena's consciousness of inferior rank is intermingled with her romantic feelings. This would be normal enough in the circumstances, but the presentation is equivocal and suggestive. As with her namesake in *A Midsummer Night's Dream*, the sense of a fixation doubtfully related to its object is strongly conveyed, although Demetrius' jilting of her focuses the first Helena's thoughts on her own delusion: 'Things base and vile, holding no quantity,/Love can transpose to form and dignity' (*MND*, I.i.232–3). Her successor's declaration of one-sided passion, which is made a surprise to us by the red herring of her supposed grief for her father, appears more naïve; in her first soliloquy, she lamely idealizes Bertram's 'arched brows, his hawking eye, his curls' (*AWW*, I.i.94), evidently incapable of seeing the decidedly earth-bound young man behind the divine image. This is the cataloguing rhetoric of the love- and grief-blinded Imogen, who cannot tell the body of Cloten from that of Posthumus: 'this is his hand/His foot Mercurial, his Martial thigh' (*Cym.*, IV.ii.309–10). It is also Hamlet's mode of idealizing his father ('Hyperion's curls, the front of Jove himself,/An eye like Mars' (*Ham.*, III.iv.56–7)) – a parallel reinforced by the *Hamlet*-echoes over Helena's tears. Yet those tears, in most un-Hamlet-like fashion, she brusquely strips from her father's memory: 'What was he like?/I have forgot him' (*AWW*, I.i.81–2).

Her transcendental rhetoric makes it all the more remarkable that Helena is simultaneously capable of acknowledging her love as a cult: 'But now he's gone, and my idolatrous fancy/Must sanctify his reliques' (97–8). Apparently, it is not that she cannot recognize Bertram for what he is, but that she does not care. What matters is possessing, or, rather, not possessing him. Unlike the first Helena, who, under the spell of romance, can see no farther than the possibility of getting a glimpse of Demetrius or a kind word from him, this heroine thinks practically and, as they are said to say in advertising, globally. Though her theme is despair, her initial analysis of her dilemma in terms of social barriers is already rich with the potential for taking things into her own hands: ' 'Twere all one/That I should love a bright particular star/And think to wed it, he is so above me' (85-7). When Helena goes on to speak of '[t]h' ambition in my love' (90), she effectively presents the two impulses as intertwined. The word 'ambition' is bound to resonate powerfully, as it does when it returns in the letter professing guilt for her '[a]mbitious love' (III.iv.5).

In her second soliloquy, Helena ignores Bertram entirely and speaks (again, most unlike Hamlet) only of the gain to be achieved by bold action:

> Our remedies oft in ourselves do lie,
> Which we ascribe to heaven. The fated sky
> Gives us free scope, only doth backward pull
> Our slow designs when we ourselves are dull.

> (I.i.216-19)

The political overtones of such thinking do not depend on the echo of the tempting Cassius ('The fault, dear Brutus, is not in our stars,/But in ourselves, that we are underlings' (*JC*, I.ii.140-1)). The idea harks back to Tamburlaine and Richard III, and points forward to Edmund: it is heady – and dubious – company. Even more questionable is her appeal to appetite as self-justifying: 'What power is it which mounts my love so high,/That makes me see, and cannot feed mine eye?' (220-1). One is reminded of Aaron's self-injunction to 'arm thy heart, and fit thy thoughts,/To mount aloft with thy imperial mistress' (*Tit.*, II.i.12-13). Helena proceeds to spur herself on to 'strange attempts' (*AWW*, I.i.224) with a rationalizing spirit worthy of Lady Macbeth. The discourse of politics and power has strongly emerged from, and all but erased, that of romance.

For Helena, then, love is at least partly a vehicle, not for social climbing, but for achievement and control. It is both a measure of and a response to powerlessness and dependency, at once revealing and filling an existential vacuum. 'Ambition' may describe an aspect, and a consequence, of that response, but it is an inadequate term for the underlying impulse of self-assertion.

159

Helena's love is, rather, a rough counterpart of Hamlet's revenge, which supplies him, willy-nilly, with mission and meaning after the multiple displacements caused by his father's death. In so far as romance is the only sphere of action open to Helena, she is similarly more chosen than choosing. Yet her actions associate, as in *Measure for Measure*, the acquisition of power with the domination of the thoughts and feelings of other characters. And because love becomes something that Helena uses, not something that uses her, its implicit status as the transforming subversive energy of comedy is itself subverted.

Between Helena's soliloquies of impotence and resolution falls the famous dialogue with Parolles concerning virginity. This bantering exchange superficially exemplifies the sort of clowning elsewhere associated with comic processes. Yet Parolles is a thoroughly tainted representative of disruptive energy, as his subsequent career confirms.[11] It is promising that he is a 'notorious liar' (I.i.100), 'a great way fool, soly a coward' (101) – from this alone, one might expect a Falstaff. What disqualifies him is his calculating interest and success in gaining others' (especially Bertram's) high opinion of him:

> Yet these fix'd evils sit so fit in him,
> That they take place when virtue's steely bones
> Looks bleak i' th' cold wind. Withal, full oft we see
> Cold wisdom waiting on superfluous folly.

> (102–5)

The trickster, when he takes on the role of *miles gloriosus*, is transparent. Everybody sensible sees through Falstaff, as he well knows. For Hal's purposes, there is no need for such empty pretences to valour to be taken seriously and punished – quite the contrary. Falstaff's lies – even his claim to the conquest of Hotspur – can safely be encouraged: the final repudiation focuses on other vices. As the texts shift from Falstaff to his successor Pistol, however, the increase in social menace goes hand in hand with an increased potential for imposing upon others, notably Fluellen: accordingly, there must be a public undeceiving. Parolles represents a further evolution in this direction, and his exposure is made correspondingly more pointed and severe. However, like Pistol's, his distinctive dialect merely preserves the outward form of subversiveness. Parolles is voluble without the traditional clown's linguistic spontaneity; in this sense, too, he is true to his name: he is only words, and his lack of originality in manipulating them would be evident to an audience familiar with the affected 'witty' style of the courtier. In fact, lively inventive wit of the sort wielded by Portia and Rosalind, Beatrice and Benedick, is sparse in *All's Well* – as, for that matter, in *Measure for Measure* and *Troilus*. The later plays, it seems, are less concerned to provide even their romantic leads with a verbal screen of subversive energy.

Certainly, Helena's wit in her exchange with Parolles is coldly mechanical, maintaining the distance established by her opening comment. Moreover, it only thinly veils her inversion of her position of powerlessness – a position of which virginity becomes the index.[12] Parolles begins like Lucio accosting Isabella: ' 'Save you, fair queen! . . . Are you meditating on virginity' (106–10). But whereas Lucio's parodic *Ave*, 'Hail, virgin, if you be' (*MM*, I.iv.16), initiates a sexual discourse that Isabella perceives as inherently threatening, Helena instead takes up the challenge in its own terms by responding, 'Ay' (*AWW*, I.i.111), and requesting advice for protecting virginity against men. Assured that there is no defence, she turns to thinking offensively: 'Is there no military policy how virgins might blow up men?' (121–2). She regards virginity as an instrument of self-realization, considering how 'to lose it to [one's] own liking' (150–1) and rejecting Parolles's advice to cast it away: 'Not my virginity yet' (165).[13] These obvious anticipations of her strategy with Bertram are interesting for the attitude towards sexuality that they establish. For Isabella, as well, virginity is a source of personal power, but that power consists merely in self-withholding: hence, the implicit challenge she poses to Angelo (whose response to her ostentatious purity is not so different from the Duke's to his own), as well as her helplessness in the face of the Duke's final proposal. Helena, by contrast, can envisage the timely loss of virginity as a means to an end. This is, of course, the premise of the bed-trick, and her manipulation of Diana – we should not forget that she and her mother are paid for their co-operation – becomes emblematic of Helena's exploitation of virginity itself. Even as her role as central manipulator links her with the Duke, therefore, she also unites the two aspects of virginity-as-power that are split in *Measure for Measure* between Isabella and Mariana. (The figure of 'pure' virginity – Diana – is left over as a sort of residue, an empty shell.) It is her affiliation with Mariana that most obviously qualifies Helena's triumph. For however she may succeed to her own satisfaction in possessing the body and subduing the psyche of her husband, she too is ultimately putting herself in a legally subordinate and personally unenviable position. Mariana's plea to the Duke is, after all, pitiable in its self-delusion: 'I crave no other, nor no better man' (*MM*, V.i.426).

One problem for women reduced to using their sexuality as an instrument of power is that the 'prize' traditionally defined as a token of power by men is to be given away only once. Isabella's absolutist chastity contains an anxious cognizance of this fact, as does Helena's 'policy'. Yet it is left to the third central female figure in this trio of texts to articulate her predicament in explicit terms of sex-as-power: 'Achievement is command; ungain'd, beseech' (*Tro.*, I.ii.293). Ironically, Cressida's fate involves not only losing control of her sexuality, as does Isabella, but having the power of virginity turned against her, also in the traditional way, by the imposition of the category of 'whore'. Her situation sheds further light on Helena's successful exercise of sexual power. What chiefly distinguishes Cressida from the other two heroines, and ultimately bears responsibility for her downfall, is her susceptibility to a man who desires her. Isabella has at least precluded the dangers of such reciprocity by cutting off her own sexual feelings, although this does not protect her from 'honourable' sexual possession. On the other hand, Helena's conspicuously unrequited love serves her well throughout. Setting her sights, focusing her susceptibilities, on a reluctant object guarantees that her 'honour' will be kept intact and makes possible an identification of self-gratification with self-realization. She is free to determine the rules of the game, and from the first they pointedly and self-protectively include marriage.

Helena's jests with Parolles contrast, not only with the meeting of Lucio and Isabella, but also with Cressida's banter:

> *Pan.:* You are such a woman, a man knows not at what
> ward you lie.
> *Cres.:* Upon my back, to defend my belly, upon my wit, to
> defend my wiles, upon my secrecy, to defend mine
> honesty, my mask, to defend my beauty, and you, to
> defend all these; and at all these wards I lie, at
> a thousand watches.
>
> (*Tro.*, I.ii.258–64)

The theme is the same – the defence of the sexual self – as is the military lexis. Yet beneath her 'wit', to which she assigns a similar distancing and protective function, Cressida is clearly in the grip of a subversive impulse expressed in the contradictory message of sexual openness. That this contradiction is not mere hypocrisy, a 'cover' for a promiscuous appetite, is established by the acute sense of her particular dilemma projected in the ensuing soliloquy and elsewhere. Cressida finds herself responding sexually to real and pressing overtures made on terms – marriage is never mentioned – that (literally) threaten her integrity: 'I have a kind of self resides with you;/But an unkind self, that itself will leave/To be another's fool. I would be gone' (III.ii.148–50). Given the productive implications of self-loss and amorous folly in the early Shakespeare, the disastrous consequences of this vulnerability would seem to mark a thorough reversal of perspective, although, as my later discussion will stress, the social context and the projections of Troilus must be taken into account. For the moment, what stands out is the radically dissimilar self-command of Helena, whose love is, in effect, pure initiative. Her guard with Parolles is always up. Her bawdy dialogue issues in a soliloquy of awesome single-mindedness. Bertram, apparently, is a safe and useful vehicle for her impulses of aspiration precisely because he has no interest in her. It helps her cause even that he is such a cipher as a character. He is mere raw material, however unwilling, for her shaping imagination, and in finally shaping him into a husband as acquiescent, at least, as the nonplussed Isabella or the shamed Angelo, that imagination thoroughly reshapes the world around her.

For attached to Helena's scheme are large implications of social and political renewal. This again affiliates her with Vincentio, but again with an inversion reflecting her primary sphere of action: the Duke's renovation of his image and his state is made to depend upon the suppression of sexual activity; Helena's injection of new life into the play's community is represented in sexual terms, in keeping with her later initiating of Bertram. The powerful overtones of sexual revival in her healing of the King – overtones that resonate with ancient myths of the wounded ruler – have been amply documented. What still calls for comment is the way in which this dimension, far from genuinely revitalizing the play-world, merely co-opts male power on behalf of Helena's project. To start with, the cure itself involves her adaptation to her own *will* of her father's - a reminiscence of Portia's use of the casket-device to acquire Bassanio. A further ramification here is that, despite having 'forgotten' him emotionally, Helena is pointedly bringing her father's legacy into conflict with Bertram's own inheritance - his social status: 'She had her breeding at my father's charge - /A poor physician's daughter my wife!' (II.iii.114–15). Similarly, having rejected heaven's power - God the Father - in her second soliloquy, Helena makes a show of submission to divinity, and so appropriates it, when it comes to persuading the King: 'But most it is presumption in us when/The help of heaven we count the act of men' (II.i.151-2).

The two defunct earthly fathers have been juxtaposed since the first scene, as they are within the memory of the King, whose body and mind are the arena chosen by Helena for the contest. She gains her opportunity much in the manner of Bassanio, by giving and hazarding all she has, but here sexuality, not wealth, is the language of power. As her reward will be a husband of her choosing, so the first part of her proposed penalty for failure is precisely what Cressida suffers after taking the ultimate risk with Troilus: 'Tax of impudence,/A strumpet's boldness, a divulged shame,/Traduc'd by odious ballads' (II.i.170-2). In binding Bertram's substitute father to her will by her success, she harnesses the authority of patriarchy itself. The King's threatening–reasoning speech to the refractory Bertram supports the lexis of state supremacy - 'I must produce my power' (II.iii.150) - with Biblical cadences evoking the wrathful Father. 'Obey our will' (158), he charges,

> Or I will throw thee from my care for ever
> Into the staggers and the careless lapse
> Of youth and ignorance; both my revenge and hate
> Loosing upon thee, in the name of justice,
> Without all terms of pity.

> (162-6)

The play-world's need for renewal, figured forth in the King's illness, is notoriously represented by the entropic lassitude of the older generation[14] - once more, the inverse of the corrupt sexual excess that serves as the Duke's excuse for reform in *Measure for Measure*. The world-weariness of the Countess, Lafew, and the

King himself is coupled with a melancholy nostalgia for better days and better men (witness Lafew's 'finding out' of Parolles). There is, then, a reminiscence of Illyria, as well as of the contrast between Duke Frederick's court and the 'golden world' of Arden. What France desires, it would seem, is an injection of the erotic energy Helena alone could be said to possess, and this might imply an openness to subversion. Yet France is also of two minds, as is clear from the character who embodies the state. The King is interested in rejuvenation but not transformation. His imposition of Helena upon Bertram, as he attempts to bend human feelings with the apparatus of state power, improbably makes the latter's refusal the truly subversive element in the scene. There is an analogy to the conflict between Cordelia and Lear, whose language the offended King anticipates: 'Do thine own fortunes that obedient right/Which both thy duty owes and our power claims' (II.iii.160–1). The King's adoptive son must, as Cordelia is supposed to do, sacrifice his sense of himself in order to display gratitude; he must also surrender control of his sexuality in order to act out the King's own feelings for Helena, which implicitly exceed gratitude. In short, the King's recovery strengthens rather than disrupts existing social relations and assumptions about power. Sexuality is appropriated by reaction.

The Countess herself, sympathetic though she is as a promoter of romantic consummation, seeks to revive the past at the cost of ignoring present realities and conflicting personal claims. Her son, indirectly identified as a 'second husband' in the play's first lines, can be retained by making Helena her 'daughter'. Helena's objections to the premature gift of this role in Act I, Scene iii, ostensibly relate to the obstacle thereby implied to a marriage with Bertram. But the existential aspect of her design lends depth to her violent reaction ('Methought you saw a serpent' (141)), as well as to the suggestion of incest. It is one thing for Helena to make the Countess her mother on her own terms, another to accept the subordinate position of, in effect, the Countess's agent and surrogate. Hence, too, her failure to take the Countess into her confidence concerning her journey to Paris. While she solemnly vows to tell the truth ('by grace itself I swear' (220)), it is hardly the whole truth. Nor, when she sets off to put her Florentine scheme into practice, does she share her thoughts with the Countess, any more than with the audience. She is even willing to let the kind old woman suppose her dead and suffer a grief as great as '[i]f she had partaken of [the Countess's] flesh, and cost [her] the dearest groans of a mother' (IV.v.10–11). Quite simply, Helena must die as the Countess's adoptive daughter in order to be reborn as Bertram's wife in her own right.

The incest-motif is usually taken up in narrow psycho-sexual terms and from Bertram's point of view. To regard it from his mother's, and to link it with the King's surrogate fatherhood, is to release its broader implications of stagnation and oppression. What is most incestuous about this play-world is its resistance to growth, change, and difference – in short, to the processes of time that are elsewhere allied with the disruptive force of love. Confirmation of this pattern is Lafew's proposal, to which the Countess assents, that his daughter should take the dead Helena's place with Bertram. This is a closed system, seeking to preserve itself intact by allowing renewal only in its own image, and Helena's 'ambition' entails an assault on that system, rather than mere gratification within it. Having appropriated the power of patriarchy, she must then put patriarchy itself in its (subordinate) place. This involves breaking those bonds between mother and son, son and surrogate father, that would keep her the conduit of others' psychic projections.

Like the other late clowns, Lavatch serves as an index of the progressive displacement and enervation of the subversive. He lags behind Feste in verbal energy while exceeding him in jadedness – Lafew aptly terms him a 'shrewd knave and an unhappy' (IV.v.63). His similarly ambiguous position in the household differs from Feste's in being a matter less of current than of expired licence: 'My lord that's gone made himself much sport out of him. By his authority he remains here, which he thinks is a patent for his sauciness, and indeed he has no pace, but runs where he will' (64–7). Even the impotent disruptions of an 'allow'd fool', it seems, belong to the past – as they do, indeed, in Shakespeare's comic canon. At the same time, there is an anticipation of the Fool in *Lear*, who, since Cordelia's banishment, 'hath much pin'd away' (*Lr*, I.iv.74). Folly and youth are made interdependent by the Countess herself in bantering with the clown: 'To be young again, if we could, I will be a fool in question' (II.ii.38–9). Over the course of *All's Well*, moreover, Lavatch visibly diminishes in sexual energy; his early plan to wed Isbel, in which he was 'driven on by the flesh' (I.iii.29) in the manner of Touchstone, is abandoned after his visit to court, which draws him further into the atmosphere of superannuation: 'The brains of my Cupid's knock'd out, and I begin to love, as an old man loves money, with no stomach' (III.ii.14–16).

The change in Lavatch reflects not only the evolution of Bertram's sexuality (Wheeler 1981: 52–4), but, more broadly, Helena's neutralizing and controlling of disruptive forces, including that sexuality. The letter from Bertram that Lavatch delivers in this scene is brashly assertive and defiant, but this bravado, like that of Parolles, rings hollow and ends with a running-away: 'I have sent you a daughter-in-law; she hath recover'd the King, and undone me. I have wedded her, not bedded her, and sworn to make the "not" eternal. You shall hear I am run away' (III.ii.19–22). The reality of his defeat is contained in 'undone', with its mixed sexual messages. The claim to independence – 'not bedded her' – is syntactically embedded within the restriction of being 'wedded'; the 'not' is overshadowed by its homonym. Helena's next move will involve forcing Bertram to acknowledge his own subtext, just as Parolles's brave words will be turned against him.

Parolles is, quite implausibly, made a scapegoat for Bertram by characters desperate for the hero's reform, beginning with the Lords who arrange Parolles's exposure as an object lesson. As a ritual cleansing the business is mere travesty, compared to the outcasting of Falstaff by the Prince whom *he* 'misled' or Fluellen's purging of Pistol on behalf of the new socio-political order. Far from stage-managing it, this young reprobate actively resists his own symbolic purification. When his jocular fear that he will 'hear . . . hereafter' (IV.iii.97) of his amorous adventure is eventually realized, he parades his impenitence. Yet his presumed reformation through the disgrace of Parolles becomes the basis of the rehabilitation proposed for him by his mother, Lafew, and the King. Lafew assures the Countess, 'your son was misled with a snipt-taffeta fellow there' (IV.v.1–2) – that is, essentially, an imitation of true courtiers like himself. In response, her slippery pronouns betoken a readiness to pile the designated victim with her son's most wilful faults: 'I would I had not known him; it was the death of the most virtuous gentlewoman that ever nature had praise for creating' (8–10). Perhaps the most significant fact about the scapegoating is that Helena has nothing to do with it;[15] it marks the emergence of an independent scheme potentially in conflict with Helena's own – a threatening counter-mine.

The older generation's mourning of Helena is superficially touching, a display of emotional sensitivity, but it also confirms that the revival of their world on their own terms depends on her supposed death. Bertram receives the King's approval when he claims to have loved Lafew's daughter before Helena's intervention, even while he shrewdly pays homage to, and claims posthumous affection for, his lost wife. Helena's memory is conveniently appropriated all round, but most convenient of all is her disappearance from the scene. Having failed to renew itself by using her alive, the social order makes the most of her death. In fact, in the language of forgiveness employed by the time-obsessed King ('Let's take the instant by the forward top;/For we are old' (V.iii.39–40)), she herself becomes scapegoat-in-chief, by her death making possible Bertram's spotless revival: 'The nature of his great offense is dead,/And deeper than oblivion we do bury/Th' incensing relics of it' (23–5). The effect is to expose Helena's ongoing role, alive or dead, as outsider in this structure, and hence the need for the manipulative magic of her own rebirth to break that structure down. Only then can she emerge, not as the saviour designated by Countess or King, but as the saviour self-created. This time, she must deprive her chosen instrument not only of the liberty to choose, but of free will itself.

This is the impact on her dramatic world of Helena's second miraculous exercise of power, and an explanation for its otherwise unnecessary deviousness and complex orchestration. To the point here are the seemingly superfluous 'follow-up' tricks of analogous manipulators. Portia gains the day by defeating Shylock; she acquires psychological power through the ring-business. Vincentio has Angelo dead-to-rights early in the play, should he choose to reveal himself; the bed-trick hits his opponent, as it were, below the belt. Even more appositely, the climax of the Duke's pageant – the revelation of Claudio's safety – puts Isabella in a position very like that of Bertram. His much-discussed response to Helena's disclosure – 'If she, my liege, can make me know this clearly,/I'll love her dearly, ever, ever dearly' (V.iii.315–16) – is simply inaccessible as an index of 'real' feelings. The point is that feelings have been made irrelevant, for *ending* well here depends on the suppression of the very capacity for subversion, including even Shylock's capacity to remain unharmonized. Bertram's statement is the equivalent of Isabella's helpless silence, Angelo's constructed relief, and its conditional formulation is less important than his implicit confession of a dependence on Helena for clear knowledge. Like Vincentio, then, Helena succeeds in irresistibly imposing the mechanism of comic transformation. And all the more clearly, paradoxically, because love is her vehicle, she demonstrates that such a resolution has no need of subversive energy – no need, even, to fear it or to crush it, since it is simply beside the point.

As before, the King's role is symbolically central. It was a comparatively easy task for Helena, using her father's remedy, to restore him to health. Now, with her own arts, exercised through Diana, she must reduce him to impotent and infantile foolishness: 'Take her away, I do not like her now./To prison with her; and away with him' (281–2). In much the same way does Angelo throw up his hands before the confusion instigated by Pompey:

> This will last out a night in Russia
> When nights are longest there. I'll take my leave,
> And leave you to the hearing of the cause,
> Hoping you'll find good cause to whip them all.
>
> (MM, II.i.134–7)

The King is already implicated in the puzzle by way of his ring; he is further drawn in through the 'tangled chain' of Diana's riddling sexual accusations. After answering the King, 'By Jove, if ever I knew man, 'twas you' (287), she goes on, in accusing Bertram, to weave her knot ('not') to include even Lafew:

> He knows I am no maid, and he'll swear to't;
> I'll swear I am a maid, and he knows not.
> Great King, I am no strumpet, by my life;
> I am either maid, or else this old man's wife.
>
> (290–3)

The comprehensive absurdity is functional. All are punished. Diana acts as the 'friend' who performs Rosalynde's magic for her in Lodge's novel, embodying Helena's realization of the desire, which has gone hand-in-hand from the first with her desire for Bertram, for a 'military policy how virgins might blow up men'.

IV

Troilus, of course, may be regarded as precisely so blown up, but to consider him primarily as a victim, even of his own emotions, is to rely on his self-portrait, and this entails accepting the emblematic destinies, too, of Cressida and Pandarus. It is to take as the play's last word – and very few critics now do so – his view of Cressida's falseness, his scornful repudiation of Pandarus ('Ignominy, shame/Pursue thy life, and live aye with thy name!' (V.x.33–4)), and his moral triumph as monopolistic incarnation of Truth: ' "As true as Troilus" ' (III.ii.182). Closure would thus accrue to his speech of fatalistic yet heroic defiance after Hector's death, his assumption of the role of 'wicked conscience' (V.x.28) to the Greeks – the very posture, in other words, which Chaucer's precursor romance pointedly refuses to accept as closure, taking the reader on to Troilus' death and recognition of earthly vanity, including the vanity of his love for Criseyde. Despite his bitterness and disillusion, the play ends on Troilus' own terms, and we might as well accept as conclusive and innocent the final readings imposed on their respective texts by Vincentio and Helena. What the picture chiefly fails to convey is the implication of Troilus in both the shaping of destiny and the sense of ultimate vanity, a sense which in Shakespeare is less formulaic and far more radical than in Chaucer, with no platform of eternal verity to offer a secure spiritual perspective. Only superficially is Shakespeare's fool-for-love the antagonist of the counter-subversive Ulysses. He is an actor in his own right – one who out-Bottoms Bottom in uniting two roles in one but without interrogating the premise of his tragic-love script: 'What is Pyramus? a lover, or a tyrant?' (*MND*, I.ii.22).

The subversive status of Pandarus is difficult to fix, hence particularly revealing. He is the energetic agent of the sexual impulses of others; there is no mistaking his pleasure both in the role of bawd and in bawdry itself – witness his obscene performance for Paris and Helen in Act III, Scene i, with Paris's comment: 'He eats nothing but doves, love, and that breeds hot blood, and hot blood begets hot thoughts, and hot thoughts beget hot deeds, and hot deeds is love' (128–30). Certainly, sexuality is his natural medium – he virtually swims within it, and at the end, with the turning of the tide, he is left high and dry, a fish out of water. It is easy, too, to compare him to Pompey as a debased descendant of the sex-promoting subversives of the earlier plays. Again, the role of bawd, so prominent in the textual imagination of this cluster of plays, *deforms* Puck's role as facilitator of a more broadly based communion. However, in contrast with

Measure for Measure, where Pompey stands for a sexuality diseased *ab origine,* Pandarus has the excuse, as it were, of the distorting pressures of war, the same pressures that foster the frenzied decadence of the doomed courtiers and render all human bonds desperate and precarious. In this respect, Pandarus is the counterpart of the physically mis-shapen Thersites, the truth-telling fool who seems to be squeezed into one self-discrediting dimension less, for a change, by the stigmatizing bias of his text than by the murderous stupidity around him. By contrast, Lucio's slander, however it may hit home at times, comes out of unseen 'dark corners'. Against a lavish background of grotesque war and love, Thersites and Pandarus emerge as more nearly normal – the living refutations, respectively, of the postures of chivalric honour and of Troilus' claim, 'In all Cupid's pageant there is presented no monster' (III.ii.74–5).[16]

But there remains a fundamental and provocative difference between Thersites and Pandarus – a point that equally distinguishes the latter from such spokesmen for a diseased sexuality as Pompey and Lucio. Pandarus' identification with sexual drives is not part of even a superficially disruptive stance: on the contrary, that he fits so smoothly into his debased aristocratic milieu is part of the satirical point. In sharp contrast with the Greek trouble-maker, there is no whiff of the Vice about him. This renders problematic not only his subversiveness, but the very basis of his fictional identity. After all, the sexual forces that constitute Pandarus as a character are located outside him. He initiates nothing. Apart from his dealings with Troilus and Cressida, he appears only in the scene with Helen and Paris, when he is on Troilus' business, and then he puts himself at the service of their lubricity. If he is, as Paris claims, comprised of 'love' (in the sense of 'hot deeds') such composition reflects the doings and desires of others. Notoriously, any 'motive' for promoting the central liaison as energetically as he does is difficult to locate, yet the lack of one is conspicuous.[17] Despite his descent into the 'hold-door trade' (V.x.51) in his epilogue, where he claims to reflect (and threatens to infect) his '[b]rethren and sisters' (51) amongst the audience, Pandarus is clearly not out for material gain. Even if we choose to posit a buried sexual attraction to Troilus, we are dependent on textual suggestions of vicarious pleasure that merely reinforce his derivative status.

It is apparent from the start, and from any critical perspective, that Pandarus offers a down-to-earth counterpoint to Troilus' romanticism.[18] In the first scene, he actually drives the poetically love-sick prince to talk frankly of achieving the 'stubborn-chaste' (I.i.97) Cressida, although Troilus goes on, asking Apollo for inspiration, to paint his longing in vivid colours:

> Her bed is India, there she lies, a pearl;
> Between our Ilium and where she resides,
> Let it be call'd the wild and wand'ring flood,
> Ourself the merchant, and this sailing Pandar
> Our doubtful hope, our convoy, and our bark.

> (100–4)

The counterpoint continues to be heard in Troilus' metaphors, which, stubbornly materialistic and possessive in a way that recalls Bassanio's image of the Golden Fleece, have given pause to many commentators. The blunt fact is that, however loftily he conceives his feelings, Troilus is setting up his own kind of bed-trick, and it is this fact that Pandarus, cutting through the lovers' professions of eternal loyalty, is made textually responsible for articulating: 'Whereupon I will show you a chamber, which bed, because it shall not speak of your pretty encounters, press it to death' (III.ii.207–9). Troilus' sordid, falsely subversive agent emerges as an index of the displaced darker side, not only of his idealism, but of his very claim of susceptibility to subversive passion, and so of his boast to be 'as true as truth's simplicity,/ And simpler than the infancy of truth' (169–70).

Janet Adelman (1980) has taken farther than other critics the idea of Cressida's betrayal as produced, even required, by Troilus' psycho-pathology. She locates his glaring defensiveness in the infantile quality of his love, a fantasy of union with the maternal ideal, whose ambivalence is actualized by sexual consummation; by projecting his sense of 'soilure' upon the real Cressida, Troilus can keep his maternal fantasy alive – hence his notorious insistence on dividing her in his exchange with Ulysses: 'This is, and is not, Cressid!' (V.ii.146). In Adelman's view, Troilus' sexual ambivalence prefigures Othello's, with the difference that Shakespeare here allows the text itself to be shaped by Troilus' fantasy.

However, by putting sex before power, in classic Freudian terms, even Adelman's argument plays into Troilus' self-justifying hands, stressing his openness to subversion (in the form of neurotic helplessness) and down-playing his manipulative aggression. The military context of the love-story might alone suggest that the question of power takes precedence. So does the treatment of sex-relations in the other Problem Plays – especially in the case of Helena, which is forfeited as a parallel if Troilus' psychological dynamic is traced to a gender-specific root. Only by returning the love-affair to its place within a network of intersecting subversive and counter-subversive forces can we appreciate the multiple resonances of Troilus' destructive eroticism. And this leads to a rather different view of the relation between his initial idealization and eventual demonization of Cressida.

Whereas love in its subversive aspect entails a disruption of identity, a loss of self, Troilus, in love and out of it, displays, in the guise of vulnerability, a regard for self amounting to narcissism.[19] He is fiercely self-protective, governed by a need to place identity beyond subversion. His obsession with Cressida may be seen as a means to this end – self-aggrandizing sexual manipulation comparable to that practised by Vincentio and Helena. Unlike those characters, however, Troilus is not in a position to do much about his dramatic universe, which imposes inordinate demands on the youngest son of Priam and brother of Paris to perform as warrior and lover – related areas of insecurity, as Adelman demonstrates in analyzing Troilus' argument that Helen must be kept for honour's sake (Adelman 1980: 134–6). Time looms as the deadly enemy of human meaning,[20] even while it is also, paradoxically, the only possible guarantor of that meaning. The sense of futility is reinforced, from outside the text, by the audience's knowledge of history and, from within it, by Cassandra's.

What Troilus can hope to control is his self-image within this confining structure. Given her parallel uncertainties about her situation and identity, Cressida makes the perfect opponent in a one-sided struggle for moral mastery. The adolescent Troilus effectively constructs a *rite de passage* by which he can initiate himself into a secure sense of worthy manhood.[21] This entails integrating himself with his 'timeless' historical–literary destiny, the myth that has formed around him of chivalric perfection and Troy's 'second hope' (IV.v.109) – a myth that, by definition, can come into its own only when the 'first hope' is eliminated. That myth, as retailed (second-hand) by Ulysses, perfectly accords with Troilus' projected self – down to the sense of unrealized promise, doomed to be endlessly deferred:

> The youngest son of Priam, a true knight,
> Not yet mature, yet matchless, firm of word,
> Speaking in deeds, and deedless in his tongue,
> Not soon provok'd, nor being provok'd soon calm'd;
> His heart and hand both open and both free,
> For what he has he gives, what thinks he shows,
> Yet gives he not till judgment guide his bounty,
> Nor dignifies an impure thought with breath.

(96–103)

Yet the myth has a long way to travel from our first encounter with it in the puffery of Pandarus, deflated by Cressida's mockery. That mockery is itself exaggerated, ironically, but it reveals the threat she poses to Troilus by her knowledge of a gap between the person and the persona. Cressida's real disloyalty consists in wanting the self that Troilus must put behind him.

It should now be clear that Pandarus is necessary less because of his persuasive powers than because he protects Troilus from the *truth* of what he is doing, 'going between' in this sense too. Yet as the agent of the first phase of the project – for as with Vincentio and Helena, there are two distinct stages involved – he inevitably becomes the scapegoat for what Troilus chooses to interpret as betrayal, as he moves on to consolidating his moral and spiritual hegemony within a society that, with Hector's death, is as thoroughly doomed as was his love. In martyrdom there is power, as Isabella well knows, and as Helena amply proves. Indeed, in that Troilus will construct his subversion-proof self by repudiating sexuality, he is psychologically linked with Isabella. For his is also, in the final analysis, an erotics of suffering under the cover of self-sacrifice:

> Th' impression of keen whips I'ld wear as rubies,
> And strip myself to death, as to a bed
> That longing have been sick for, ere I'ld yield
> My body up to shame.

(*MM*, II.iv.101–4)

For Isabella, too, the idea of self-sacrifice is intertwined with the need to sacrifice someone else. A major difference is Troilus' access to male prerogatives. Like Bertram, he participates in the

174

character-type of the soldier who acquires power over (hence protection from) women through degrading knowledge of them, carnal and otherwise.[22] Yet he also exploits Cressida's false – superficially, at least – perception of his own behaviour as stereotypically masculine.

Don Juanism is a notion foreign to the courtly-love ethos, which is the ostensible cultural premise of the play-world, thanks partly to Chaucer's poem. For the medieval Troilus, as for Shakespeare, sex forms a natural part of a nonetheless idealized passion. It is 'that a lover most desires', as Ariosto says of the 'faithfull loving' Sacrapant (1.51). However, the English Renaissance version of the romance tradition preferred its heroes chaste, and Shakespeare's presentation – of Troilus himself, of Pandarus, and of the morals and mores of *this* Troy – enforces an opposition between spiritual and carnal aims. Despite his idealizing rhetoric, the Shakespearean Troilus, as he sets sail for Cressida's bed, would hardly be capable of the tender (if naïve) consideration displayed by Chaucer's hero:

'But herke, Pandare, o word, for I nolde
That thow in me wendest so gret folie,
That to my lady I desiren sholde
That toucheth harm or any vilenye;
For dredeles me were levere dye
Than she of me aught elles understode
But that that myghte sownen into goode.'
(Chaucer, *Troilus and Criseyde*, 1.1030–6)

His artificial and self-delusive fusion of the romantic and the physical exposes the later figure as, in effect, taking refuge from responsibility in his literary heritage.

This is the context, then, for Cressida's resistance to Troilus' artificial idealism, however much she counts, and stakes, on the depth of his passion. Criticism has amply documented her defensiveness, her sense of vulnerability, her reluctance to become engaged. Specifically, her observation that '[a]chievement is command; ungain'd, beseech' recognizes a sexual politics of male conquest in her milieu as she knows it, and as Shakespeare portrayed it. Yet Troilus insists on establishing faithfulness as the currency of psychological power with his extravagant challenge to her to match his own 'integrity and truth', his 'purity' and 'simplicity' (III.ii.165, 167, 169). She responds, 'In that I'll war with you' (171), and he eagerly takes up her metaphor: 'O virtuous fight,/When right with right wars who shall be most right!' (171-2). In effect, he manoeuvres her into outdoing his vow by agreeing to be made a model of falsehood if she should fail him. Only Cressida 'must give and hazard all [she] hath', as the subversive power of love requires.

So it is hardly surprising that Cressida should later put Troilus' conduct into the category she feared – and was encouraged to fear – it might belong in.[23] Troilus' detumescence of urgency, his bland eagerness to part after their tryst, fit the 'love 'em and leave 'em' pattern, as she immediately recognizes: 'You men will never tarry./O foolish Cressid! I might have still held off,/And then you would have tarried' (IV.ii.16-18). This statement need not be taken as 'chilling in its implication that Troilus is only one of many' (Adelman 1980: 136 n.21). Rather, it marks a return to the wry and wistful wisdom of her early soliloquy – wisdom that hardly needs, in this society, to have been gained by sexual experience. One may compare Desdemona's sighing exclamation, 'O, these men, these men!' (Oth., IV.iii.60) – also a response to a male faithlessness that is being projected upon her.

In the stressful scene of parting Cressida is fearfully alert to signs of Troilus' failure to match her love, and she finds them in his insistence on renewing, despite what for her has been the ultimate proof of commitment, the earlier 'war' of faith. His lack of faith in her clearly indicates his own shallow feelings. Her outburst, 'O heavens, you love me not' (IV.iv.82), arguably constitutes the emotional pivot of the scene. The self has been ventured and lost, her hopes destroyed of a sexual relation different from the cruelly exploitive models around her, as well as of a sanctuary from the broader context of destruction. Adelman aptly notices Cressida's reduction to silence by the end of the scene as the object of competition between Troilus and Diomedes (Adelman 1980: 127). The 'chance of war' (Prologue 31) has played into both their hands.

The male imposition upon Cressida of the role of wanton, beginning with the kissing episode and Ulysses' subsequent reading of the 'language' (IV.v.55) of her body, has been widely recognized.[24] The other side of the coin is her internalization – simultaneously self-destructive and self-protective – of Troilus'

176

betrayal. She now blames her own sex – that is, herself – taking the cynicism of men for granted and deploring the intervention of 'error', the disruptive principle: 'Ah, poor our sex! this fault in us I find,/The error of our eye directs our mind' (V.ii.109-10). For his part, Troilus' one-sided interpretation of her scene with Diomed ironically fulfils his earlier promise to 'give [her] nightly visitation' (IV.iv.73). He watches and 'reads' and raves, but he never thinks of communicating with her. His insistence on partitioning her ('This is, and is not, Cressid') – a reminiscence of her earlier self-division for his sake – dramatizes his own integrity in the predictable guise of subversion, with his 'soul' (V.ii.147) divided by the 'madness of discourse' (142). He is transparently seeking, not union, but separation.

Despite her disillusion and his silence, Cressida writes to Troilus of love. When he tears up the letter with a Hamlet-like contempt for any language but his own – 'Words, words, mere words' (V.iii.108) – he silences her conclusively, in a *reductio ad absurdum* of the principle that, as French puts it, '[i]nconstant women are central to male rhetoric' (French 1981: 159). But Troilus also commits an act of theatrical violence beyond even his previous mediation of her speech and actions: he actually denies the audience access to her words. This confirms that the stylistic distancing of Cressida in the latter part of the play, far from endorsing Troilus' view, functions as an index of her isolation and suppression. In so far as there is 'a radical inconsistency of characterization' (Adelman 1980: 120), it is the creation of yet another internal dramatist. Again, there is an instructive contrast with Chaucer's poem, where Criseyde recedes more drastically than in the play, as the narrator retreats into ignorance ('Ther is non auctour telleth it, I wene' (*Troilus and Criseyde*, 5.1088)) and charity ('Ne me ne list this sely womman chyde/Forther than the storye wol devyse' (5.1093-4)). There Troilus writes pleadingly and often to her and longs to believe her coldly evasive responses. The vulnerability, and the narrator, are unequivocally on his side.

The ultimate irony of Cressida's discovery of Troilus as the typical seducer is not that it plays his psychological 'game' and produces the betrayal he seeks, but that it is not true. Unlike Bertram – and of course his own 'shadow' Pandarus – Troilus is far from cynical about the sex-act, which, on the contrary, serves as a focus of romantic fantasy. Thus the mythology of anticipation reaches its climax in explicitly sexual terms, as he waits, at once Romeo- and serpent-like, in Cressida's orchard:

Th' imaginary relish is so sweet
That it enchants my sense; what will it be,
When that the wat'ry palates taste indeed
Love's thrice-reputed nectar? Death, I fear me,
Sounding destruction, or some joy too fine,
Too subtile, potent, tun'd too sharp in sweetness
For the capacity of my ruder powers.
I fear it much, and I do fear besides
That I shall lose distinction in my joys,
As doth a battle, when they charge on heaps
The enemy flying.

(III.ii.19–29)

This is a speech that might have furnished Jonson with inspiration for the grotesquely solipsistic sexual fantasies of Volpone and Sir Epicure Mammon. Troilus is wholly in the grip of his imagination, but what it imagines is itself. Ominously, his bizarre elaboration of the standard equation of sex with death first brings out the initiatory overtones of the experience, then gives way to the metaphor of combat. Infantile his love certainly is, but in celebrating the self-sufficiency and exclusivity of a transcendental sensuality, he expresses less a desire for the maternal than a nostalgia for the illusion of omnipotence.

As is well known, Troilus' response to the discovery that the lovers must part – 'How my achievements mock me!' (IV.ii.69) – contrasts sharply with Cressida's wild desperation: 'O you immortal gods! I will not go' (94).[25] Yet while he echoes Cressida's earlier complaint that men treat love as conquest, he does so with a tantrum-like frustration, registering an impact on himself of a kind alien to a Don Juan. For Troilus, the 'achievement' itself is not the be-all and end-all, but a means of 'mocking' him into a form of absolute self-sufficiency. His agent, left to impart the news, imparts also the irrelevance of Cressida's response – 'the young prince will go mad' (75) – and her exit in helpless tears is abruptly juxtaposed with his return in a false guise, 'acting' for the benefit of Paris, Diomedes, and the rest. This theatrical marking of a new identity accompanies a transfer of his emotional investment from possessing Cressida to giving her up, as he adapts his former rhetoric of anticipated possession to the idea of (self-)sacrifice: 'And to his hand when I deliver her,/ Think it an altar, and thy brother Troilus/A priest there off'ring to it his own heart' (IV.iii.7–9).[26]

Cressida's penalty for mocking Troilus' myth is to be mocked by it. She is not wrong in intuiting that he does not love her. But in view of that fact, she could hardly anticipate that his loss of her would lead, not to a replacement myth of new conquest, but to a more powerful myth of loss and betrayal that remains squarely focused on her. Troilus has put the very principle of emotional responsibility towards another (that is, an Other) – a principle perceived as subverting the stability of the self – safely into the past. There it remains beyond change, part of the pure and secure memory that he himself will shortly become, self-extricated from the 'wallet at his back' (III.iii.145) into which Time, according to Ulysses, that cynical and so ultimately less dangerous arch-manipulator, puts 'alms for oblivion' (146).

7

TRAGIC HEROISM: THE 'FORGERY OF SHAPES AND TRICKS' AND THE WRITING ON THE WALL

Crossing the traditional moralist barrier, various psychoanalytic critics of Shakespeare link Cressida and her near-contemporary Ophelia by way of their lovers' similarly conflicted sexuality.[1] An approach through subversion and counter-subversion broadens this link, incorporating the sexual dimension, which must largely be filled in from outside the text, into the visible pattern of power-relations. In *Hamlet*, too, a self-professed 'passion's slave' (III.ii.72), under pressure to define himself in terms of 'manhood', uses his love-interest to put behind him love itself and the threatening relatedness it involves. In aid of this process, Ophelia is bewhored and repudiated – Hamlet denies even the previous existence of emotion ('I never gave you aught'; 'I lov'd you not' (III.i.95, 118)) – then '*divided* from herself and her fair judgment' (IV.v.85), by which point she has internalized the licentiousness that he earlier imputed to her. When she is safely out of reach – less equivocally so, as '[o]ne that was a woman' (V.i.135), than the character who 'is, and is not, Cressid' – emotional commitment can be paraded in the past tense and in superlatives. Hamlet's arithmetic ('Forty thousand brothers/ Could not with all their quantity of love/Make up my sum' (269–71)) has all the self-discrediting distance of Troilus' protest, when Ulysses shrewdly questions whether, in effect, his display 'denote[s him] truly' (*Ham.*, I.ii.83): 'Never did young man fancy/With so eternal and so fix'd a soul' (V.ii.165–6). Ophelia resembles Cressida even in being more crudely manipulated by an older male relative who purports to have her welfare at heart but who sets her up as victim and finally joins her as scapegoat. In approaching this most problematic of tragedies, linked with the Problem Plays in so many oblique ways (and often considered one of them), to compare the two women as victims offers a perspective, however partial, of chilling clarity. Conversely, *Hamlet*'s greater realism, its hero's introspective habits, the open conflict within him between, as it were, love and war, and Ophelia's clear status as a side-issue all combine to dissect the dynamic that is folded in on itself in *Troilus*, where, more elusively, it is 'love' that denies love.

Hamlet also acknowledges this dynamic, which has been gathering momentum since the middle comedies and histories, as tending towards tragedy. Not even the 'problem comedies' could do this, given their 'happy' endings, while *Troilus* sidesteps the issue: Cressida's fate is not Ophelia's, while tragic closure is pointedly deferred for Troilus himself. At the same time, *Hamlet* continues to portray mechanisms of self-construction that are generally presupposed in the later tragedies. The protagonists of those plays come on stage with fully formed identities to defend – identities, of course, ready to crumble – and with an implicit claim to hegemony over their worlds. By contrast, Hamlet resembles those internal dramatists in the middle plays and late comedies, both male and female, who fence with the trickster before our eyes. Not that he seeks this match, any more than, apparently, he seeks that with Laertes: rather, he is challenged by the very epitome (if not incarnation) of subversiveness marginalized.

If Ophelia comes to embody, for Hamlet, a threat to the self whose duty is revenge, the obverse is his admiration for her heroically vengeful brother: 'For by the image of my cause I see/ The portraiture of his' (V.ii.77–8). When Hamlet appears in her closet to mime a ritualistic pathetic farewell, he re-enacts the annunciatory mission of the ghost itself, looking, she reports, '[a]s if he had been loosed out of hell/To speak of horrors' (II.i.80–1). He is ostentatiously confronting Ophelia's subversive love with a conflicting – and stronger – subversive claim. Yet this identification with the spirit of vengeance involves 'but the trappings and the suits' (I.ii.86) of subversiveness. It forms part of a staged fiction, the 'antic disposition' (I.v.172), whose conception went hand-in-hand with a momentary acknowledgement of his task, much as it might accord with his hostilities, as a terrible burden: 'The time is out of joint – O cursed spite,/That ever I was born to set it right!' (188–9).

That sentiment is never repeated. Hamlet is ready enough to accuse himself of lethargy, even of cowardice, in failing to act against Claudius, but he never again rebels against his assigned purpose in life. Nor does he deny his commitment to life itself, despite his wish, in the first soliloquy, 'that the Everlasting had not fix'd/His canon 'gainst self-slaughter' (I.ii.131). In so far as the 'To be, or not to be' soliloquy raises the 'question' of suicide and presents such 'action' as attractive, it does so in a safely impersonal way and works round to establishing cowardice as an excuse for all passivity. The dynamic has been succinctly described by Paul Tillich: 'Anxiety strives to become fear, because fear can be met by courage' (Tillich 1952: 39). Regardless of any extratextual 'source' of such anxiety, Hamlet's emotional investment of the killing of Claudius with ultimate meaning is transparently a fabrication – and inadequate to motivate the deed. His 'real' feelings have gone underground as unacceptable to that part of him that has, in a state of near-hysteria, internalized the ghost's message:

> Yea, from the table of my memory
> I'll wipe away all trivial fond records,
> All saws of books, all forms, all pressures past
> That youth and observation copied there,
> And thy commandement all alone shall live
> Within the book and volume of my brain,
> Unmix'd with baser matter.

> (I.v.98–104)

In effect, the 'antic disposition' that Hamlet makes so much of, scattering his disruptive energy in all directions, dramatizes for his own benefit his assimilation of the force that has overturned his identity, erased his past self. Hamlet stays in erratic motion so as to keep one step ahead of the ghost, aligning himself with its subversive thrust, lest he again become the object of subversion. His success may be measured by the spirit's second appearance, when Hamlet, having just passed up the opportunity of killing Claudius at prayer, is venting his hostility and frustration upon his mother, contrary to orders. Visible only to Hamlet, clad in a nightgown instead of armour, and altogether less authoritative, the ghost is prevented from doing any real chiding by Hamlet's anticipation of its purpose: 'Do you not come your tardy son to chide?' (III.iv.106ff.). Hamlet boldly displays his bloodthirsty persona – 'Do not look upon me,/Lest with this piteous action you convert/My stern effects' (127–9) – and the spirit 'steals away'

(134), as if exorcised. Never again is Hamlet's commitment challenged. He has succeeded in establishing himself as heaven's 'scourge and minister' (175) at the very point when he is about to be shipped off to England with no reasonable prospect of accomplishing his appointed task.

All he is doing, in fact, is submitting himself to danger, and this is the other side of the 'antic disposition', which (unless one strains the evidence) is stripped of the self-defensive rationale possessed by its counterpart in earlier extant versions of the story. The foolish-threatening behaviour that proves Hamlet's commitment to the role of revenger has the contrary effect of alerting and provoking Claudius. This is also true of the play-within-the-play, a triumph that leaves him at a conspicuous loss for a sequel. 'Now could I drink hot blood' (III.ii.390), he claims, but instead he turns aside: 'Soft, now to my mother' (392). The actual killing that follows is of Polonius – a blind act of violence which, in retrospect, he interprets as a near-miss, hence proof of his capability. His spontaneous 'Nay, I know not' (III.iv.26), when asked what he has done, gives way to contemptuous confidence: 'Thou wretched, rash, intruding fool, farewell!/I took thee for thy better' (31-2). The epithet 'fool' here, followed by Hamlet's jesting with the corpse, betrays the counter-trickster. This is Hamlet's conclusive outdoing of another figure whom he has perceived as a subversive threat – in effect, a rival, because closer to the 'real thing' than himself. It is not, in the end, enough to outfool '[t]hese tedious old fools' (II.ii.219), or to banish them: 'Let the doors be shut upon him, that he may play the fool no where but in's own house' (III.i.131-2). The match with the trickster, like the contest with Claudius that it displaces, is a matter of life and death. Thus, too, Hamlet gleefully paints his displacement from opportunity into jeopardy as a contest in cunning and blood, characterizing the King's naïve agents as if they were the King himself: 'But I will delve one yard below their mines,/And blow them at the moon. O, 'tis most sweet/When in one line two crafts directly meet' (III.iv.208-10). There is no parallel elsewhere for such intense identification with the subversive principle in something like its multiplicity – as if to exorcise the threat by consuming it, or by being consumed.

For Hamlet's highly public demonstrations of disruptive energy imperfectly mask not only his inability to execute the ghost's command, but the continuing influence of his original suicidal impulse, now gone underground. Only by dying can he escape his unfulfillable responsibility, but he can face death only in the self-fashioned guise of the foolish-passionate revenger, the blindly loyal son.[2] The serene faith he comes to profess in 'a divinity that shapes our ends' (V.ii.10) is indistinguishable, in practice, from a suicidal fatalism, and under this new camouflage he continues to send the same double messages. His letter to Claudius begins by combining a romance-like image of miraculous rebirth with a distinct note of menace – 'You shall know I am set naked on your kingdom' (IV.vii.43-4); he then appends the postscript 'alone' (52). He insults Laertes at Ophelia's grave, then agrees to the fencing match, despite his premonition and the suspicious circumstances. Only when he learns that he is doomed does he turn on the King – 'Then, venom, to thy work' (V.ii.322) – freed to avenge his own death rather than his father's.

The graveyard scene unites, first in the ultra-insouciant Gravedigger, then in the skull of Yorick, that standard pair, the Fool and Death, in a way that supports Blum's (1983: 265) perception of 'la possibilité donnée au fou de dire la vérité et de transformer la mort en vie'.[3] And 'la vérité' includes the fact that the transformation works, always and at the same time, both ways. Not far in the background lurks that seemingly supernatural horseman who exceeded Claudius' imaginative 'forgery of shapes and tricks' (IV.vii.89) but who puts the trick that will deal death to Hamlet into the King's head. Laertes makes his name into an exclamatory paradox: 'Upon my life, Lamord' (92).

The scene thus gives concrete embodiment to the link between Hamlet's playing of the fool and his attempt to turn the tables on mortality itself. Using Horatio as his audience, Hamlet stages yet another pageant, this time of the mastery of death, with yet another contrary subtext. What he presents as the last barrier to action – the gruesome reality of the grave – is equally the last barrier to annihilation. The more he attempts to appropriate the Clown's knowledge of the meaninglessness of death, the more he imports a conviction of the meaninglessness of life: 'Why may not imagination trace the noble dust of Alexander, till 'a find it stopping a bunghole?' (V.i.203-4). Even for Horatio, the romantic in arch-rationalist guise, this is reason taken to an extreme – 'to consider too curiously' (205). The opening dialogue between the Clowns has just proved the absurdity of curious reasoning in the face of death. In quibbling over Ophelia's responsibility for her own end – while ironically failing to mention the person ultimately responsible – they illustrate at once the cost and the futility of Hamlet's drive to monopolize subversiveness. Yet that drive will shortly reassert itself with hysterical desperation when Hamlet challenges Laertes to a duel of passion over her corpse.

Hamlet has matched himself with, and eliminated, the subversive in various vulnerable forms. The Gravedigger is the thing itself – at once 'lying' and truth-telling, endlessly poised, singing, on the threshold between life and death.[4] Yet Hamlet's response to this incarnation of liminality is to shut the door and lean upon it. And when that figure brings back from the dead the memory of his father's jester, as if extracting the subversive essence of the ghost whom Hamlet has nearly succeeded in laying, the Prince puts Yorick, too, back into the grave as a conventionalized emblem of human vanity. The death-grin is polysemous; it will laugh at mortality with the trickster's 'infinite jest' (V.i.185), if Hamlet will let it. Instead, he makes it echo his earlier attack on the threatening sexuality of the woman soon to take the jester's place in the grave: 'Now get you to my lady's chamber, and tell her, let her paint an inch thick, to this favor she must come; make her laugh at that' (192–5).

Hamlet thereby commits the same misreading of the jester's message as that less sophisticated, but less desperate, misappropriator of subversive tactics in *Love's Labor's Lost*, who pronounces it a thing impossible '[t]o move wild laughter in the throat of death'. As his blindness betrays his surrender to the very threat he pretends to have mastered, so it ensures that the final jest will be on himself. When he asks whom the grave belongs to, he is met with truth-telling equivocation: 'Mine, sir' (119). The Clown, it emerges, became grave-maker on the day that saw both old Hamlet's greatest feat of heroism and young Hamlet's birth. Clearly, Hamlet, about to pit his subversive energy against death by leaping into someone else's grave, is on the verge of his own.

I

The intrusion of various subversive elements at 'crucial moments' (Weimann 1978: 244) in the later tragedies is hardly a critical secret; nor are the frequent intimations of liminality. But it remains an underemphasized fact that a surfacing of the trickster, in the form of clown, fool, or servant, occurs at a liminal moment in every one of them. In two cases – the Clown in *Othello*, the Fool in *Timon* – the motif is so attenuated as to risk seeming pointless, and hence cuttable in performance. Aufidius' roisterous servants cannot easily be dropped, since they confront Coriolanus, but their banter and bravado are thinly sketched, and they are soon reduced – this is precisely the point – to chattering fans of the new alliance. Yet each of these three manifestations of lower-class subversive energy, mere textual hiccoughs though they may be, is not only associated with a turning point in the fortunes of the tragic hero but also liminal in the literal sense: they all have to do with thresholds, even more concretely than does the maker of 'houses' that 'lasts till doomsday' (*Ham.*, V.i.59). So, by definition, does the far-from-negligible Porter of *Macbeth*, while two other significant figures manifest a liminality that, while purely figurative, is powerfully so. The Clown in *Antony and Cleopatra* comes closest to *Hamlet*'s Gravedigger in explicitly mediating between life and death, though he is farthest from him, I shall argue, in his significance for the play. The best-known Fool of all, unique in the group for his sustained (if abruptly curtailed) presence and his attachment to a particular character, is widely taken to interpret between Lear and his unconscious.

Needless to say, these figures are not the only, or even the principal, sites of subversion in the late tragedies. Apart from the tragic heroes themselves, a wide range of characters exert disruptive influence on the action. Some have thrust upon them a subversiveness that remains wholly in the eye of the beholder; others have their subversive labels, even if attached by the protagonist, contextually confirmed. The supernatural sphere, though linked with Macbeth's imagination, lends authority to the Witches, as well as to Banquo's ghost. Iago and Edmund flaunt their Vice-heritage – Iago in diabolic terms – while Lady Macbeth invokes demonic forces. The mobs in *Coriolanus*, like those in *Julius Caesar*, are repositories of violent energy, though it is Caius Martius who turns that energy negative.[5] *Timon* designates as formal subversives the cynic Apemantus and, *en passant*, Alcibiades' courtesans and the Banditti. Finally, and crucially, there is Cleopatra, whose 'infinite variety' (*Ant.*, II.ii.235), intense sexuality, and responsibility for an Antony 'transform'd' – for better and worse – '[i]nto a strumpet's fool' (I.i.12–13), mark identification with the trickster-archetype, rather than mere participation in it. It is this transformative power, ultimately, of which Enobarbus is in awe: 'vildest things/ Become themselves in her, that the holy priests/Bless her when she is riggish' (II.ii.237–9). Such numinosity is the key to a treatment of the subversive unique in the canon.

At the core of each of these plays, by generic definition, lies the 'larger-than-life' *agon*, both inward and outward, of a central male character. The external subversive elements function to construct the internal struggle, too, in terms of the trickster-principle. Typically, the protagonist falls victim to a subversive threat, which he then internalizes in a self-destructive form – jealousy, madness, heroic fury, and so forth. By itself, this is merely to supply new vocabulary for the old 'slaves of passion'.[6] But 'passion', in these tragic heroes, is already beyond the pale, wholly negative. By going a layer deeper, cutting below tragic passion to subversiveness itself, with its potential for creation and destruction, it is possible to expose the hero's vulnerability as reflecting his prior exclusion of disruptive energy. As Richard III is made monstrous by his world's failure to break its closed cycle of bloodshed, so the microcosms that are the tragic protagonists project outside themselves the deformed and dangerous incarnations of the form of subversion most threatening to them. They are possessed, in short, by what they refuse to own.[7]

In this context, the liminal comic figures gesture towards forfeited possibilities, wrong turnings, neglected truths. At once engaging and morally neutral, they alone recuperate the trickster's native ambiguity as a positive value. And they do, after all, serve to impart a momentary 'relief' – not from tragic tensions (those they actually enhance), but from tragic ideology. In contrast with the 'allow'd' fools of the romantic comedies, they stand outside, not only the social structure, but the textual process; they are tangential and ephemeral. Only Lear's Fool figures in a sustained way; the Clown in *Othello* appears twice, the rest once. Only the Clown in *Antony and Cleopatra* – an important exception – actively contributes to the plot. Otherwise, these are the most extreme displacements of the subversive impulse in the canon. From that position, they help to deconstruct those forms of disruption already skewed by tragic bias.

Othello's Clown gets only a few lines to speak, but he is, in his first appearance, the general's door-keeper – an ineffectual one, considering the pending invasion of his master's hearth and home. It is by his agency that the disgraced Cassio first seeks access, via Emilia, to Desdemona, although Iago – two-faced Janus himself – immediately arrives to take charge of the business, his pronouns slipping ominously from his wife towards Desdemona herself:

> I'll send her to you presently;
> And I'll devise a mean to draw the Moor
> Out of the way, that your converse and business
> May be more free.
>
> (III.i.36–9)

Not only does the Clown thus figure at the beginning of the end, but the motive for his appearance is significant. He has been sent to stop the music that is Cassio's peace-offering: 'to hear music the general does not greatly care' (16–17). Whether a matter of mood or of preference for 'the shrill trump,/The spirit-stirring drum, th' ear-piercing fife' (III.iii.351–2), the response is ominous, especially given the custom of having music on the wedding-morning. Apart from the Shylockean overtones, this foreshadows the discord promised by Iago: 'O, you are well tun'd now!/But I'll set down the pegs that make this music' (II.i.199–200). Also suggested is Othello's deafness to an honest confession of folly – folly into which 'honest' Iago could dupe Cassio so readily and destructively because, like Othello himself, he has prided himself on self-control: 'To be now a sensible man, by and by a fool, and presently a beast!' (II.iii.305–6).[8] Having produced Cassio as 'honest fool' (353), Iago has reason to defend wine – using the lexis of witchcraft – as 'a good familiar creature, if it be well us'd' (309–10).

Iago's crossing of Othello's threshold is decisive. At the top of Act III, Scene ii, he himself serves as Othello's messenger, and he returns in time to appear as the general's only companion early in the next scene, when Cassio and Desdemona are discovered together. The agent of disruption who began by manipulating – deforming – the mode of carnival before the closed doors of Brabantio has made himself horribly at home. Anticipating his displacement of Cassio and Desdemona, the tragically biased subversive has effectively displaced the neutral figure of folly as door-keeper, controlling access to Othello's inner being. And when that figure appears again, in Act III, Scene iv, he has effectively been incorporated into Iago's scenario. Despatched by

Desdemona to summon Cassio – 'Tell him I have mov'd my lord on his behalf, and hope all will be well' (18–20) – he is ironically doing at once her bidding and her enemy's.

Many critics would agree that what Iago actually brings home to Othello is the latter's own doubts and fears, whose destructive potency reflects their repression. So central is the dynamic of subversion, however, as to obviate the need to fix the psychological grounds of Othello's vulnerability – those areas of self-doubt he glancingly acknowledges (his lack of Venetian charm, his blackness, his age) or, according to some commentators, conceals (a horror of sexuality[9]). What matters is that Othello's notorious self-mythologizing takes aim, as an existential strategy, at the multivalent trickster himself. Othello's story-telling is an attempt to contain and control – in words, in the past – nature's 'infinite variety', its capacity for the unexpected and improvisatory (hence the term *'lusus naturae'*), figured forth in terms of elemental destruction and monstrous aberration: 'the Cannibals that each other eat,/The Anthropophagi, and men whose heads/Do grow beneath their shoulders' (I.iii.143–5).[10]

Othello's public account of the wooing, as Greenblatt has stressed (1980: 237–9), makes Desdemona's love wholly dependent on the pseudo-magical power of the self projected in these narratives. Ultimately more *telling* is the fact that his love for her is made conditional on her response: 'She lov'd me for the dangers I had pass'd,/And I lov'd her that she did pity them' (167–8). Inevitably, when the cornerstone of his reconstructed identity appears to shift, there is a complete collapse – 'Othello's occupation's gone' (III.iii.357); the failure of the magic spell renews the 'witchcraft', now focused (through another doubtful narrative) on the handkerchief as symbol of loyalty. Othello has mythologized his love as a 'content so absolute' (II.i.191) that it transcends time itself, cherishing Desdemona as 'such another world/Of one entire and perfect chrysolite' (V.ii.144–5) – superlunary and non-human. As his feelings for her (not hers for him) will keep 'chaos' at bay ('when I love thee not,/Chaos is come again' (III.iii.91–2)), so his loss, not of the woman she was, but of what she has represented – 'I have no wife' (V.ii.97) – means cosmic upheaval: 'Methinks it should be now a huge eclipse/Of sun and moon, and that th' affrighted globe/Did yawn at alteration' (99–101).

Ultimate darkness and terror, then, belong to 'alteration'. It is

precisely Othello's downfall, and Iago's invariable argument –
even to Roderigo ('She must have change, she must' (I.iii.351-2))
and even regarding Othello ('These Moors are changeable' (346))
– that change comes with time, which Iago well knows cannot be
stopped. The key distortion that Iago at once mirrors and
promotes lies in Othello's association of change exclusively with
loss, death, 'chaos' conceived as mere destruction. The heroic self
may be enshrined in the past, but Othello still sees life as a one-
way trip: the vigour of youth is 'defunct' (I.iii.264); he is
'declin'd/Into the vale of years' (III.iii.265-6). In this context,
Iago has hit on the fatal flaw in Desdemona's status as immut-
able possession – namely, her own possession of desire, that
stubborn measure of separateness, physicality, and participation
in time: 'That we can call these delicate creatures ours,/And not
their appetites!' (269-70). Appetite inherently looks to the future
– a fact that Iago also exploits with Roderigo, wallowing in a
present of unfulfilled desire: 'Our bodies are our gardens, to the
which our wills are gardeners; so that if we will plant nettles or
sow lettuce . . . why, the power and corrigible authority of this
lies in our wills' (I.iii.320-6). The trickster has no trouble
making a 'fool' of Roderigo (383), but it is the trickster deformed,
twisted into the fantasy – Othello's fantasy – of controlling the
future implied by appetite.

The challenge of 'alteration' is perceived differently by
Desdemona – in terms of acceptance of time as a fertile medium,
offering infinite opportunity, if also uncertainty and the
potential for loss: 'The heavens forbid/But that our loves and
comforts should increase/Even as our days do grow!' (II.i.193-5).
She doubly weakens her position when she unwittingly opposes
to Othello's idealized version of their wooing (delivered, incidentally, in her absence) her ingenuous account of

> Michael Cassio,
> That came a-wooing with you, and so many a time,
> When I have spoke of you dispraisingly,
> Hath ta'en your part.
>
> (III.iii.70-3)

What Othello needs to memorialize as a single miraculous
moment that put a stop to 'alteration' is here revealed as an
ordinary process within time – a process ominously associated

both with Desdemona's skill in Venetian courtship and, in particular, with Michael Cassio.

The instrument for achieving magical power over time naturally becomes the scapegoat for the loss of such power. In transferring his commitment to the role of revenger, Othello in effect reverts to the warrior's imaginative power over death through the dealing of death – a reversion also seen in the crises of Macbeth and Antony. Though he disguises his assault on time by identifying himself with a timeless 'cause' (V.ii.1), he talks of preventing future betrayals and of renewing his love if Desdemona could be made changeless through death: 'Be thus when thou art dead, and I will kill thee/And love thee after' (18–19). The very realization that he cannot undo the deed, once done, becomes a backhanded self-stimulus to action. Finally, Othello's suicide involves an explicit resumption of his soldier-identity, a remythologizing of his past self in the cause of not merely fixing time but abolishing it.

It is Iago's representation of flux, therefore, that constitutes the most basic level of his threat to Othello. Like nature's mutability, the ability to improvise, which Greenblatt identifies with Iago (1980: 227–37) and which identifies Iago as a trickster-figure, is full of danger in itself – for what it is, not merely for what it does. His pervasive falseness expresses Othello's refusal to accommodate the trickster in his own guise, as after all he has failed to make Iago his lieutenant, interposing the man who helped to get him Desdemona. The lies that will gain that place at the price of mutual destruction are not pure invention, but the dark side of the truth that is the trickster's stock-in-trade. This is clearest when Iago is toying with Roderigo; for when he is at work upon his chief victim, his most vicious insinuations are overshadowed by the multiple 'fantastical lies' (II.i.223–4) that feebly bind, not Desdemona to Othello, but him to her.

II

The drive towards some form of transcendental perfection more obviously underlies the ostensible motives of the other late tragic protagonists; for them, too, subversion entails indications, and ultimately proofs, of the futility of that goal. In fact, given the inevitability of such action and reaction, it is possible to situate this dynamic at the core of tragic determinism in the late

Shakespeare, as the mechanism by which character becomes fate. This position receives support in cultural-historical terms from the concept of 'self-fashioning' as propounded by Greenblatt in his early work, especially his observation that 'any achieved identity always contains within itself the signs of its own subversion or loss' (Greenblatt 1980: 9). This view usefully intersects with Goldberg's, cited earlier, that 'hegemonic control is an impossible dream, a self-defeating fantasy' (Goldberg 1987: 244). Greenblatt's model, however, implicitly allows for the tragic trajectory, the *final* 'defeat' of the 'self', and, albeit from a collectivist perspective, suggests the mechanism whereby the productive potential of subversion is thwarted – in effect, the constitution of the trickster as 'other': 'the alien is perceived by the authority either as that which is unformed or chaotic (the absence of order) or that which is false or negative (the demonic parody of order)' (Greenblatt 1980: 9).

The pattern is easier to see where the heroes are explicitly their own worst enemies, actively pursuing the impossible in ways that guarantee their own ruin, in contrast with Othello's patent victimization and his apparently modest ambition for a happy marriage. Only in *Lear* is there another trickster–villain of Iago's ilk, and he is displaced onto the subplot, where he acts so as to ensure that his father reaps what he sowed (namely, wild oats): Gloucester, like Othello, merely wants things in the domestic sphere left the way he thinks they are, ignoring unfinished business. Otherwise, those external elements that become associated with the subversion of the hero (as distinct from the transient figures of folly) develop their disruptive power in response to his initiative. In seeking to manipulate his world, he effectively constructs the subversive in terms of interference, resistance, betrayal, mockery. Such contrary elements project an unacknowledged inward critique of that vision, a critique that inevitably widens into open self-conflict, reabsorbing the externalized, marginalized challenges. This helps to explain why even the clearly labelled agents of subversion tend to be profoundly equivocal, to use a term that applies, significantly, both to the Witches of *Macbeth* and to the protagonist's response to them.

Indeed, the Witches, who 'look not like th' inhabitants o' th' earth,/And yet are on't' (I.iii.41–2), and who have an obvious connection with Macbeth's thoughts,[11] furnish a paradigm of the process that elsewhere, more complicatedly, involves unequivocally terrestrial relationships. In appearing to offer a means of realizing the inner vision, then becoming its enemies, they follow essentially the same pattern enacted by Cordelia in the imagination of her father when he is confronted with her equally equivocal silence. Lear's perception of subversion is all but instantaneous; Macbeth takes the whole play to resolve negatively the weird sisters' initial potential for either 'good' or 'ill'. Yet both characters are merely switching from one projected interpretation to another. Macbeth is more right than he knows when he denies the very possibility of unitary meaning: 'This supernatural soliciting/Cannot be ill; cannot be good' (I.iii.130-1). The first sign of his fall is his insistence on reading this language by the light of reason instead of taking it on its own mysterious terms, whereas Banquo allows for the subversion of 'reason' (85) and accepts the contradictory gender-signs as impossible to 'interpret' (46).[12] (This is not to deny the equivocal presentation of Banquo, but merely to ally it with the equivocation of the Witches.) Fittingly, Lady Macbeth is introduced as the reader of her husband's letter, the active supporter – and, of course, translator into action – of his own biased translation. Her one-sided internalizing of the subversive 'word of promise' (V.viii.21), whose other side will claim its due in the form of nightmares and madness, complements Macbeth's refusal to acknowledge it as part of himself.

By incarnating the trickster-archetype in explicitly liminal terms, the Porter serves as a foil to this aspect of the Witches, who cross not only moral boundaries but those of gender, time, and nature itself. Yet their very liminality, which in itself might neutrally suggest infinite possibility and potential for transformation, has been distorted and restricted by passing through the lens of Macbeth's imagination. His one-sided response is already reflected in their intention to encounter him, as well as in their destructiveness. Theirs is no Puck-like delight in mischief for its own sake: vindictiveness and pleasure in killing inform their introductory exchange (I.iii.1-29). The trickster's 'promise' of change and growth within the flux of time is harnessed to Macbeth's compulsion to be, not merely king, but 'perfect,/Whole as the marble, founded as the rock,/As broad and general as the casing air' (III.iv.20-2). The need to 'give and hazard' the self in order to find it becomes a mere matter of risk-taking, including the risk of 'the life to come' (I.vii.7). Rebirth is reduced to the acquisition of new titles, new power.

Conventional though the role of comic devil may be for a subversive clown, the Porter's allegory obviously exposes the moral consequences of such distortion: the castle has become hell; Macbeth and his wife have damned themselves in this world, regardless of the next. They participate, too, in the various crimes exemplified by the Porter's imaginary clients – equivocation, treason, theft. More puzzling but most provocative is the first case, that of a 'farmer, that hang'd himself on th' expectation of plenty' (II.iii.4-5). The murderous couple certainly expect 'plenty', and they are in a sense hanging themselves, but it is significant, too, that the sin at issue is despair. As with the other late tragic heroes, the text is pointedly reticent about motives beneath the drive to restructure the play-world – a drive for which the text's own term, 'ambition', is conspicuously inadequate. What such a drive does imply, here as elsewhere in the canon, is a response to existential vacuum, and, to this extent, despair is very much to the point. Yet lest we should apply the model of Richard III rather than that of Hamlet, the Porter also makes it clear, by his own example, that these protagonists are far from possessing the trickster's characteristics, beginning with his self-delight. Trapped in the mimeticism of Shakespeare's late tragic style, they cannot rewrite their texts, even at their own cost. Whereas Richard carries his witches within him and lives the Porter's fantasy – 'Down, down to hell, and say I sent thee thither' (3H6, V.vi.67) – the monsters they make of themselves are doomed to remain pitifully and terribly human.

In their different ways, then, both Macbeth and his wife appropriate the transformational potential of disruptive energy without acknowledging its claims on themselves. And in proportion as those claims are denied, they return in forms that challenge the projected vision. The emblem of this process is the ghost's disruption of the banquet by which the new royal selves are to be consolidated.[13] Thereafter, Macbeth's tyrannical paranoia constructs representatives of the threatening side of the subversive in an attempt to keep its 'promise' pure and to outrun his conscience. This dynamic of exclusion finally prompts nature itself (with human assistance) to apply disruptive mechanisms – the moving of Birnan wood, a man not born of woman – so as to confront Macbeth with what he has refused to integrate.

Only in the last scenes does Macbeth's language at all come to grips with the subversive principle, for the first time since he faced the puzzle of 'good' and 'ill'. He suspects 'th' equivocation of the fiend/That lies like truth' (V.v.42-3) and finally resolves, 'And be these juggling fiends no more believ'd,/That palter with us in a double sense' (V.viii.19-20). Yet still the trickster is wholly 'other', and he 'lies like truth' without also telling truth like lies. Again Macbeth throws his shield before his body, but literally now: anxiety has become fear, and fear is met by courage.

The Porter does not merely furnish moral commentary on the larger action; he stops it in its tracks, interpolating a substitute world of play and improvisation in momentary defiance of the tragic momentum. By delaying the entry of Macduff and Lennox, the Porter does what Macbeth can never do: he makes time stand still. And in this textual gap he recreates, fleetingly, the forfeited potential of excluded comic energy, the mode of carnival with its celebration of physicality, including death itself, as the key to regeneration.[14] This meaning, too, is comprehended in his request to the play's agents of redemption – as well as to the audience, who might otherwise be carried too smoothly from Duncan's death-knell to the knocking at the gate to the alarm-bell: 'I pray you, remember the porter' (II.iii.20-1).

Delay also figures in the two other instances of subversive threshold-activity in the late tragedies, although these interruptions are less clear-cut, the interrupters farther removed from the trickster-archetype. When Aufidius' servants try to eject Coriolanus, when the Fool distracts the servants of Timon's creditors on his doorstep, the sudden shifts of perspective at these climactic moments, as confrontation is deferred, provide a blurred glimpse of the disruptive energy that is *not* being allowed a regenerative function in these tragic worlds. For where that energy manifests itself elsewhere, it comes, like the Witches, coloured by the role assigned it in that personal drama contrived by the hero to take him over a psychic threshold of his own.

Coriolanus is the starkest of the late tragedies, not only in style and action, but also in its depiction of the hero's ultimate subversive enemy. Caius Martius' transcendental ambition is not bound up with a plan of action; it is not premised on the active contribution of others to a personal or political ideal. He comes to need the people's voices, but the consulship belongs to his mother's absolutist vision, not to his:

Vol.:   I have lived
To see inherited my very wishes
And the buildings of my fancy; only
There's one thing wanting, which I doubt not but
Our Rome will cast upon thee.

Cor.:   Know, good mother,
I had rather be their servant in my way
Than sway with them in theirs.

(II.i.198–204)

On the contrary, his is frankly a vision of exclusiveness and independence, founded on a narrow concept of manhood and sustainable only through self-isolation. It is menaced by his humanity itself, whose dangerous sign is weakness, emotional and physical.[15]

As with Othello and Macbeth, the inevitable inner challenge to the fabricated ideal is projected outward and endowed with subversive energy. Robert N. Watson (1984) convincingly depicts Coriolanus as a dramatist who stages confrontations in order to support his self-image (146); in particular, he 'assaults the citizens as a way of externalizing, and thus resisting, an internal contaminant' (160). This process is complicated, however, by the role of Volumnia. She provides not only the kind of counter-subversive reinforcement of 'manhood' that is the specialty of Lady Macbeth, but also, unwittingly, the secret undermining practised by Iago. On the one hand, she is the undisputed founder and continuing patroness of Coriolanus' obsessive courage and contempt; on the other, she now wants him to alter course and resists his constitution of the plebs as 'other'. She herself thus takes on a subversive taint in her son's eyes, and there is good reason, apart from the much-discussed ambivalence in the relationship,[16] why her criticism should connect with the most basic threat to his self-image. For prior to her dehumanizing of him came her creation of his humanity.

Ultimately, it is only through death itself, the medium which has mediated his relations with the world, that Coriolanus can render himself invulnerable. Indeed, his actions from the point of his banishment lead him in this direction so consistently as to convey, as with Hamlet, a suicidal undertow beneath the heroic commitment. This death-wish – aimed squarely at the essence of his mother's creative power – is at once the root and the extension of his political self-destructiveness, with its objectified rebellion against Volumnia.[17] The subtext of self-destructiveness closely shadows the discourse of heroism, as when Menenius asserts, 'His nature is too noble for this world' (III.i.254), and praises his ability to 'forget that ever/He heard the name of death' (258–9). When Coriolanus cries, 'I banish you!' (III.iii.123), his turning of the fact inside-out mirrors an inner reversal: he will make war on himself, as on his nurturing city and nurturing mother, in the guise of self-assertion. Thus he proceeds, in a sequence that gives concrete embodiment to the boundary between reality and illusion, to re-image his enemy as his friend.

Our sense of Coriolanus' search for death is strong as he enters the house of Aufidius, who will eventually become, by trickery virtually forced upon him, the hero's executioner. Coriolanus' disguise marks a self-conscious suspension of his invincible identity – 'Then know me not,/Lest that thy wives with spits and boys with stones/In puny battle slay me' (IV.iv.4–6) – and in the soliloquy that precedes his encounter with the servants, he lays himself uncharacteristically open to fortune: 'If he slay me,/He does fair justice' (24–5). When he discloses himself to Aufidius, he goes farther; if his old antagonist has no stomach for new wars against Rome, he declares,

> I also am
> Longer to live most weary, and present
> My throat to thee and to thy ancient malice;
> Which not to cut would show thee but a fool.
>
> (IV.v.94–7)

The range of choices offered Aufidius – he may define himself as ally, murderer, or 'fool' – picks up the surprising language of contingency which Coriolanus, standing on the threshold, applies to the 'slippery turns' (IV.iv.12) of the world:

> so, fellest foes,
> Whose passions and whose plots have broke their sleep
> To take the one the other, by some chance,
> Some trick not worth an egg, shall grow dear friends
> And interjoin their issues.
>
> (18–22)

Michael Goldman notes Coriolanus' 'attempt at self-authorship' (Goldman 1985: 157) and distance on his own feelings here. But more remarkable is the accompaniment of his self-recreation, in a way reminiscent of initiatory rituals, by a symbolic return to chaos, dangerous but rich with the potential for new beginning. This matches the revelry in the house, with the First Servant calling for 'Wine, wine, wine!' (IV.v.1). When one includes the erotic language with which the two enemies unite, especially Aufidius' account of his dream (122ff.), the resemblance to *Romeo and Juliet* becomes insistent: 'My only love sprung from my only hate!' (*Rom.*, I.v.138). Coriolanus is like Romeo, incited by the trickster-like Mercutio to attend his enemies' feast, where the discovery of his name may be death, but where he finds love.

Yet this is to put the most positive construction, that of Coriolanus himself, upon the encounter, as well as to ignore the eavesdropping presence in the earlier tragedy of Tybalt, the trickster's nemesis, who heralds the fatal consequences of Montague–Capulet miscegenation. In his own view, Coriolanus has exposed himself to subversiveness, in the form of two out of three of Aufidius' choices, and not only overcome it but enlisted its power on behalf of his martial self: 'I banish you!' The reality is brought out by a more subtle parallel to Macbeth's second encounter with the Witches, when he seeks them out in their cave 'to know,/By the worst means, the worst' (III.iv.133–4), as he prepares to cross another threshold: 'I am in blood/Stepp'd in so far that, should I wade no more,/Returning were as tedious as go o'er' (135–7). What Coriolanus gets from his agent of disruption is a similar promise of, in effect, immortality, which only thinly veils the certainty of treacherous destruction. As with Macbeth, his blindness to the negative 'reading' confirms the link between the inner and outer challenges to the constructed self. The trickster has not been enlisted, but further displaced; as Aufidius' servants rally round the 'rarest man i' th' world' (IV.v.161), their rhetoric becomes a conspicuously pallid reflection of carnivalesque energy: 'Let me have war, say I, it exceeds peace as far as day does night; it's sprightly, waking, audible, and full of vent' (221–3).

Even the critic who has made the most of the protagonist's previous encounters with the subversive as staged and manipulated takes at face value the power-relations of the most artificial scene of all – the highly ritualistic series of supplications that culminates in Coriolanus' yielding to his mother. According to Watson, Volumnia 'subverts her son's ambitious project by forcing him to confront its latent Oedipal content'

(Watson 1984: 175).[18] Superficially, Rome and mother prevail; but, again, who is banishing whom? Beneath the surface, it may be argued, the subversion and the forcing work the other way. Far from signalling her 'triumph', Volumnia's failure to respond to her son's apparent capitulation is a response to its fatal implications – an especially complex version of the silence that elsewhere marks women manoeuvred into powerlessness. This hero makes his mother, not only the scapegoat for his tainted flesh and feelings, but also his escape route. Coriolanus guarantees his own death, but Volumnia will bear the responsibility: 'But, for your son, believe it – O, believe it – /Most dangerously you have with him prevail'd,/If not most mortal to him. But let it come' (V.iii.187–9).

The last words echo Hamlet's suicidal fatalism, and there is common ground with his treatment of Gertrude, but the closer analogy is with Troilus, especially given the filial dimension of the latter's relation with Cressida. To construct a subversive female emblem for his physicality similarly clears the road for Coriolanus' union with the masculine myth of transcendental heroism, the self as 'eagle' (V.vi.114), that is his historical destiny. It remains only for Aufidius to discharge the role he has been cast in, gathering the forces of violent treachery and provoking the anger that enables the 'nature . . . too noble for this world' to 'forget that ever/He heard the name of death'. The epithet, 'boy of tears' (V.vi.100), duly recapitulates in maternal terms the susceptibility to subversion, the taint of humanity, so that it can be destroyed forever, much as Othello conjures his subversive shadow, the 'turban'd Turk' (*Oth.*, V.ii.353). As Othello renews his faded warrior image, Coriolanus appeals to the 'annals' (113) recording his feats at Corioles. He, too, might as well have a concealed weapon to use against himself. The 'lawful sword' (129) that he wishes he could employ against 'six Aufidiuses, or more, his tribe' (128) – the elusive and manifold trickster – would not serve his deepest purpose.

Timon, one might say, does not so much cross a threshold as have his threshold crossed for him.[19] The first encounter with his creditors, by way of their servants, occurs as, with Alcibiades, he returns for his dinner after hunting, confident of his accustomed power to come and go as he pleases: 'So soon as dinner's done, we'll forth again' (II.ii.14). There is a parallel to the blindly self-indulgent Lear in Goneril's palace (I.iv), calling for his dinner and about to be jolted by the reality of his position – a reality mediated by another Fool. Lear will be expelled over alien thresholds he had thought his own, having actually given his own away, and he never does get the dinner he calls for. For Timon, there is a stay of execution, the space occupied by the interlude of the Fool, and the reckoning (literally) comes when he and his faithful Steward re-appear at his door. At Flavius' request, the servants walk apart so that the revelatory conversation can take place. More curiously, Apemantus takes the Fool off when Timon appears, despite their earlier exchange:

> *Apem.:* . . . Fool, I will go with you to Lord
> Timon's.
> *Fool:* Will you leave me there?
> *Apem.:* If Timon stay at home.

(88–91)

Perhaps this was mere jest – the equation of Timon and Fool is vintage Apemantus. Or perhaps it becomes obvious to Apemantus that Timon is not staying at home. In any case, Apemantus for once passes up the chance for a cynical dig, thereby suggesting the redundancy now of the subversive message that philosopher and Fool have to offer: their arguments have been displaced by the ineluctible lesson of hard cash – that is, the lack of it.

Timon soon internalizes that message in a way reminiscent of Lear's madness, which also has no need either of the Fool, who silently vanishes, or of Edgar, whom he had perceived as a 'good Athenian' (*Lr*, III.iv.180). Such internalization is signalled when Timon bursts out of his house to confront the obstreperous servants, who are at the point of forcing their way in:

> What, are my doors oppos'd against my passage?
> Have I been ever free, and must my house
> Be my retentive enemy? my jail?
> The place which I have feasted, does it now
> (Like all mankind) show me an iron heart?

(III.iv.79–83)

Festivity, linked with the freedom of his threshold, has been turned against itself; the lavish banquets of the old days will be ritually undone by an anti-feast: 'invite them all, let in the tide/ Of knaves once more; my cook and I'll provide' (116–17). The next move is to a threshold-less cave and the identity of Misanthropos, with humanity stigmatized in festive terms: 'Therefore be abhorr'd/All feasts, societies, and throngs of men!/His semblable, yea, himself, Timon disdains' (IV.iii.20–2).

This anti-self represents Timon's thorough identification with the subversive outlook formerly represented by Apemantus, whose place is on the margins of the feast – at 'a table by himself' (I.ii.30). Thus Apemantus himself now complains, 'Men report/ Thou dost affect my manners, and dost use them' (IV.iii.198–9). In so far as it reveals the cynic's own affectation, the accusation rebounds on his head, but he is also on to something. The encounters with conventional figures of disorder – Alcibiades' whores, the Banditti – involve Timon in veritable contests of subversiveness, and indeed the Banditti are done out of theirs in a way that anticipates Autolycus: 'H'as almost charm'd me from my profession, by persuading me to it' (450–1). Moreover, Timon resists modifying his vision to accommodate his steward's loyalty; when he is forced to retract his claim that 'I never had honest man about me, I; all/I kept were knaves' (477–8), he merely attempts to remould the man in his own new image: 'Hate all, curse all, show charity to none' (527). Now it is the Steward's challenge to that image that poses a subversive threat, and Timon is far from open to it.

In no other tragedy of Shakespeare is the collapse of the protagonist's self-image made so mechanical, absolute, and, to adapt Apemantus, extreme: 'The middle of humanity thou never knewest, but the extremity of both ends' (IV.iii.300–1). But then nowhere else is that self-image directly dependent, without mediation, upon an appropriation of the spirit of carnival, the emblems of disruptive energy, even the trappings of divinity.[20] The falseness of the appropriation is reflected in the cynicism of Timon's flatterers and false friends, but it is Timon himself who, carrying the role of Christ through to its appointed end, sets up his own betrayal. When cornered, he takes refuge in an image of himself as foolish victim – 'Unwisely, not ignobly, have I given' (II.ii.174) – that bears a resemblance to both the self-portrait of Othello as 'one that lov'd not wisely but too well' (*Oth.*, V.ii.344) and Lear's claim to indulgence as 'a very foolish fond old man' (*Lr*, IV.vii.59). All three lay claim to the innocence of folly. Timon stands alone, however, in having projected this role from the start. Apemantus has been an indispensable presence at the feast, precisely because of his persistent accusations of folly. Yet Timon is no fool in the true sense. His indulgence of festivity has itself been 'affected' (in contrast, say, with Sir Toby's) because it has involved, not self-abandonment, but self-fabrication. And the essence of this process has been what Lear attempts in his first scene – the buying of love through giving.[21] Timon has been building towards the moment when he proclaims the triumph, couched in the lexis of spirituality, of his self-delusion:

> And in some sort these wants of mine are crown'd,
> That I account them blessings; for by these
> Shall I try friends. You shall perceive how you
> Mistake my fortunes; I am wealthy in my friends.

> (II.ii.181-4)

In keeping with the pattern elsewhere, then, the falseness of Timon's own project effectively constructs the falseness of his friends, converting debtors into creditors in a self-destructive inversion of Portia's manipulations of Antonio, Bassanio, and Shylock. While exploiting the outward forms of folly so as to set himself above his fellow men, he prepares a fall that will confirm his moral monopoly in the diametrically opposite role of subversive cynic, *below* all men. In their roughly analogous stagings of self-betrayal, Troilus and Coriolanus are assisted by female figures who can be made the focus and locus of their own irrationality. Timon faces the tougher challenge of constituting the whole human race as 'other'. As Apemantus' pivotal role reveals, the continuity between Timon's 'extremities' consists in his relation to the principle of subversion. Narrowly self-protective as he is from start to finish, his opening and closing postures both 'affect' the energy of disruption, in its positive and negative aspects respectively. In the last analysis, it is precisely this artificial distinction that reveals the falseness of both claims. The Fool in his pure form, who follows 'sometime the philosopher' (II.ii.122), momentarily intervenes between crime and consequences but never crosses Timon's threshold.

The rather more prominent Fool in *Lear* has acknowledged status as the epitome not merely of truthful folly but of truthful folly marginalized – something easier to see here, evidently, than with the 'allow'd' fools of *Twelfth Night* and *As You Like It*. Moreover, to the extent that this marginalization reflects his master's attempt to exclude from consciousness the truths that the Fool tells, a form of liminality, too, may be taken for granted: when the Fool speaks, his voice comes to Lear distortedly across the barrier Lear has erected against all that menaces his vision of the world. Initially, royal power suffices to actualize that vision, albeit with revisions: he can banish the objections, silent and raucous, that he designates as subversive. Eventually, after successive retrenchments, the vision can be sustained only as fantasy, although Lear's madness, alternating between extremes of despair and mania, internalizes 'in his little world of man' (III.i.10) the same fluctuation between vulnerability to subversion and aggressive counter-assertion. At the extreme poles of Lear's engagement with reality and his withdrawal from it, the Fool has no place. His mediation belongs to the phase of dynamic interaction between Lear's illusions and the external forces of disillusion. And, as has often been observed, when Lear awakens from madness he takes over the Fool's role himself. As Farnham puts it, presuming that the Fool's 'sapience' has been thoroughly absorbed, 'there comes a time when he needs no longer to be a separate self of Lear' (Farnham 1971: 119) – a view that meshes, paradoxically, with Willeford's perception of Lear's acknowledgement of folly in terms of a necessary differentiation of the formerly conflated roles of king and fool (Willeford 1969: 213–23).

Such a bond between the protagonist and an explicit figure of folly is unique in the late tragedies. But then so is Lear's participation in a prolonged dialogue between truth and self-deception that strongly implies a teleology of redemption. More than any of the tragic heroes except Antony, Lear seems always within reach of a capacity to '[s]ee better' (I.i.158). His sight improves in frank terms of the recognition of folly ('Beat at this gate, that let thy folly in/And thy dear judgment out!' (I.iv.271–2)), to the point where he redefines himself as 'foolish fond old man'. From this perspective, the increase in his intimacy with the Fool points towards the sort of self-realization that leads audiences and critics to reject the ending as unbearably painful, essentially because poetically unjust.[22] That ending, of course, by way of Lear's resonantly enigmatic cry, 'And my poor fool is hang'd!' (V.iii.306), sets the seal on the Fool's much-discussed function as stand-in for Cordelia during her absence in France.

The mediating ministrations of Kent and Edgar, whose disguises loudly proclaim the disruptive energy imputed to them by others, shed light on this link. The Fool functions, it would seem, in a parallel way, keeping Lear in touch with the subversive principle he had sought to banish with Cordelia. For Kent and Edgar, however, foolishness is never more than skin-deep – a cover for their resistance to the genuinely disruptive practices of Goneril, Regan, and Edmund. To Lear and Gloucester they offer protection, reinforcement, and comfort, not creative confrontation. Kent's reckless disruptiveness flatters Lear's non-existent '[a]uthority' (I.iv.30); Edgar's claim to transformative power is exposed by his decision to 'trifle' with Gloucester's 'despair' in order to 'cure it' (IV.vi.33-4) – an echo of Vincentio's rationale for keeping Claudio's survival from Isabella. 'Think that the clearest gods . . ./. . . have preserved thee' (73-4), he enjoins – an illusion that depends on the repudiation of his former disguise: it is one thing to be possessed by the 'fiend', another thing to be one. The identification of the Fool with Cordelia tends to render his subversiveness similarly toothless: after all, commentators stress the affectionate support, not the abrasiveness, in his relation with Lear; the Fool's 'nuncle' modulates into Cordelia's 'dear father'.

In this light, the Fool's inextricability from his master's thought-processes reflects not Lear's openness and susceptibility but his continuing control and resistance. Ultimately, the Fool is less the 'bur' that will 'stick' to Vincentio than the clown that will 'go along o'er the wide world' with Celia. He, too, stands firmly with Lear against Goneril and Regan, who frankly demand that Lear accept his weakness and folly, his age and mortality. Implicitly, moreover, as Edmund does with Gloucester, they insist that their father should take responsibility for the unacknowledged darker side of his role as patriarch. This includes the familial jealousies that he, like Gloucester, has fostered as a form of emotional tyranny: they are built into the idea of the love test, his 'darker purpose' (I.i.36), and so bound up with his display of royal power. The extreme cruelty practised by the children considered 'illegitimate', together with the vulnerability of their fathers, manifests the extreme displacement by Gloucester and Lear alike of threats to patriarchal absolutism.

So when Lear admits to foolishness, it is only to a part of what the Fool represents, and this limited admission excludes the rest. Instead of recognizing the Fool as kin in the deepest sense – king and clown as a dynamic unit – he takes his cue for repentance from Kent's ultimately comforting accusation that he has blurred an essential binary opposition: 'To plainness honor's bound,/ When majesty falls to folly' (I.i.148-9). Confessing a mistake – a mere misprojection of the subversive, a mis-aiming of the 'shaft' of his anger (143) – makes a convenient substitute for reclaiming all that has been excluded from consciousness. Only at one moment on the heath does the transformative potential of the Fool show signs of prevailing – not in Lear's Timon-like recourse to the comfort of misanthropy, but when he prays for the '[p]oor naked wretches, wheresoe'er you are' (III.iv.28) in a way that acknowledges his responsibility. Yet like Gloucester's proto-socialist plea, on similar grounds of feeling as a way of seeing, that 'distribution should undo excess,/And each man have enough' (IV.i.70-1), Lear's fragile self-questioning collapses into renewed escapism. The critical blow is precisely the appearance of a poor naked wretch, not whereabouts unknown but right at hand. The Fool's attempt to help Lear keep his balance – 'Prithee, nuncle, be contented' (III.iv.110) – proves useless. The deeper irony is that Edgar's enactment of 'the thing itself' (106), the occasion for Lear's most explicit revelation of his underlying fear, is a superficial posture. Even though, in putting on the trappings of wretched mortality in order to save his life, he symbolically enacts the Fool's deepest message, Edgar will find it disturbingly easy to wield against his subversive brother not only his sword but his exclusive righteousness.

When Lear eventually concedes his status as 'foolish fond old man', he does so only in Cordelia's wholly indulgent presence. It is a renewal of his initial plea for her 'kind nursery' (I.i.124), and she obliges, as she would not do earlier, by granting him shelter from threatening reality. When they are captured, he strikes down her proposal to confront Goneril and Regan with a renewed fantasy of transcendence through her nurturing: 'No, no, no, no! Come let's away to prison:/We two alone will sing like birds i' th' cage' (V.iii.8-9). Lear has internalized a partial notion of folly only to recuperate a child-like irresponsibility.[23] The Fool's disappearance marks both this internalization and the suppression of the subversive threat. The visionary triumph over mutability – 'we'll wear out,/In a wall'd prison, packs and sects of great ones,/That ebb and flow by th' moon' (17-19) – confirms that the ultimate target of his counter-subversion here, as in the beginning, is the fact of mortality itself. He has aimed to gain power over death by pre-empting it – 'that future strife/May be prevented now' (I.i.44–5) – and retreating into a world beyond time, a second womb.[24] From this perspective, the final tableau seems inevitable – the surfacing of death as the ultimate subversion, no imitation now but truly the 'thing itself', with time reasserting its power through the failure to 'send in time' (V.iii.248).[25] Lear's insistence on banishing the Fool's traditional (if often invisible) companion, on splitting his twofold significance – 'la possibilité donnée au fou de dire la vérité et de transformer la mort en vie' (Blum 1983: 265) – has proved as destructive as the division of his outer kingdom.

III

It is the key to *Antony and Cleopatra*'s pivotal importance for my argument that, in the one late tragedy widely considered to cross the tragic frontier into the realm of romance, anticipating in style and ethos Shakespeare's final tragicomedies, the hero shares top billing with the chief subversive. Part of the title's point is that he shares much more – more, often, than he wishes to or than he will acknowledge. Notoriously, it is Antony's susceptibility to Cleopatra's disruptive energy – coded as sexuality but dynamically multivalent – that leads to his destruction. Without necessarily enforcing a moralist stance – the Roman reading of Antony's fate – the late tragic pattern points to the derivation of that energy from subversive forces within the tragic hero. But Cleopatra maintains from the start a claim to incarnate the trickster, not merely to reflect him, and that claim is justified by her extraordinary metamorphosis after Antony's death, when she applies the trickster's transformative power to Antony's spirit resurrected in herself. The tempestuous relation between the lovers finally issues in a form of Neoplatonic synthesis – a view supported by recent critical emphasis on the breaking-down of gender boundaries.[26] It is as if Othello were to free himself from Iago by venturing the loss of his 'occupation', the experience of 'chaos', for the sake of a guilty Desdemona. But then Desdemona's innocence is inextricable from the presence of Iago and has the ultimate effect of writing her out of the story; Cleopatra combines the two roles, making and remaking history for both herself and Antony.

Clearly, the centrality of Cleopatra marks a radical departure from the general tragic policy of marginalizing the subversive. The function of the Clown changes accordingly, in a way that anticipates the role of such figures in the universe of Shakespearean romance, despite his resemblance to other tragic agents of 'comic relief', those transient incarnations of a 'pure' subversiveness and liminality. In fact, a case can be made that the play's transitional status, its divided generic loyalties, are grounded in the conflict between tragic and romance versions of the dynamic of subversion. Well before the Clown appears – and his late appearance is part of the point – the play's extensive mythological apparatus throws that conflict into relief. Moreover, the very episode that specifically foreshadows the epiphanies of romance dramaturgy (albeit in a minor way) serves to focus Antony's evolving relation to the subversive principle. Again, a structurally marginal element is used to provide perspective on the trickster, but this time it is not the trickster who is marginalized.

Until Act IV, Scene iii, the universe of *Antony and Cleopatra* is down to earth. The characters' unusually frequent allusions to the gods do not compromise the picture of human beings as strictly on their own. There are not only no ghosts but more remarkably, given the setting, no omens or dreams. The Soothsayer's fortune-telling (for the waiting-women and later for Antony) is as close as the play has come to suggesting a metaphysical dimension at all. So when, on the eve of the penultimate battle, Antony's sentinels are surprised by supernatural music from 'hoboys . . . under the stage' (IV.iii.12, stage direction) and then interpret, ' 'Tis the god Hercules, whom Antony lov'd,/Now leaves him' (16–17), our own surprise comes partly from the breaking of a pattern – and for so little apparent reason. The scene is only twenty-one lines long and contains no major characters – nor, indeed, any with names. It does not advance the action. Yet Shakespeare's substantive alterations to his source for the narrative, Plutarch's *Life of Antony*, mark the scene as a site of textual redefinition. As is well known, he changed both the position of the scene and its content: in Plutarch it is not merely music but the noise of revelry that is heard, and the god is Bacchus.

Not that all patterns are broken. The scene's brevity, abrupt change of setting, and reliance on minor characters are all typical of the method of the play – there are, after all, fifteen scenes in Act

IV. This one, moreover, has straightforward dramatic functions: it serves to indicate the passing of time, while providing pre-battle atmosphere. Most important, it feeds into the dominant thematic line in an obvious way. As it happens, the next day's victory will be Antony's, but the writing is on the wall. He has been slipping increasingly into defeatism, punctuated by outbursts of ineffectual aggression (the flogging of Thidias has taken place three scenes earlier). The desertion of his followers will soon culminate in the defection of Enobarbus. What could be more appropriate than that the very spirit of heroic valour should take leave of him? It is easy to ignore the scene's status as a turning point, not only in the hero's fortunes, but in the presentation of the lovers.

Love makes the natural critical point of entry into the play's mystical counter-current. Amongst commentators along these lines, there is general agreement that, as Roger Stilling puts it, in death the bond of love 'is restored and paradoxically affirmed' (Stilling 1976: 288). But Eugene Waith insists that the transforming power of Cleopatra's words and feelings actually produces a 'recreation' or 're-discovery' of Antony's image – 'an image which owes as much to the ideals of romance as to the older heroic ideal' (Waith 1962: 114–15).[27] And Adelman, who demonstrates more broadly that the play's hyperbole 'begins to invoke our belief, in spite of all reason' (Adelman 1973: 117), confirms that romance is very much to the point, and not just because of the values portrayed.

In so transforming Antony (and herself), Cleopatra completes the mythologizing process whereby the plausibly mimetic representations we have followed converge with their own legend. This was always implicitly their destination, as it was their starting point, and the clearest sign of arrival is their own consciousness of that legend as their ends approach. Enobarbus, ironically, talks of earning 'a place i' th' story' (III.xiii.46) through the very loyalty he will shortly abrogate. Antony dies counting himself 'a Roman by a Roman/Valiantly vanquish'd' (IV.xv.57–8), while Cleopatra takes action so as to deny degrading material to the 'quick comedians' (V.ii.216). And Caesar, whose obsession has been with history all along, must finally concede:

No grave upon the earth shall clip in it

A pair so famous. High events as these
Strike those that make them; and their story is
No less in pity than his glory which
Brought them to be lamented.

(359–63)

The play has decisively moved beyond tragedy into a world like
that of Shakespeare's final plays – a world whose essential
quality is, in Adelman's phrase, a 'sense of the participation of
the mythic in human life' (Adelman 1973: 80).

This implies that the apotheosizing rhetoric of the protagonists opens up a genuine alternative to the bitter reality that
seems to undercut it. In fact, there is a springboard effect, with
the transcendental impulse actually gaining creative potency
from the ironic tension. The absurd fact that Cleopatra is not
dead helps to project Antony's imaginings into their own
legitimate sphere, where they match the imaginary nature of her
death:

Eros! – I come, my queen! – Eros! – Stay for me!
Where souls do couch on flowers, we'll hand in hand,
And with our sprightly port make the ghosts gaze.
Dido and her Aeneas shall want troops,
And all the haunt be ours.

(IV.xiv.50–4)

The grotesque physical elevation of the wounded Antony does
not mock, but adds impetus to, Cleopatra's fantasy of divine
strength (exercised through the trickster-god), as does her coming
back to earth, a self-acknowledged 'fool':

Had I great Juno's power,
The strong-wing'd Mercury should fetch thee up,
And set thee by Jove's side. Yet come a little –
Wishers were ever fools – O, come, come, come.

(IV.xv.34–7)[28]

Even Dolabella's mild but firm insistence on Antony's human
proportions in the face of her extravagant myth produces
balance, not deflation – a sense of two valid perspectives side by
side:

Cleo.: Think you there was or might be such a man
As this I dreamt of?

Dol.:   Gentle madam, no.

(V.ii.93–4)[29]

As Cleopatra goes on to confirm, much more than mere dreaming is involved. Her imagination has penetrated to the region of the gods, tapping the creative energy of nature itself: 't' imagine/An Antony were nature's piece 'gainst fancy,/Condemning shadows quite' (98–100). 'Shadows' reaches out to include all mortal actors on the world's stage. By the time Cleopatra's senses actually present her with Antony's image and voice, he is endowed with a god's-eye view: 'I hear him mock/ The luck of Caesar, which the gods give men/To excuse their after wrath' (285–7). And when she joins him, there is no trace of her old impulsiveness or changeability. She is 'marble-constant' (240) in making herself 'fire and air' (289).

When Antony and Cleopatra leave behind heroic, and heroically flawed, humanity for the pantheon, they make the same transition that Hercules himself once made. But to become a god means to serve none. To serve, moreover, as Antony has done – blindly, erratically, without a secure sense of independent identity – bespeaks less service than possession. In fact, there is a powerful sense in the departure scene of more than a simple parting. It is as if the god, as it 'now leaves him', is relinquishing the body it had inhabited. And this has important implications in terms of the human qualities associated with the god.[30] An internalized god suggests a demand for exclusive and absolute fealty by a part of the self that cannot be properly known or assessed. Such service is doomed to failure: other parts of the self, other gods denied, will, subversively, have their due. And so they have had, of course, in Antony's alternate worship (for which he regularly condemns himself) of his 'great fairy' (IV.viii.12), whose 'beck', as he complains, 'might from the bidding of the gods/Command me' (III.xi.60–1). In this context, the externalization of the god manifests a liberation necessary for psychic balance. And if this comes only after the keenest spiritual torment – a veritable crucifixion, with Antony agonizingly suspended between Roman and Egyptian 'thoughts' – such a death, such chaos, must logically precede rebirth. For him, too, 'desolation does begin to make/A better life' (V.ii.1–2). The transformation from tragedy to romance, then, is signalled even before the finality of loss energizes the lovers' imaginations. A new dimension of the universe is unfurled; they are stepping unawares through the looking-glass.

If the departure of Hercules marks, not the collapse of Antony's warrior identity, but the re-placing of a god where a god belongs, it is easier to understand the sudden alleviation of his despair. He has not lost his allegiance to Hercules, as his martial spirit and heroic performance in the battle – that is, both words and deeds – indicate. But the cycle of obsession, lapse, and anger has been broken, at least for the present (there will be a reversion, with fatal consequences). The measure of his self-reconciliation is his reconciliation to his goddess of pleasure, his accommodation of her disruptive energy. Up to this point, he has been vacillating wildly between extremes. Both Thidias and Cleopatra have been lashed – she perhaps more brutally, though only verbally – as a displacement of self-flagellation. The text presents Antony's feelings of failure in a familiar code, through his painful sense of his own age and Caesar's youth. The manic phase that follows shows him trying to recapture a youthful persona – 'Let's have one other gaudy night' (III.xiii.182) – and boasting of his power over death through the dealing of death: 'I'll make death love me; for I will contend/Even with his pestilent scythe' (192–3). So to 'outstare the lightning', to be thus 'furious' (194) – these are Enobarbus' terms – clearly evinces Herculean possession; only in this way is he 'Antony again' (186), and although Cleopatra may keep his revels company, she cannot truly be with him.

This changes, literally, overnight. When Cleopatra helps to arm Antony on the morning after the god's departure, it would take an uncompromising moralist indeed to deny value to their unstrained communion, which is all the more remarkable for the realism on both sides. Antony's farewell looks the future straight in the eye – 'Fare thee well, dame, what e'er becomes of me./This is a soldier's kiss' (IV.iv.29–30) – as does her comment afterwards on their hopeless position: 'He goes forth gallantly. That he and Caesar might/Determine this great war in single fight!/Then, Antony – but now – Well, on' (36–8). It is the time of Antony's extraordinary – because neither impulsive nor self-dramatizing – act of spiritual generosity: the forgiving of Enobarbus. And his exuberant homecoming incorporates a frank acknowledgement of age into its renewed self-confidence: 'What, girl, though grey/Do something mingle with our younger brown . . .' (IV.viii.19–

20). The inner victory is as temporary as the outer one, but perhaps all the more significant because of this.

It is later, when he presumes Cleopatra has betrayed him in the final battle, that Antony has his most notoriously Herculean moment:

> The shirt of Nessus is upon me; teach me,
> Alcides, thou mine ancestor, thy rage.
> Let me lodge Lichas on the horns o' th' moon,
> And with those hands, that grasp'd the heaviest club,
> Subdue my worthiest self. The witch shall die.
>
> (IV.xii.43–7)

By seeing Antony's reversionary loss of control, not merely as a mimetic tracing of the classical model,[31] but as a dynamic of counter-subversion – the god taking over again, re-imposing a sense of the failed heroic ('worthiest') self as exclusively valid – we can better appreciate the distortion of his vision. To start with – and this error begets the others – he is wrong about Cleopatra this time. But his lack of openness to her excuses and, more broadly, to her love, contrasting as it does with his earlier forgiving of her cowardice, helps make the point that her culpability is virtually beside the point. She is, in fact – not merely in his imagination – unpredictable and unreliable: this is the key to her transformative potential. Her 'infinite variety' is the essence of her love-divinity, and, as the Clown points out, when one meddles with dangerous creatures one must accept their natures: 'the worm will do his kind' (V.ii.262–3). Certainly, she is part witch, but to see only her black magic is to use the eyes of the god that hates her.

Even in deceiving him about her death, as she used to do about her humour ('If you find him sad,/Say I am dancing' (I.iii.3–4)), Cleopatra is being true to herself; in projecting his own feelings of inadequacy, of self-betrayal, upon her, Antony is not. The initial form of his despair in the suicide scene seems calculated to signal that identity has become elusive, impossible to grasp, because the heroic self-image has again claimed hegemony: 'Here I am Antony,/Yet cannot hold this visible shape' (IV.xiv.13–14). It is, in effect, the validity of the other self that Mardian insists upon when he turns aside Antony's Herculean thrust, 'She has robb'd me of my sword' (23), a statement whose narrowness is emblematized by its notorious phallicism. Mardian's reply –

212

suggestively, he earlier expressed his concept of sexuality in terms of '[w]hat Venus did with Mars' (I.v.18) – defines love as interpenetration: 'No, Antony,/My mistress lov'd thee, and her fortunes mingled/With thine entirely' (IV.xiv.23–5).[32]

It takes the subversive fiction of Cleopatra's death to exorcize Hercules again, and Antony's terms point clearly to the god's identity: 'Now all labor/Mars what it does; yea, very force entangles/Itself with strength' (47–9). The effect is to restore the god to its rightful position as emblem, not of the whole man but of his heroic side, which is now free to coexist again harmoniously with his love: masculine and feminine are symbolically in balance, as they will be in Cleopatra when she kills herself in fact. The ultimate sign of restoration is Antony's reaction when Cleopatra's real act of deceit – the one which has cost him his life – is revealed. Surely this would provoke the classically Herculean hero (and perhaps even lesser beings) to recrimination. Yet Antony has no sense of wearing the 'shirt of Nessus' now, and, significantly, the text furnishes no explanation for this acceptance. It provides only a powerful impression of Antony as inwardly at peace once more because acknowledging his dual loyalty. As after the earlier departure of the god, this self-possession expresses itself in his desire to be with Cleopatra ('Bear me, good friends, where Cleopatra bides' (131)), his kindness to his followers, and his noble patience in the face of death. He is on his way to securing the 'new heaven, new earth' (I.i.17) that his love could not generate when he boasted of its power in the first scene.

The renewal of Antony's love, in contrast with classical precedent, leads Waith to conclude that the 'meaning of Antony's tragedy does not lie entirely in the Herculean pattern' (Waith 1962: 120). Yet part of that pattern, as Waith himself expounds it, is the fable of Hercules' Choice of Virtue over Pleasure. Although this fable was extremely popular among Renaissance moralists[33] (and has thus proved useful for modern commentators of the same persuasion), John Coates (1978) and Barbara Bono (1984: 160–1) have valuably applied it to the play in terms of the interest it also held for Renaissance Neoplatonists. Still, in continuing to see Hercules as the 'complete man', an ongoing model for Antony's evolution, both critics in effect drift back into the moralist mainstream.

According to Edgar Wind's (1967) classic study of Renaissance mythology, the rejection of dialectical process implicit in the Choice of Hercules made the hero, for proponents of mystical synthesis, an emblem not of completeness but of limitation. Wind cites the views of such figures as Ficino and Pico that the 'Platonic initiate' would see through and supply (from outside the myth) the very 'absence of any transcendent alternative' that made the fable useful in moral teaching (205). Moreover, Ficino presents Hercules as having offended against the principle of the *triplex vita* (*contemplativa, activa, voluptuosa*) and so as justly punished by the gods he neglected (Wind 1967: 82). The popularity of the syncretic ideal may be judged by the ubiquitous use of the Judgement of Paris motif to flatter princes – notably including Elizabeth, as in Peele's *The Arraignment of Paris* (Wind 1967: 82-3). More to the point, however, as has been recognized, is the prominent myth of the union of Venus and Mars to produce Harmony, *discordia concors*.[34] This ancient mystical idea captured the imagination of Renaissance Neoplatonists and inspired a great many pictorial representations of Venus associated in various ways with Mars's armour (Wind 1967: 85-96). The concept amounts to a rebuttal of Hercules' choice-making in closely comparable terms.

Of special relevance is Plutarch's exegesis of this myth in his essay on Isis and Osiris, which appeared in Holland's English translation in 1603. The formative importance of this text for Shakespeare's play has been securely established, thanks to Michael Lloyd (1959) and the development of his observations by Bono (1984: 199-213), but an important point has been missed. The Stoic distinction endorsed by Plutarch – 'the generative and nutritive Spirit, is *Bacchus*; but that which striketh and divideth, is *Hercules*' ('Of Isis and Osiris', 1304) – confirms the limitation built into Antony's link with Hercules. Hercules, for Plutarch, blends into the figure of Typhon, the death-principle that perpetually opposes the creative union of Isis and Osiris (the latter identified with Bacchus):

> the Aegyptians evermore name *Typhon, Seth*, which is as much to say as ruling lordly, and oppressing with violence. And after their fabulous manner they say, that *Hercules* sitting as it were upon the Sunne, goeth about the world with him; . . . they put the power of *Osiris* in the Moone. They say also, that *Isis* (which is no other thing but

generation) lieth with him; and so they name the Moone,
Mother of the world; saying, that she is a double nature,
male and female.

(1304)

It strikingly suits the emergence in *Antony and Cleopatra* of a
transcendental 'third term', transforming the heroic through the
disruptive energy of eroticism, that a myth of choice should yield
to one of creative union. The importance of this displacement is
suggested by Shakespeare's extensive manipulation of his primary source. By changing the identity of the departing god, he
emblematized the effect of the departure itself, restoring to
Antony the fertile multiplicity of Bacchus–Osiris. Thus one text
of Plutarch cancels another, the Neoplatonist philosopher
superseding the moralist–historian. Shakespeare also invented
the arming scene that follows, infused it with a highly symbolic
harmony, and sustained its imagery in the lovers' exultant
reunion after the battle:

> O thou day o' th' world,
> Chain mine arm'd neck, leap thou, attire and all,
> Through proof of harness to my heart, and there
> Ride on the pants triumphing!

(IV.viii.13–16)

Perhaps most significant, though, is the alteration of the
sequence of events as its stands in Plutarch. There the victorious
sally of Antony, mentioned merely as a minor skirmish, precedes
the 'gaudy night' and the departure scene; the apparent omen of
defeat is made contiguous with the final debacle. In its new
position, where it unexpectedly heralds not defeat but victory, the
departure scene transgresses tragic form and destabilizes the
moral régime associated with it.

While the arming scene is rich with Neoplatonic overtones,
and the new sequence is powerfully suggestive, there is still
nothing inherent in the departure of Hercules to challenge the
narrowly judgemental understanding that would come so readily
to the orthodox moralist. It may be argued, however, that the
entrapment of such opinion is part of the process of exposing it
as inadequate. Certainly, the soldiers' responses constitute a
caveat against overconfident interpretation:

1 Sold.: Music i' th' air.

3 Sold.:   Under the earth.
4 Sold.: It signs well, does it not?
3 Sold.:   No.
1 Sold.:   Peace, I say.
        What should this mean?

(IV.iii.13–15)

Moreover, the gathering power of the lovers' non-worldly triumph generates two pointed revisions of judgements made according to the Herculean perspective. In deciding to desert Antony, Enobarbus accurately takes his measure, as he has done throughout, on the premise of the incompatibility of Virtue and Pleasure. But he finds that he has offended against principles that transcend that distinction – against, in effect, Antony's godhead, manifested in his bountiful forgiveness. 'Your emperor/Continues still a Jove' (IV.vi.27–8), according to the soldier who brings him the news. Enobarbus' fatal seizure of melancholy comes close to being a second numinous event: its affinities are with the curse of Cain, the despair of Judas.

Caesar, too, consistently applies the Herculean model. He even provides Antony with a goddess of Virtue, in the person of Octavia, to dramatize Antony's falling-off. Caesar's final acknowledgement that the lovers' fame matches his own involves a forced retreat from his concept of immortality through worldly victory: 'her life in Rome/Would be eternal in our triumph' (V.i.65–6). His ambition has amounted to a challenge in terms of the Choice of Hercules. It was an important feature of the fable (as influenced by the story of the dream of Scipio) that Virtue offered the hero immortality, while the association of Pleasure with death was often explicitly portrayed. The spiritual victory of Antony and Cleopatra over death, sealed by Cleopatra as *Venus victrix*,[35] uniting in herself now masculine and feminine, signals a transcendence also of a moralistic eschatology.

It appears, then, that in initiating the counter-current of triumph and beauty as the lovers go to their doom, Shakespeare used the Hercules scene as a sort of pivot, suspending in it the play's central paradox. That this paradox is developed through Neoplatonic resonances hardly constitutes Shakespeare as a mystical adept. After all, the same pattern was frankly used by Ben Jonson about ten years later as the core of his masque, *Pleasure Reconciled to Virtue*. There the mystical union of the two contraries is figured forth in a series of dances designed by Daedalus, who possesses the lore of 'sacred harmony' (Jonson, *Pleasure Reconciled*, 215).[36] Coates has pointed out the general relevance to Shakespeare's play (1978: 46-7). But what the masque throws into relief is precisely the limited role of Hercules. The hero's function as 'active friend of Virtue' (147) is rendered redundant. Mercury, appearing as instrument of a higher wisdom, praises him, but then effectively relieves him:

> But now
> The time's arrived that Atlas told thee of: how
> By unaltered law, and working of the stars,
> There should be a cessation of all jars
> 'Twixt Virtue and her noted opposite
> Pleasure.
>
> (165-70)

Hercules does not go on to play a new part - he is simply superseded. And when the dancing begins, Daedalus puts the choice-motif in context, as representing a necessary early stage on the way to integration:

> First, figure out the doubtful way
>   At which awhile all youth should stay,
> Where [Pleasure] and Virtue did contend
>   Which should have Hercules to friend.
> Then, as all actions of mankind
>   Are but a labyrinth or maze,
> So let your dances be entwined.
>
> (228-34)

After the labyrinth of human actions comes that of beauty, in which the contraries are even more intricately interwoven. What remains, as Daedalus introduces the final dance, is to celebrate their union in erotic terms: 'It follows now you are to prove/The subtlest maze of all, that's love' (270-1). That is the celebration, too, of *Antony and Cleopatra*.

To return briefly to the Clown, it should now be evident that his appearance on the boundary between life and death with the worm whose 'biting is immortal' (V.ii.246-7) marks the fulfilment of subversive potential - the Fool's capacity 'de transformer la mort en vie'. The Gravedigger's lesson was lost on Hamlet, his riddling style twisted to a contrary purpose. This clown alone, of all the figures of folly in the late tragedies, has power to affect the action, by the significant means of enabling a necessary 'next step' to take place. He pays his fleeting visit from the margins to the very centre of his text, contributing precisely that element of plot that is required, not only by the tragic, but by the counter-tragic, momentum – the means to Cleopatra's end. He represents the logical extension and fulfilment of her trickster-nature, reminding us of its roots in the physical, of the physical's association with death and decay, and of the role of death and decay in renewing life – the process celebrated in the Neoplatonic rhapsody of Paracelsus:

> Decay is the midwife of very great things! It causes many things to rot, that a noble fruit may be born; for it is the reversal, the death and destruction of the original essence of all natural things. It brings about the birth and rebirth of forms a thousand times improved. . . . And this is the highest and greatest *mysterium* of God, the deepest mystery and miracle that He has revealed to mortal man.
>
> (Paracelsus, *Selected Writings*, 144)

At such a moment, it is fitting that Cleopatra's flesh-and-blood vulnerability should briefly show itself in a childlike form reminiscent of Juliet's fearful fantasy about waking in the tomb (*Rom.*, IV.iii.15ff.): 'Will it eat me?' (271).

The Clown's punning and malaprop speech is rich with paradoxes conflating life and death, breaking down barriers in a way that harks back to the comedy of the tragedy of *Pyramus and Thisby*. His jocular references to women, superficially anti-feminist and supportive of the moralist reading, more deeply serve to invest the feminine with a potent numinosity. When he answers Cleopatra's question about 'any that have died on't' (249), his sexual word-play not only matches but extends hers, linking female sexuality with the production of truth out of falsehood:

> I heard of one of them no longer than yesterday, a very honest woman – but something given to lie, as a woman should not do but in the way of honesty – how she died of the biting of it, what pain she felt. Truly, she makes a very good report o' th' worm.
>
> (250–5)

He and Cleopatra are speaking dialects of the same language. In contrast with Hamlet's forced engagement of the Gravedigger, there is easy communication between them. It is together that they pose their riddle of 'new heaven, new earth' to Caesar, the 'universal landlord' (III.xiii.72) and master of unitary meaning. And though Caesar may, with advice, deduce the asp – the means – he remains without an answer as to the end.

8

THE TRICKSTER MADE SPIRIT AND THE 'TRICKSY SPIRIT'

From this study's perspective (as of course from others), three of Shakespeare's late romances group themselves naturally together, while *The Tempest* stands significantly apart. If *Antony and Cleopatra* generates myth under the influence of disruptive energy, the thoroughly mythologized worlds of *Pericles*, *Cymbeline*, and *The Winter's Tale* express the absorption and assimilation of that energy. That is, they evince, to return to Pelton's formulation – which might as well be describing the awakening of Hermione's statue – 'the ultimate holiness made the moving power of ordinary human life' (Pelton 1980: 283). Not that the plays' 'ordinary human life' always feels itself so moved. The powers ruling these worlds signal their presence, not only through theophanies, prophecies, and the miraculous coincidences characteristic of romance, but also through the apparently pointless disruption of mortal purposes, even of seemingly stable and happy existences. Yet an ultimate purpose is invariably revealed, and existence itself emerges as a veritable rite of sacralization dependent on openness to subversion. Naturally enough, Jupiter speaks with resounding authority on the subject – and with the trickster's voice: 'Whom best I love, I cross; to make my gift,/The more delay'd, delighted' (*Cym.*, V.iv.101–2).

On the other hand, as is especially clear in the middle comedies and Problem Plays, it is a far more problematic matter for '[o]ne of their kind,that relish[es] all as sharply/Passion as they' (*Tmp.*, V.i.23–4), to appropriate such authority, even in a worthy cause:

> All thy vexations
> Were but my trials of thy love, and thou
> Hast strangely stood the test. Here, afore heaven,

I ratify this my rich gift.

(Tmp., IV.i.5–8)

Prospero may stand 'afore heaven', instead of being suspended in it, and the 'love' in question may be terrestrial (Ferdinand's for Miranda), but there is no mistaking the encouragement offered by *his* slippery discourse for Ferdinand's own: 'So rare a won-d'red father and a wise/Makes this place Paradise' (IV.i.123–4). What disqualifies Prospero even as an ally of the trickster-godhead is that, however he may subject others to disruptive energy, employing his 'tricksy spirit' (V.i.226) for the purpose, he keeps such energy rigorously at a distance when it threatens him ('that foul conspiracy/ Of the beast Caliban and his confederates/ Against my life' (IV.i.139–41)) or his: 'do not give dalliance/Too much the rein' (51–2). In fact, his proves the most radical of counter-subversive stances, because it comes in the guise of a wisdom that, exceeding the range even of Vincentio's friarly counsel, is marked as transcendental and superhuman.

I

As the example of Caliban suggests, the final romances, like the late tragedies, comment on the subversive dynamic through formal embodiments of disruption. Yet in this respect, too, *The Tempest* stands out as a special case, given the Ariel–Prospero–Caliban triangle. In the three earlier plays, the tragic pattern is more simply inverted. Instead of being marginalized, such figures are integrated into the main action, to the degree that, paradoxically, their disruptive energy tends again towards ineffectuality. Because, in a way recalling the early comedies, they are in league with the governing powers of the universe, their subversiveness becomes the dramatic equivalent of punch-ing a pillow. Like the Clown in *Antony and Cleopatra*, they supply their catalytic services on textual demand.

This is readily seen in the two sets of humble characters who perform rescues from the sea – the playing-field, in the romances, of an apparently arbitrary Fortune. Thus the Fishermen in *Pericles*[1] and the rustics who inhabit the sea-coast of Bohemia (that frankly impossible place produced by inverting the locales in Greene's *Pandosto*) mediate between the spheres of human vulnerability and human possibility, as well as between life and

death: 'Die, keth 'a? Now gods forbid't, and I have a gown here!'
(*Per.*, II.i.78–9); 'Now bless thyself: thou met'st with things
dying, I with things new-born' (*WT*, III.iii.113–14). In *The
Winter's Tale*, this scene also serves as a transition from the
destructive to the creative half of the play, bringing to life the
bear-motif of Du Bartas and *Richard III* with its implication of
chaos as matrix.[2] In both rescue scenes, the vehicles of subversive
energy have familiar distinguishing marks: satirical mockery,
foolish truth-telling, 'honest mirth' (*Per.*, II.i.95), and a mixture
of idealism and cynicism. In turn, they associate such energy
with nature itself. The Fisherman who offers life to Pericles
follows up with a vision of carnival bounty actually com-
prehending Lent and Mardi Gras: 'Come, thou shalt go home,
and we'll have flesh for holidays, fish for fasting-days, and,
moreo'er, puddings and flap-jacks, and thou shalt be welcome'
(II.i.80–3). This is the verbal counterpart of *The Winter's Tale*'s
sheep-shearing festival, which celebrates nature's creative energy
while acknowledging its cyclicality.[3]

The prolonged theatrical attention given pastoral Bohemia
tends to obscure the parallel with the Fishermen. Indeed, they
quickly recede in our sense of the action, as Pericles' tribulations
begin again. Yet the compressed symbolic technique of the
earlier play helps to clarify the contribution of the Clown and
Shepherd. The Fishermen, like the Bohemian countrymen, act of
their own volition to save the helpless life – there is a pivotal
moment of choice. But when they recover Pericles' rusty armour,
which at once gives him an entrée into the new world and
partially restores his continuity with the old, they are fulfilling
the will of a higher power. His words anticipate the language of
Cymbeline's Jupiter: 'Thanks, Fortune, yet, that after all thy
crosses,/Thou givest me somewhat to repair myself' (II.i.121–2).
A similar transition is built into the evolution of events in *The
Winter's Tale*, as the Clown and Shepherd are caught up by
forces so much larger than themselves as to appear quite terrify-
ing. The culmination is their incorporation into the restructured
community. Amongst the multiple miracles that conclude the
play, it is easy to overlook their own attainment of the impossible
status of 'gentlemen born' (*WT*, V.ii.128ff.). As usual, the
superficial absurdity points to a truth: no other lower-class
characters in Shakespeare cross the socio-dramatic barrier, if only
to remain, appropriately, objects and sources of 'honest mirth'.[4]

What immediately terrifies the peasants is not what an audience begins to sense – the gathering momentum of romance fulfilment – but the tyranny of 'authority', which the Clown terms a 'stubborn bear' (IV.iv.802), thus unwittingly acknowledging the romance link between the human and the natural. At this point, however, 'authority' takes the form of the latest imposture of Autolycus. The effect is to assimilate the rogue's role, too, into the larger pattern – a process that he himself begins to intuit. Thus the career of the character who, more explicitly than any other in the late romances, incarnates the trickster-archetype, imitates and comments on the transformation experienced by his dupes.

Autolycus, with his thieving Mercurial heritage, his shape-changing, his festive bawdiness, and above all his energy, blatantly advertises his carnivalesque subversiveness, complete with creative potential:[5] 'And when I wander here and there/I then do go most right' (IV.iii.17–18). Carroll effectively portrays him as an emblem of the 'power of "making" which comes to dominate the last half of the play' (Carroll 1985: 211) and observes that the ballad of the singing fish (IV.iv.275–81) 'provides an exuberant mockery of virtually all transformation' (212). But Autolycus merely describes this song; equally significant is another that he actually sings, taunting his fellow-singers with a secret that never gets revealed: 'Get you hence, for I must go/Where it fits not you to know' (IV.iv.297–8). Autolycus is surreptitiously announcing his intention of disappearing with their purses, but the text is also glancing mockingly at his disappearance as a force within it. The Clown speaks truer than he knows: 'We'll have this song out anon by ourselves' (309).

The effect of making Autolycus so openly an emblem of the trickster-principle is precisely to point up his out-tricking by the dramatic universe itself, which frankly appropriates his disruptive energy for its own redemptive purposes. Three successive soliloquies track his developing anxiety as to his role, and when the trickster takes to doubtful introspection, he is, by definition, on the way out, as the case of Falstaff has shown. Coincidences that play too conveniently into his roguish hands challenge Autolycus' self-image as marginal outsider, at odds with the world. From gloating over his deceptions (IV.iv.595ff.), he shifts, after overhearing Camillo's scheme and acquiring the Prince's clothes, to a smug view of the universe as aligned with his interests: 'I see this is the time that the unjust man doth thrive. . . . Sure the gods do this year connive at us, and we may do any thing extempore' (673–7). 'Extempore' nicely conveys the improvisatory nature of the identity Autolycus revels in. But there is an uneasiness, too. For the 'Prince himself', in being 'about a piece of iniquity: stealing away from his father' (678–9), is intruding on his territory. Beneath his bravado, Autolycus is unsure about the course that suits his character and so, it follows, about that character itself: 'If I thought it were a piece of honesty to acquaint the King withal, I would not do't. I hold it the more knavery to conceal it; and therein am I constant to my profession' (679–83). When circumstances – this time his overhearing of the Clown and Shepherd – actually threaten to divide him from his dishonest nature ('Though I am not naturally honest, I am so sometimes by chance' (712–13)), he is grateful to discover a self-interest that conceals the reversal of the balance of power between himself and the ascendant trickster, Fortune: 'If I had a mind to be honest, I see Fortune would not suffer me: she drops booties in my mouth' (831–2).

The fact is that there is no longer any place in this dramatic world where the disruptive impulse, as Autolycus embodies it, can gain a foothold. His displacement is enacted when he is reduced to hearing at second-hand about the discovery of Perdita's identity – a secret that he was the unwitting means of transporting to Sicilia. He rationalizes his failure to capitalize on his position, but the truth is brought home by the entrance of the transformed peasants. His fate is pointedly the opposite of the humiliating exclusions of Falstaff, Pistol, and Parolles. Rather, it is the 'punishment' over which Elbow gloats at Pompey's expense: 'Thou art to continue now, thou varlet, thou art to continue' (*MM*, II.i.191–2). Autolycus is to be integrated, vices and all, into the new dispensation: 'I'll swear to the Prince thou art a tall fellow of thy hands, and that thou wilt not be drunk; but I know thou art no tall fellow of thy hands, and that thou wilt be drunk' (V.ii.163–6). To be thus pre-empted, thus spoken for, is a form of silencing, but for once the trickster shares his silence with others. Thus, at the Shepherd's revelation concerning Perdita, '[t]here was speech in their dumbness, language in their very gesture' (13–14). Thus Paulina, an internal dramatist at last who does the subversive work of the gods themselves, re-creating life from death, imposes a silence that produces first a moving, then a speaking Hermione. The reduction of the voluble Autolycus to bland formulas of obedience ('I will prove so, sir, to my power' (169)) manifests a universal articulation of Pelton's 'ultimate holiness'. Autolycus' stock-in-trade is now free-for-all: 'Such a deal of wonder is broken out within this hour that ballad-makers cannot be able to express it' (23–5).

Pericles offers a rough equivalent of Autolycus in the form of Boult and company. The *demi-monde* of Mytilene serves to complete the picture of the trickster, much as Autolycus' villainy supplies an essential aspect of pastoral Bohemia. And despite Marina's more sinister victimization, the brazenly inverted morality of the brothel crew is similarly laden with the numinous potential of anti-masque and misrule, reinforced by a discourse of religious parody:

> *Boult*: Worse and worse, mistress, she has here spoken
> holy words to the Lord Lysimachus.
> *Bawd*: O abominable!
> *Boult*: She makes our profession as it were to stink
> afore the face of the gods.
> *Bawd*: Marry, hang her up for ever!
>
> (IV.vi.132–7)

The very echo of Pompey ('Indeed, it does stink in some sort, sir' (*MM*, III.ii.28–9)) marks the distance from the devitalized sexuality of *Measure for Measure*. Boult's brief picture of the prospective clients drooling at the description of Marina (IV.ii.98ff.) renders a more vivid account of the sexual impulse as such than does all the cynical banter of the earlier brothel-world. Pompey has an insouciant consciousness of his own corruption that is quite foreign to Boult, who, even when he agrees to help Marina out of the brothel instead of raping her, maintains his world-view unshaken. Her sermon on the evil of his life fails to inspire repentance, in contrast with her earlier impact on Lysimachus; it is the list of her marketable talents to which he responds: 'But can you teach all this you speak of?' (IV.vi.188).

To read the brothel scenes only in the narrow moral terms of Marina herself is to miss their contribution to her spiritual power. The dramatic method is, of course, highly emblematic, with Marina not only embodying the magic of virginity, but enacting a myth of descent into the underworld. Howard Felperin has compared Valdes to Dis, Marina to Proserpina

(1967: 390). I detect, as well, an inversion of the legend of Orpheus, coloured by that of Arion – Gower's model for the poet as redeemer in the *Confessio Amantis*, the play's primary source.[6] The music of Marina's speech charms the human beasts around her; through it she redeems a future husband from the underworld, just as she will later wake her father from his living death. But such redemption requires an underworld in the first place, as creation presupposes chaos, and we are specifically prepared by Leonine – in lines that strangely anticipate Paulina – to link her experience with the same destructive–creative element that first gave her life and took her mother: 'There's no hope she will return. I'll swear she's dead,/And thrown into the sea' (IV.i.98-9). In the larger romance scheme, Marina's landing at Mytilene has more in common than might be supposed with the Fishermen's succour of her father.

So integral is disruptive energy to the play-world of *Cymbeline* that two of its notable representatives, the rude mountaineers, do not merely succour and nurture the blood royal but contain it. Going the Clown and Shepherd one better, they are revealed as 'princes born' from the start. The organic influence of their natural environment is, as with Perdita, elevated and transformed by their equally natural nobility: 'nature prompts them/In simple and low things to prince it much/Beyond the trick of others' (III.iii.84-6). Yet they combine Perdita's role with that of her putative father and brother. Their rebelliousness is enriched by a becoming touch of the peasant roughness they complain of: 'We are beastly: subtle as the fox for prey,/Like warlike as the wolf for what we eat' (40-1). In dealing with Cloten, who is crudity personified, Guiderius draws, even from the height of instinctive high birth, on a low comic style:

> *Clo.:*   Thou villain base,
>   Know'st me not by my clothes?
> *Gui.:*   No, nor thy tailor,
>   rascal,
>   Who is thy grandfather! he made those clothes,
>   Which (as it seems) make thee.
>
>   (IV.ii.80-3)

The basis of the brothers' alignment with the Clown and Shepherd, however, is structural. When she wanders into their cave, symbolically descending into the underworld, they nourish the starving and despondent Imogen with food, hope, and family – an anticipation of Posthumus' dream. Thus they, too, mediate not only between nature and civilization but between life and death, as is confirmed when they preside over the first stage of her experience of death and rebirth. Their famous elegy applies the familiar view of death as natural subversion: 'Golden lads and girls all must,/As chimney-sweepers, come to dust' (IV.ii.262–3).

The return from the dead of the odious Cloten, made Posthumus by his clothes, brings Imogen into confrontation (if not exactly face to face) with this reality. He thereby continues his own subversive function, contributing his disruptive energy and his liminality to the larger pattern, even as his danger is neutralized. The image of his 'clotpole' floating 'down the stream/In embassy to his mother' (IV.ii.184–5) includes this positive significance.[7] There is a parallel, then, especially considering his sexual violence, with the brothel-crew in *Pericles*. Yet Cloten, as Belarius insists, remains a Prince – this is, indeed, how he finally gets to lie with Imogen – and his assault on social decorum, his disruption of class barriers, is part of the point, like the translation of the Clown and Shepherd into 'gentlemen born'. Obviously, a Prince who acts like a stereotypical peasant is a far cry from peasants who gain nobility, but both phenomena belong to a universe that not only tolerates but thrives on the principle of transgression. Cloten must be disposed of, but not before his subversiveness is fully assimilated.

That subversiveness is all the more valuable dramatically because it is manifold, ramifying throughout the text in potently symbolic ways; as Murray M. Schwartz puts it, he serves as a 'touchstone for the play's sexual and social anxieties' (Schwartz 1970: 222). Apart from enabling Imogen to come to terms with the loss of Posthumus, he serves as a displacement of Posthumus' Othello- and Leontes-like self-subversion. Appropriately, for a displaced trickster, he is deformed and monstrous; appropriately, for Posthumus' *semblable*, the distortion is inward. Yet he makes visible the jealous murderous shadow-side that Posthumus can only neutralize by recognizing it as an image of himself, whereupon he gains access to other nurturing selves within him.[8] Such recognition finally comes in his extraordinary acceptance of responsibility for Imogen's supposed death when he still believes her guilty – the same test that Othello fails and that Antony passes.

At the political level, too, Cloten is a recognizable subversive type – the ambitious trouble-maker who makes history but writes himself out of the text. The war between Britain and Rome leads, not to the isolationist supremacy he had asserted ('Britain's a world/By itself' (III.i.12–13)), but to an harmonious peace based on interdependence. Yet the familiar pattern is significantly varied in the matter of self-sufficiency: in all the harm that he does, or tries to do, Cloten is his mother's agent, the concrete projection of her abstract malice. His disappearance opens the way to the purging of the political and social order of its secret internal enemy. In this context, his defeat by Guiderius marks the transition from a subversive energy unacknowledged, and so made deformed and dangerous, to such energy openly exercised and accommodated: the mountaineer-princes come out of hiding; in lending their vitality to their country's cause, they lend it also to the ensuing revelations and reconciliations.

The only vehicle of subversive energy in *Cymbeline* who keeps a stable identity, secure within his social niche, is Posthumus' (First) Jailer. His is a brief appearance at a typically liminal moment, but the transition he marks is not, significantly, the one that he himself supposes. He comes to usher Posthumus to execution, and their banter highlights the prisoner's new state of mind after his vision – his sense of the fulfilment, though in an unexpected way, of his earlier intuition: 'Most welcome, bondage! for thou art a way,/I think, to liberty' (V.iv.3–4). Posthumus had previously longed for death merely as punishment and escape; now he seems free of his inner bonds and prepared for death as an experience in itself, an experience that he, unlike the Jailer, professes to understand. His spiritual freedom is manifested by his descent into the 'foolish' style. In marked contrast with Hamlet's response to the Gravedigger, he outfools the subversive voice of mortality ('I am merrier to die than thou art to live' (171)), absorbing the Jailer's reminders of death's unknowability – the source of fear to Hamlet – into a confidence like Cleopatra's:

> . . . how you shall speed in your journey's end, I
> think you'll never return to tell one.
> *Post.:* I tell thee, fellow, there are none want eyes to
> direct them the way I am going, but such as wink

and will not use them.

(182–7)

Posthumus has made himself the truer trickster in grasping the secret of the grave, and the threshold he crosses takes him beyond death to a miraculously renewed life. As with Autolycus, the larger processes of the play leave the Jailer behind precisely by integrating his message; his soliloquy seems beside the point:

> I would we were all of one mind, and one mind good. O, there were desolation of jailers and gallowses! I speak against my present profit, but my wish hath a preferment in't.

(203–6)

That wish has already been granted, including his 'preferment'.

Once the central dynamic is identified, a variety of disruptive agents and circumstances fall into place in the subversive economies of these three plays. Indeed, the frequent blurring of the distinction between agent and circumstance further reflects the tight control exercised over these worlds by their ruling powers. The fairy-tale enlists fairy-tale villains – Antiochus, Dionyza, Cymbeline's Queen – then disposes of them as tokens of the spiritual growth of the protagonists. They are as much instruments of the subversive principle as the bear or the storms at sea. The exceptional villain is Jachimo, whose relative independence matches the unusual mimeticism with which Posthumus is portrayed. As with Othello,[9] the element of fantasy and possessiveness in Posthumus' love begets a subversive reaction, of which Jachimo serves as the vehicle – responding, as does Iago, with equally flimsy because strongly desired 'ocular proof' (*Oth.*, III.iii.360). As Posthumus is finally redeemed by the disruptive influence of his conscience, so Jachimo's conscience undoes his subversiveness. Self-subversion is taken a step farther by Leontes, who becomes his own secret enemy, then projects this role onto his wife and friend. Here, too, a rich psychological context is supplied (so rich that critics have not reached a consensus about it), but the violent outbreak of his delusion also makes it equivalent to the arbitrary deprivations of wife and child by which the gods of *Pericles* challenge the one 'whom best [they] love' to accommodate the subversive principle. Leontes' failure to take responsibility for the inner forces that threaten him results in his terrible punishment and long atonement. Meanwhile, Polixenes enacts a reprise of his friend's crime; in projecting upon the young lovers his own sense of subversion by time and age, he makes his kingdom, too, a potentially tragic site. (It again becomes fortunate that Bohemia has a sea-coast.)

Finally, it is worth touching on the manipulative charade of the good King Simonides, who is doing the heavens' own work – no doubt they *will* 'make a star of him' (*Per.*, V.iii.79) – in playing the counter-subversive opponent of his daughter's match in order to promote it. Such a role is also adopted, of course, by Prospero. However, this parallel only makes more urgent the need to come to terms with that self-made 'god of power' (*Tmp.*, I.ii.10) as an element injected into a dramatic system that seems, as it were, to have been working very well on its own.

II

By 1611, when *The Tempest* was probably written, audiences had reason to count on certain basic returns from romantic comedy or tragicomedy, thanks in good measure to Shakespeare himself. Above all, Sidney and Jonson notwithstanding, they could expect to travel widely – in place, in time, in the realm of imagination generally. The ultimate liberation offered was not from the pessimism of tragedy, not even from the 'real' world, but from the tyranny of narrative logic itself. So much is at least implicit in most recent criticism of Shakespeare's last plays, and it implies the institutionalization of the subversive principle, the installation of the trickster as presiding spirit. I wish to propose that *The Tempest* takes these conventions farther than its predecessors in order to interrogate them. The ostentatiously fantastic indices of the 'wonder' proper to romance prove, in the end, as insubstantial as Prospero's spirit-actors and, like them, vanish into thin air to leave disturbing resonances.

For *The Tempest* is, in its basic terms, overwhelmingly a play of confinements, manipulations, and intimidations. With a surprising reversion to the neoclassical unities, Shakespeare creates a single setting – one which, however exotic and fancifully populated, proves claustrophobic for audience, inhabitants, and castaways alike. Far from being allowed to 'use [its] wings' (*WT*, IV.i.4) or even to '[travel] in divers paces with divers persons' (*AYL*, III.ii.308-9), time marches strictly to Prospero's tune. The logic of the action – similarly Prospero's own – is rigorous and inexorable, helping to give the romance content a treatment that Felperin terms 'anti-romantic' (1972: 264). And in harnessing the characteristic romance ornaments – song, dance, spectacle, the supernatural – so tightly to that action, *The Tempest* suppresses its own vital signs at the basic theatrical level. When Ariel is finally set free 'to the elements' (V.i.318), the play is over. It is precisely 'to the elements' that the marvellous – and the subversive – naturally belong in the three preceding romances.

Coups de théâtre were hardly Shakespeare's stock-in-trade, especially not the sort that perceptually 'dislocate', as Joan Hartwig puts it (1972: 139), rather than merely surprise. Apart from the opening of *The Tempest*, the most notable examples form parts of conclusions: the Abbess Aemilia's revelation, Falstaff's delayed bounce from Shrewsbury field (surely he should not mug his fall), the awakening of Hermione's statue. These widely disparate events all involve restorations, and they have a similar structural impact reflecting the assertion of the subversive principle: an entire level of dramatic reality is suddenly added (or, in Falstaff's case, restored). In *The Comedy of Errors* and especially *The Winter's Tale*, this new dimension at once redeems the past and bestows a future: 'Hastily lead away' (V.iii.155) are Leontes' final words, and, according to Frye, they 'summon us like a beckoning to a new and impossible world' (Frye 1965: 117). The death-threatening storm in *The Tempest*, followed as it is by the revelation of Prospero's supernatural control, might seem similarly expansionary. But the common view that an audience is thereby introduced to what Dawson calls 'the classic pattern of romance, where apparent disaster is metamorphosed into serenity and reunion' (Dawson 1978: 158) needs closer scrutiny. Such a reading assumes that we are just as dependent as Miranda upon Prospero's assurance that '[t]here's no harm done' (I.ii.15). We might as well be equally susceptible to his sleeping-spell.

Dawson does point out that we are conscious of the storm 'as an illusion, and Miranda is not' (1978: 158). This perception may usefully be extended. We are also conscious of the genre implicit in that illusion: both sea and storm recognizably belong to romance convention, and even the much-praised 'realism' –

which amounts to an overdetermining plethora of 'authentic' details – does not put Prospero's tempest in a different category from the one described in *The Winter's Tale* (III.iii.88ff.), or that portrayed in *Pericles* (III.i), or, for that matter, the analogue in the Digby *Mary Magdalene*. Such recognition automatically brings with it a sense of *natural* magic, of romance's limitless possibilities. To open the play this way is to announce its world as completely open. What does it matter if the deaths are 'real'? – the promise of compensation, of redemption, inheres in the genre. From this angle, the widening of perspective to show Prospero's manipulation actually constricts, counter-subversively, an audience's confidence in romance affirmation. The effect, then, is nearly opposite to that of the statue scene. Instead of puffing up soufflé-like, infused with wonder, the structure collapses, the wonder explained away from the start. Instead of being given – and left with – a sense of infinite future, we are funnelled into a strictly measured present, where we shall have to spend the rest of the play. The romance world is no longer identical with the dramatic world at large; it is set off and labelled as such – firmly, to use the New Historicist term, contained. So the question arises: if that world is not free to generate its own magic, what is that magic worth?

The question is kept current by friction between the symbolic mode and the insistent realism of much of the presentation. This realism, far from being superficially theatrical, as in the storm scene, offsets the strain of conspicuous theatricality. Prospero's world may run on supernatural energy, but the 'unities' are employed – in contrast with their use in *The Comedy of Errors* – so as to enforce a consciousness that its constraints are close to those of our own. The symbolic pattern is essentially that of *The Winter's Tale*, yet sixteen years' worth of spiritual development is here accomplished in three hours. The realism extends to the more remote corners of characterization. Many commentators deal with Ariel and Caliban as if they indeed 'were . . . human' (V.i.20), while Sebastian and Antonio break through the shell of caricature through sheer grittiness. Significantly, this involves their fidelity to an irreducible subversive core. They are the deformed trickster-presence within the court party, and they conspicuously decline to lend their energies to the cause of transformation by becoming grist for Prospero's mill. When his magic lapses, they require the practical power of blackmail to

232

keep them under control, and they retain the capacity to deflate his new symbolic order with a mockingly materialist perspective:

Seb.:   Ha, ha!
      What things are these, my Lord Antonio?
      Will money buy 'em?
Ant.:   Very like; one of them
      Is a plain fish, and no doubt marketable.

                                            (V.i.263–6)

Style in *The Tempest* is highly politicized. By resisting, as they alone do, the lexis of wonder that expresses Prospero's hegemony, Sebastian and Antonio undermine not only the final harmony, but the method that has procured it.[10]

It is natural that Prospero himself, whose role is all-encompassing, should stand at the centre of the play's realism. At the same time, he puts a special obstacle in the way of mimetic analysis, as the Epilogue retrospectively acknowledges: 'Now my charms are all o'erthrown' (Epilogue 1). We respond to him first and foremost as mage, tending to accept, on the spectacular evidence, his claim to incarnate the trickster-godhead. Yet here again the contemporary audience, familiar with magician characters who are mostly magic and little character, would find its generically conditioned expectations challenged. Prospero's notorious 'irascibility' is pivotal. A conventional trait of magician figures (Kermode 1966: lxiii), it outgrows its formulaic origin by attaching itself to a wide spectrum of shifting thoughts and feelings – bitterness about the past, solicitude over his daughter, pessimism regarding Caliban. In fact, by varying the context, the object, and the degree of manipulation actually called for, Shakespeare transforms Prospero's very inflexibility of manner into an instrument of unwitting self-revelation. It is one thing to put on a show of anger for Ferdinand, another to castigate Caliban, another to bully Ariel, still another to lose patience with Miranda. Similarly, his constant secretiveness, the fact that he keeps others – including the audience – almost uniformly at arm's length, becomes an actively characterizing element rather than a merely formal one.

But to approach Prospero as a multidimensional figure projecting himself in a one-dimensional way entails daunting interpretative responsibilities. It becomes inadequate to concede a smattering of human qualities to the superman. Prospero himself willingly does as much at various points, with the effect of renewing and rejustifying his magisterial status. Nowhere is this more apparent, or important, than in the fifth-Act exchange with Ariel that precedes the decision to forgive his enemies. For when Prospero allows his 'affections' to 'become tender' (V.i.18–19) by admitting that he is '[o]ne of their kind', he effectively sets up another demonstration of his superiority:

> Though with their high wrongs I am strook to th' quick,
> Yet, with my nobler reason, 'gainst my fury
> Do I take part. The rarer action is
> In virtue than in vengeance.

> (25–8)

The context here lends urgency to the critical challenge. That Prospero is 'acting' is conveyed by familiar indicators – the neatness of the pattern, his controlled tone, his manipulation of Ariel – in keeping with the impression that a cruder 'vengeance' was never part of his plan.[11] But for once – and at the play's ostensible climax – he is playing to an empty house. Ariel hardly needs controlling, as it might be argued he did earlier; on the contrary, his very willingness to serve his master makes him the most compliant possible foil. The disquieting fact is that Prospero has no one to impress but himself. The gulf thus widens between his view of all his enemies as 'penitent' (28), by which he justifies his mercy, and the incorrigible subversiveness of Antonio and Sebastian. Prospero's inflexible performance throughout the play falls into place as having been, to some degree, aimed at reinforcing a particular self-image. And this raises a logical barrier even more formidable than his secretiveness: how can his role as guide to self-knowledge in others – 'and all of us, ourselves,/When no man was his own' (212–13) – be reconciled with a lack of it in himself?

The very awkwardness of this paradox is a signal to make use of it. And there is an obvious starting point – the formal and conventional nature of Prospero's wisdom. The magical power that seems to attest his trickster-status would have manifested, for a Renaissance audience, his attainment of a set of widely recognized, if mystically elusive, spiritual truths. This aspect of his role has been stressed by a number of commentators, though without necessarily clarifying the relation between symbolism and action. Thus Frank Kermode, after discussing Prospero's art as 'a technique for liberating the soul from the passions, from nature . . . a discipline of which the primary requirements are learning and temperance', still speaks of him as outgrowing his need for magic when he 'achieves this necessary control over himself and nature' (Kermode 1966: xlviii). Now it is certainly Prospero's own view that his magic is dispensable, once he has brought his scheme to fruition, but that view is doubtfully consistent with the symbolic significance of magic in the play. If his powers exist precisely by virtue of his status as 'holy adept' (Kermode 1966: xlvii), why is another step necessary, and why should this entail discarding those powers?

Analogues from the earlier romances press these questions home. When Paulina wields her pretended magic in recognition of the spiritual power, the 'faith' at last attained by Leontes, there is no sense that this culmination needs to be exceeded or qualified. Even more to the point is Cerimon in *Pericles*, whose healing powers and heavenly connection ('The gods can have no mortal officer/More like a god than you' (*Per.*, V.iii.62-3)) place him squarely in the mage tradition. His powers, like Prospero's, involve the liberation of forces latent in nature and have been gained through intellectual and moral self-perfection, in particular through '[v]irtue and cunning' (III.ii.27) – qualities that 'immortality attends . . . /Making a man a god' (30-1). Moreover, his role as the instrument of Pericles' final miraculous reward – the restoration of his wife – links him with the process of suffering and redemption, the accommodation of the subversive principle, undergone by the hero. The concluding attribution to him of '[t]he worth that learned charity aye wears' (V.iii.94) hardly implies that he falls short of an ideal.

An audience expert in Shakespearean romance, therefore, takes up with Prospero where it is used to leaving off, in the same way that it finds itself in a milieu already made magical. If *The Winter's Tale*, in drawing romance out of tragedy, suggests what might have been possible for Lear – given a stronger heart, sixteen more years, and a loving-subversive presence like Paulina – then *The Tempest* explores, and so creates, new territory: the future to which the fulfilled Leontes eagerly turns, the hypothetical 'happily ever after'. The world of the play is premised on a completed romance pattern, as Prospero makes clear in presenting his own history in terms of the typical movement from subversion to deliverance.[12] The basic elements strikingly overlap

with those of *Pericles* – exile from power and identity, privation
at sea, charitable succour, the consoling presence of an infant
daughter. Yet the arrival at the island, the founding of the
magical kingdom, in marking the end of Prospero's sufferings
also set a limit to 'Providence divine' (I.ii.159) – the ultimate
agency of beneficence in the other romances.

The constriction of the supernatural influences and energies of
romance into a human 'god of power' is accompanied by a shift
in Fortune's function. Having independently carried Alonso's
vessel within range of Prospero's magic, Hamlet's 'strumpet'
(*Ham.*, II.ii.236) has now become Prospero's mistress:

> By accident most strange, bountiful Fortune
> (Now my dear lady) hath mine enemies
> Brought to this shore; and by my prescience
> I find my zenith doth depend upon
> A most auspicious star, whose influence
> If now I court not, but omit, my fortunes
> Will ever after droop.

> (I.ii.178–84)

Prospero is not merely appropriating but redefining, in a way
that restates the central problem: how does he, beloved of
'Fortune', now conceive his 'fortunes'? A Shakespearean con-
cordance reveals, in general, the pattern of usage documented by
the *OED*: the pluralizing of 'fortune' tends to bring the concept
down to earth, imparting materialistic connotations. In fact,
setting aside the symbolic trappings of reformation, rebirth, and
resumption of identity, Prospero's manipulations produce an
impressive total in the ledger. He will return to his dukedom on
his own (largely ceremonial) terms; his daughter will marry so as
to provide him with royal heirs; his enemies have been
humiliated and their future docility assured. It is almost as if
Cordelia's forces had won their battle and revalidated Lear's
original vision. Prospero will get Lear's lost chance to
'[u]nburthen'd crawl toward death' (*Lr*, I.i.41): 'Every third
thought shall be my grave' (V.i.312).

That comparison begins at the beginning, with Prospero's *de
facto* abdication of responsibility for his dukedom (a reminiscence, too, of Vincentio, as has often been noted). Both Prospero
and Lear have unfitted themselves for office by trying to separate
responsibility from '[t]he name, and all th'addition' (*Lr*, I.i.136)

of their positions. Prospero, however, appears to have done so, not in order to thwart the subversive menace of mortality, but for the sake of a transcendental wisdom that by definition accommodates the subversive – including, necessarily, the subversion applied by the usurpers. However bitterly Prospero looks back on his usurpation, his narrative reveals that it merely brought appearances into line with reality: 'To have no screen between this part he play'd/And him he play'd it for' (I.ii.107–8). In effect, he made a choice, and both suffered and profited from the consequences.[13] His dedication to the spiritual over the temporal engaged the forces of the romance universe, exalting him in his preferred sphere. What is so remarkable about the play's direction is not that he finally achieves Lear's goal, but that he now wants to. Prospero still claims to 'prize' his books 'above [his] dukedom' (168). Yet in extending his magical arm beyond the island to intercept the passing ship, he effectively reverses his original choice and commits himself to drowning his books for his dukedom's sake. Implicit in his decision is a return, however disguised, to the universe of tragedy, where humanity is on its own.

But of course we are not meant to detach Prospero's material interests and achievements from their 'higher' meanings. We are discouraged from doing so not only by Prospero himself, but also by Gonzalo, whose role as Prospero's secret ally thus unwittingly continues. He brackets his recital of *res gestae* between the characteristic romance responses of wonder ('O, rejoice/Beyond a common joy' (V.i.206–7)) and celebration of spiritual gain ('and all of us, ourselves,/When no man was his own' (212–13)). His obliging interpretation here is in line with his comment after Ariel's harpy-speech, when, though nothing but shallow defiance is apparent in Antonio and Sebastian, he anticipates Prospero's labelling of *all* his enemies as 'penitent': 'All three of them are desperate: their great guilt/(Like poison given to work a great time after)/Now gins to bite the spirits' (III.iii.104–6).

Gonzalo's very presence lends Prospero's treatment of the castaways an enhanced aura of beneficence. His sufferings are prominent in the account by Ariel that leads up to the act of mercy; as the spell dissolves, he provides an occasion for Prospero to display his compassionate humanity by joining him in tears (V.i.62–4). But it is Ariel's intervention when Gonzalo and Alonso are about to be murdered in their sleep that most strikingly calls attention, by its self-contradictory presentation, to his usefulness in mediating and colouring Prospero's actions: 'My master through his art foresees the danger/That you, his friend, are in, and sends me forth/(For else his project dies) to keep them living' (II.i.297–9). In sum, the role played by Gonzalo in Prospero's script is to provide assurance that it is the script of a romance, rather than of a revenge play or other self-aggrandizing exercise. And Gonzalo is uniquely equipped for the purpose by his prominence in Prospero's romance history. 'Would I might/But ever see that man!' (I.ii.168–9), exclaims Miranda, as if on cue, after Prospero has stressed the saving act of 'charity' in strongly archetypal terms (it involved the gifts of food and water, 'rich garments', and the then-all-important books (160–8)). If we knew no more of Gonzalo than this, we should have no trouble accepting him as a rough counterpart of romance rescuers elsewhere.

It is ironic, therefore, that Gonzalo is also one of the chief instruments by which romance significance is deconstructed. Even before Prospero paints his portrait, we have seen the original, and the family resemblance to Polonius is later confirmed. The Cerimon-like impulse to bring renewal out of death and disaster, to make the desert island bloom, to create a harmonious commonwealth, runs up against Alonso's intense mourning, the mocking cynicism of Antonio and Sebastian, and, most basically, his own preference of 'art' to 'matter':

> *Ant.*: His word is more than the miraculous harp.
>
> . . .
>
> What impossible matter will he make easy next?
> *Seb.*: I think he will carry this island home in his
> pocket, and give it his son for an apple.
> *Ant.*: And sowing the kernels of it in the sea, bring
> forth more islands.
>
> (II.i.87–94)[14]

Gonzalo, it turns out, is only half a Cerimon – idealistic 'virtue' without 'cunning', 'charity' that is essentially un-'learned', as is signalled by his ignorant history ('This Tunis, sir, was Carthage' (84)), even by his unassimilated Montaigne.

There is no point in trying to decide whether Gonzalo or the two egregious exemplars of 'cunning' without 'virtue' are closer to the truth about the island. Caliban has testified that, like reality at large, it is a mixture of 'barren place and fertile' (I.ii.338). The effect is to foreground the issue of interpretation. That we are attracted by Gonzalo's optimism, repelled (if titillated) by his Vice-like interlocutors, becomes a comment on our preference for romance – and on Prospero's success in severing romance from subversion. The same idealizing impulse informs Kermode's effort to excuse Gonzalo's limitations by appealing to his final summary: 'he pronounces the benediction, and we see that he was all the time as right as it was human to be, even when to the common sense of the corrupt he was transparently wrong' (Kermode 1966: xxxviii). The 'wise fool' archetype blends all-too-smoothly into Gonzalo's role of 'allow'd' romance spokesman. But a foolish 'wise' man, like Gonzalo or Polonius, is very different from a 'wise fool'. The real truths that Gonzalo tells foolishly are those that call the genre itself into question, and, in the prologue to his benediction, he hits his head on the nail: 'Was Milan thrust from Milan, that his issue/Should become kings of Naples?' (V.i.205–6).

Prospero's provision for royal descendants is, after all, the cornerstone of his project – the subtext, as events make clear, of his early declaration to Miranda: 'I have done nothing, but in care of thee' (I.ii.16). The match with Ferdinand gets his direct attention (Ariel can see to the others), and very anxious attention it is, especially on the question of chastity. The symbolic implications of this theme have been widely discussed.[15] Both Shakespearean and non-Shakespearean analogues relate the principle of desire under control, passion in harmony with reason, to the magical enhancement of natural fecundity – an idea consistent with the goal of transcending disruptive energy by integrating it. Prospero's manipulation of this symbolism is plain from the masque of spirits, which makes such values the basis of the fertility-blessings of Juno and Ceres. In encouraging yet restraining the young couple's desire, he is forging (in a double sense) an embodiment of a Neoplatonic ideal.

Only by ignoring the almost comic intensity in his manner, the realistic element, can one miss the counter-subversive counter-current. For Prospero, too, has a touch of Polonius about him:

> Look thou be true; do not give dalliance
> Too much the rein. The strongest oaths are straw

To th' fire i' th' blood. Be more abstemious,
Or else good night your vow!

(IV.i.51-4)

I do know,
When the blood burns, how prodigal the soul
Lends the tongue vows.

(Ham., I.iii.115-17)

Given its narrow limits, this is a useful comparison. Not only does it suggest the incompatibility of royal dallying with the royal marrying necessary for Prospero's scheme, but it links both men as manipulators who virtually extinguish their daughters' wills and personalities. (Prospero's pawns are formally presented as such when Prospero reveals his richly symbolic chess-tableau.)[16] Needless to say, Miranda is far from harmed materially by her role; nor is she in the least displeased by it. But then Prospero is in the extraordinary position of both constructing her character and controlling the action. And there remains something in her like Ophelia's impotence and vulnerability. Her capacity for responding independently to experiences – 'O! I have suffered/With those that I saw suffer' (I.ii.5-6) – is indeed put to sleep; she all but sleep-walks through most of her father's script. Similarly, Ophelia is granted a single outburst of spontaneous grief – 'O, what a noble mind is here o'erthrown! . . .' (III.i.150ff.) – as a measure of her repression elsewhere.

It is theatrically absurd to exaggerate (hence to oversimplify) Prospero's brutality, but his imposition of symbolic functions on other characters must be recognized as counter-subversive. And his daughter's case, the fundamental case, casts particular doubt on the validity of the symbolism. Unquestionably, the restorations of children, the marriages, the anticipations of royal issue that conclude Shakespeare's other late romances carry positive symbolic significance, but that significance is conferred by the romance universe itself in recognition of sufferings endured, lessons learnt – subversions, in short, accommodated. This is, in fact, the way things work for Alonso, according to Prospero's script. It is a different matter for one character to manipulate others, especially his children, into serving as symbols for him. Even apart from the obvious internal dramatists, the destructive effects of such manipulation pervade the canon, and the other romances actually present an initiating hamartia in these terms.

The pattern is clearest in *Cymbeline* and *The Winter's Tale.*
Both Cymbeline and Posthumus simultaneously produce and
react against Imogen's 'otherness' by demanding that she con-
form to their (conflicting) projections of her significance: like
other constructed subversives, she begins as the object of counter-
subversive manipulation. Cymbeline, in classic patriarchal
fashion, expects her to produce heirs on his terms; Posthumus
stakes his self-image on her embodiment of an ideal of
transcendent beauty and chastity – as his possession. According
to the subversive dynamic, she dies to both of them, but when her
loss is integrated she is restored – independent of their projections yet symbolically redemptive. When, in *The Winter's Tale,*
Leontes imposes upon Hermione the subversive image of
adulteress and would-be murderess, this entails repudiating his
daughter as legitimate royal issue and fixing obsessively on his
son as a guarantee of self-perpetuation through posterity. His
punishment strikes directly at his symbol-making – 'the King
shall live without an heir, if that which is lost be not found'
(III.ii.134–6) – and the universe responds to his transformation
with symbolic gifts pointedly contained within human limits:
Hermione returns, as if from the dead, but wrinkled; Perdita and
Florizel make suitable royal heirs, but Mamillius is gone forever.

The mechanism by which Pericles is plunged into his sufferings is more problematic – by the standard moral criteria, they
are undeserved.[17] Yet in light of the danger and culpability of
symbol-making itself, the far-reaching influence of the hero's
disastrous courtship of Antiochus' daughter appears fully
justified:

> I went to Antioch,
> Where, as thou know'st, against the face of death
> I sought the purchase of a glorious beauty,
> From whence an issue I might propagate,
> Are arms to princes and bring joys to subjects.

(I.ii.70–4)

The primitive style here (whether Shakespeare's or not) makes
the key elements more starkly apparent. Pericles' vision of self-
perpetuation through royal progeny amounts to a counter-
subversive assault on death. He imaginatively transforms the
woman into something more than human and consequently
blinds himself to the less-than-human reality; it takes the

ambiguity of a riddle to expose the truth of the incest. His naïve use of the symbolism of the Fall betrays his distortion. In longing '[t]o taste the fruit of yon celestial tree' (I.i.21), defying death in the process, he elevates his love-object into a virtual embodiment of immortality, while unwittingly tracing her fatal import. Deprivation of identity and abundant proof of the long reach of mortality follow discovery of the facts; subsequently, the gods thwart his efforts to re-establish his sense of self through Thaisa and Marina. He must internalize the utter loneliness and vulnerability associated with Lear's vision of Poor Tom in order to earn worldly fulfilment and symbolic immortality.

The closest analogues, then, support *The Tempest*'s own evidence against accepting Prospero's symbolization of his material gains as a valid romance culmination. Rather, as the renunciation of his magic in itself suggests, he appears to be stepping backwards, returning to the beginning of the cycle. The analogues throw into relief Prospero's manipulations of time – the relentlessly subversive medium, at once destructive and creative: 'I, that please some, try all, both joy and terror/Of good and bad, that makes and unfolds error' (*WT*, IV.i.1–2). Typically, erring romance characters constitute time as exclusively destructive; their counter-subversions are aimed ultimately against *tempus edax*. These involve, as with most of the late tragic heroes, attempts to forestall the future by reconstituting or fixing the present. After a spiritual death, characters are reborn into the flux of the present with an acceptance of both the inherited obligations of the past – its pastness – and the amorphous finitude of the future. The symbolic grant of immortality thus denotes imaginative freedom from time and death within the temporal continuum.

Again, it is remarkable how conscious of romance meanings Prospero's script shows him to be. His victims are symbolically cut off from their proposed futures and made to face the responsibilities of the past. Alonso and Ferdinand, at least, are painfully infused with a consciousness of mortality as a natural process – the theme of Ariel's 'sea-change' song (I.ii.397ff.). The royal father believes himself bereft of posterity; the son loses his source of royal identity in a way that recalls the shipwrecked Pericles, but without even his father's armour ('a shield/'Twixt [him] and death' (II.i.126–7)) to initiate his recovery (not that he has long to wait). The castaways' experiences are more clearly made the lessons of time itself by the pressure of Prospero's punctual management. When he declares, as his scheme nears completion, that 'Time/Goes upright with his carriage' (V.i.2–3), he effectively identifies his project's moving and generative force.

Prospero also thereby implies his own control over time, which he then confirms by assuring Ariel, who had prematurely requested his liberty ('Before the time be out?' (I.ii.246)), that their work is finished. Except that the temporal units are hours instead of days, this might be the voice of the primordial creator, bringing order out of fertile chaos – an allusion that helps prepare for the translation of wrath into mercy:

> How's the day?
> *Ari.:* On the sixt hour, at which time, my lord,
> You said our work should cease.
> *Pros.:*   I did say so,
> When first I rais'd the tempest.
>
> (V.i.3–6)

As ruler of the magical kingdom whose very establishment manifested his triumph over time, Prospero stands outside time as he does outside time's milieu, the play-within-the-play – until, that is, he at once puts on his own costume and discloses his manipulations. Our sense of resolution at this point, reflecting Prospero's own, should not obscure the fact that these two aspects of his role point in different directions. Primarily, he exposes the script his characters have been acting as a fabrication of his art, thus lifting them out of it and into 'reality'. But on a deeper level, by joining them as star of the show he raises the level of the illusion itself and installs it as the foundation of his new order. His outward resumption of 'true' identity is more truly a time-denying revival of an outworn self; his theatrical language renders the artifice unmistakable: 'I will discase me, and myself present/As I was sometime Milan' (85–6). This is a making good of Lear's futile threat to 'resume the shape which thou dost think/I have cast off for ever' (I.iv.309–10), and it retracts the earlier presentation of Antonio's usurpation as truth-telling rather than play-acting. Even as he symbolically grants the 'freedom' from oppressive time that his victims have supposedly earned, therefore, Prospero is turning back the clock. And even as he submits himself to the temporal current, declaring his acceptance of mortality ('Every third thought shall be my grave') and mortal frailty ('And what strength I have's mine own,/Which is most faint' (Epilogue, 2-3)), he is transferring to that world a network of manufactured consolations recognizable as hollow attempts to manipulate the future. It is not only Stephano and Trinculo who prefer stealing rich garments (symbols of romance achievement) to being kings of the isle indeed.

The elusive but powerful tragic undertones often detected in Prospero's final position – the sense that, more profoundly than he admits, his 'ending is despair' (Epilogue, 15) – make for a further comparison to *Lear*. Both Lear and Prospero respond to the prospect of extinction by projecting themselves into a world reshaped so as to insulate them from the power of death. In both cases, this world combines a political restructuring with personal irresponsibility and dependence on heirs for self-perpetuation – a standard Renaissance figuration for worldly immortality. Lear's construct, of course, soon collapses, leaving him more acutely subject to death than before. Prospero's promises to be considerably more durable, thanks to his access to magic, as opposed to mere magical thinking, in setting it up. But that very use of magic makes for deeper, if less literal, tragedy by exposing the depth of his successful self-delusion. For the wisdom manifested by Prospero's power is founded on the very knowledge that such denials of time and death are futile – in the end, death-serving. Prospero, that is, knows better, and he is actually misappropriating his better knowledge to convince himself that his created future represents a worthy extension and application of the romance ideal rather than a relinquishing of it. It is as if God were creating man in his image in order to give himself a sense of heaven on earth, while putting chaos safely behind him. Even the best wisdom signified by romance fulfilment is liable, it would seem, to corruption over – that is, in the face of – time.

What helps to obscure the ambiguity in Prospero's resumption of the dukedom is the association of that 'best wisdom', in Shakespeare's other romances, with participation in, rather than withdrawal from, social structures. However, *The Tempest*'s contradictions call into question, not the value itself, but Prospero's relation to it. Obviously, from one perspective, which happens to be Prospero's current one, the island is a place of exile and isolation, but it has also been revealed as obligingly multivalent. Revealingly, in calling it a 'bare island' in his

Epilogue (8), he echoes the cynicism of Antonio and Sebastian rather than the idealism of Gonzalo. On his own evidence, the island at least began as something very different – the locus of providential salvation and fulfilled wisdom, a commonwealth in microcosm, actively and harmoniously governed by Prospero, indeed a king and no king. And while Milan may now seem to have a symbolic monopoly on engagement with 'real' life, the terms of Prospero's return there constitute a private reality of escapism and withdrawal. Ostentatiously to repudiate, in effect, the stance of Jaques is to rally behind his project the forces of comic resolution, but there is no mistaking that a profound underlying melancholy is being gratified, not joyously cast off.

The concept of a misappropriation of the knowledge that is his power returns us to the tension between Prospero and Ariel over the spirit's longing for his promised freedom. It also recalls the unlawful 'black' magic of Sycorax, who imprisoned Ariel in a tree – as Prospero threatens to do again (with an escalation from softwood to hardwood) – because he was 'a spirit too delicate/To act her earthy and abhorr'd commands' (I.ii.272-3). Ariel is once again being constituted as something he is not. He may come labelled as 'tricksy spirit', but it is Prospero who applies the label, with a firmly possessive 'my'.[18] The spirit's subversion of the castaways is balanced by his repression of subversiveness in Caliban; in both instances he is doing his master's bidding – with a desire to please, perhaps, but never with self-delight. Puck's slippery relation to Oberon suffices to show that the trickster cannot be owned. Yet Prospero plainly needs not only Ariel's spirit-power but, in order to sustain his illusions, Ariel's loyalty. He must do more than master the subversive principle; it must justify his superhuman status by serving him willingly. In fact, he reverts to the 'divide and rule' principle familiar from the middle plays, appropriating a tame version of trickery's creative potential, while displacing and stigmatizing its destructive aspect. The frankness of the symbolism is unprecedented, and it is also, paradoxically, the key to this text's refusal to succumb to its internal dramatist, whatever the characters may do. To project not merely the hegemonic vision itself, but an understanding of it, is self-exposing, especially when the key symbols are making urgent political claims of their own.

Apart from his subversive label, the formal significance attached to Ariel is large indeed. It is part of the Neoplatonic model that the agent and symbolic embodiment of Prospero's power was liberated from nature through knowledge as part of the founding of the magical kingdom. This further identifies him with Prospero's spiritual liberation from time, so that he comes to suggest a veritable mystical equivalent of the immortal soul.[19] Ariel thus realizes, one might say, the potential of air-and-fire imagery elsewhere in Shakespeare. These elements' commonplace properties of lightness and quickness, which figure, for instance, in the Dolphin's description of his horse as 'pure air and fire' in *Henry V* (III.vii.21), are extended on two significant occasions to a heightened spirituality. The first involves a conceit in Sonnets 44 and 45 that presents the lover's two lighter elements, 'slight air and purging fire,/ . . . /The first my thought, the other my desire' (45.1–3), as going forth to his absent love, while his remaining self '[s]inks down to death, oppress'd with melancholy' (8): 'so much of earth and water wrought,/I must attend time's leisure with my moan' (44.11–12). The correspondence with the elemental associations of Ariel and Caliban is striking – it is surprising that G. Wilson Knight seems to have been the first to notice it in print (1969: 240 n.1). But more significant is the presentation of that structure in terms of freedom from, and subjection to, time and mortality. This is also a central feature of Paracelsus' concept of 'sidereal' and 'animal' bodies:

> In his earthly life, man consists of the four elements. Water and earth, of which his body is formed, constitute the dwelling place and the physical envelope of life. And I am not referring here to that life of the soul, which springs from the breath of god. . . . For we must know that man has two kinds of life – animal and sidereal life. . . . The relations between the two [bodies] are as follows. The animal body, the body of flesh and blood, is in itself always dead. Only through the action of the sidereal body does the motion of life come into the other body. The sidereal body is fire and air; but it is also bound to the animal life of man. Thus mortal man consists of water, earth, fire, and air.
>
> (Paracelsus, *Selected Writings*, 18)[20]

The notion of a spiritual entity comprised of 'thought' and 'desire' might seem at odds with some Renaissance spirit-theory and certainly does not suit the critical tradition of identifying

Ariel and Caliban with forms of reason and passion, respectively. But in fact, mimetically speaking, the play depicts both characters as mixtures, although in Ariel's case the mixture is highly refined and powerfully concentrated within the alembic of his spirit-nature. As a result, his longing for his freedom, his gratitude to Prospero, his sense of the castaways' suffering, amount to more feeling than most of the human characters display. When he finally reports than his 'affections' would soften if he were human, he exposes as hollow the more complete sensitivities claimed by his master. It is important to recognize the role of emotional excess in generating spiritual transformation elsewhere – for example, in Prospero's victims. Passion is the standard measure of the impact of the subversive, and its harmonious union with the rational carries the Neoplatonic stamp of approval. This brings us back to that earlier crossing of the barrier between tragedy and romance, Cleopatra's realization of her '[i]mmortal longings' (*Ant.*, V.ii.281) while remaining '[n]o more but e'en a woman' (IV.xv.73). That mystery elicits Shakespeare's only other use of the imagery that became Ariel: 'I am fire and air; my other elements/I give to baser life' (V.ii.289–90).

If Ariel manifests Prospero's claim to power over death, the realized potential of the trickster, Caliban inevitably suggests the aspect that remains subject to the ultimate subversion. The two characters, super- and sub-human, thus enact a version of the traditional soul–body dialogue. Apart from his general physicality, Caliban is specifically linked with those polar aspects of the body's role, sustenance of life and deprivation of life: introduced through Prospero's grudging acknowledgement of the need for his grudging services ('But as 'tis/We cannot miss him' (I.ii.310–11)), he is also his master's would-be killer. In fact, he assumes overtones of the medieval figure of Death when his recital of the ways in which Prospero may be killed, king though he is, turns into a catalogue of the manifold ways of ending life:

> thou mayst brain him,
> Having first seiz'd his books; or with a log
> Batter his skull, or paunch him with a stake,
> Or cut his wezand with thy knife.

> (III.ii.88–91)

The scenes that pair Caliban with Stephano and Trinculo

present a simultaneous comic and dangerous festivity. This is, again, the ambiguous alliance of the Fool and Death – the two figures who will triumph, according to Cerimon, if one chooses material over spiritual riches (*Per.*, III.ii.41–2), but whose transformative energy may be released if they are recognized and accommodated.

The reference to Prospero's books highlights the role of his magic in shielding him from death – the need, in short, for Ariel to protect him from Caliban. In isolation and from a distance, the subordination of Caliban might stand as a valid emblem of spiritual power over death. Again, however, the mimetic dimension helps to disclose the configuration as Prospero's projection. It may be just possible to accept Caliban's harsh treatment at Prospero's hands, but, on the political level, there is no dismissing his eloquent appeal to natural justice. Moreover, Caliban's unwilling servitude pointedly represents a falling-off from willing service. Farnham (1971: 153–6) points out that Caliban is distinguished from Shakespeare's other grotesque figures of folly, including Stephano and Trinculo, by his revolutionary spirit. That spirit specifically reflects his perception that Prospero has become a tyrant. The immediate reason for the change in their relationship, Caliban's attempt to rape Miranda, offers little room to blame Prospero. But two facts are naggingly present: first, it was eminently 'natural', at once destructive and creative, for Caliban to behave as he did; second, as with Ariel's restlessness, the spur to this action was nothing less than the inevitable passing of time, which brought Miranda to sexual maturity – a state that Prospero himself is now exploiting.

Characters in the three earlier romances work towards a relation with the subversive physical self like that which first existed between Prospero and Caliban. The body loses its sovereignty – Caliban can no longer be 'mine own king' (I.ii.342) – but it is mastered by manifest merit, not by the tyranny of counter-trickery, and its prerogatives and limitations are accepted. Thus the current enmity, however it may be rationalized in terms of 'civilization', reflects Prospero's lapsing from the ideal to which, with Ariel's reluctant support, he continues to profess allegiance. Justifying his claim would entail accepting the trickster's message of vulnerability to Caliban. In this context, Prospero's formal acknowledgement of 'this thing of darkness' as 'mine' at the end of the play joins his other acknowledgements of his mortality not only as cloaking assertion with humility – again, his possessive cuts two ways – but as ironically revealing impotence after all: he has convinced himself that he has mastered death by reconstituting reality along romance lines; in fact, he has merely revived the tragic condition, putting himself more deeply into death's power. Caliban's teeth may have been drawn for the present; he may have been manoeuvred into subservience again – 'I'll be wise hereafter,/And seek for grace' (V.i.295-6). But actually his time has come because it is time itself: 'Every third thought shall be my grave.'

It is precisely thoughts of the grave that have defined and measured the threat of Caliban before, at the play's true climax, as opposed to the climax of Prospero's romance script. The spirit-masque, designed to invest the future Prospero is constructing with the symbolic trappings of freedom from death, is violently interrupted. The naïve comments of the lovers document the subversion of Prospero's status as wise creator and superhuman manipulator of time. 'So rare a wond'red father and a wise/Makes this place Paradise' (IV.i.123-4), Ferdinand has just exclaimed, following Prospero's script; now he notes 'some passion/That works him strongly' (143-4), while Miranda elaborates, 'Never till this day/Saw I him touch'd with anger, so distemper'd' (144-5). The sudden descent into vulnerable humanity, the loss of control, have proved similarly puzzling for many commentators, but the focus of Prospero's distress – the sense of universal mortality as rendering life meaningless – is the key to its intensity. His famous elegiac speech is recognizably tragic, with no analogue in the romances nearly so close as Macbeth's 'to-morrow' soliloquy (*Mac.*, V.v.19ff.) or Lear's 'Is man no more than this?' (*Lr*, III.iv.102-3). The give-away is his most striking Lear-moment, when 'I am a very foolish fond old man' (IV.vii.59) is so powerfully echoed: 'Sir, I am vex'd;/Bear with my weakness, my old brain is troubled./Be not disturb'd with my infirmity' (158-60).

What is revealed, as the symbolic structure momentarily gives way like the 'baseless fabric of this vision' (151), is the extent to which Prospero's project has been aimed at removing the threat of the knowledge of death – at, in the most basic sense, forgetting: 'I had forgot that foul conspiracy/. . . /Against my life' (139-41). His counter-subversive response to a mere given of existence has constructed the subversive in monstrous form. The urgency

Prospero has imposed on others as manipulator of time suddenly comes back at him as time's prospective victim: 'The minute of their plot/Is almost come' (141–2). Caliban, however clumsily, has his intersecting agenda: we age, we will die, we are doomed with the trickster (to paraphrase Pelton (1980) once more) to 'touch nothing', whether we 'find joy' or not. No amount of 'nurture' can erase these terms of 'nature', yet Prospero reveals himself as deserving his own abuse of Caliban: 'on whose nature/ Nurture can never stick' (188–9). A 'holy adept' in the mystery of life must begin and end by accepting life's termination. Ariel's date is out – he should not be summonable to keep Caliban at bay.

Nor should he be called upon to furnish the fair winds that will enable Prospero to transport his secured cargo of illusion back to reality. It seems fitting that in the Epilogue Prospero makes the weather – and his success – depend rather upon the audience's judgement of him. If we consider that getting his dukedom back and pardoning the deceiver warrant our endorse-ment, we allow ourselves to be deceived as deeply as Prospero himself. Our applause must be for the chief actor in the tragedy, not for the self-styled hero of the romance it contains. If we insist on the traditional view that Shakespeare himself takes leave of something with the ending of *The Tempest*, that something must be less theatrical illusion in general – for Prospero has simply changed costume again – than the illusive hope proffered by romance. An ultimately more conservative reading might be that the developing text-of-texts which, over twenty years, had opened up issues of subversion and counter-subversion for relentless interrogation, but which then seemed to be imposing a closure called 'romance' upon that process, ends by subverting itself.

NOTES

1 INTRODUCTION

1 This is evident from – and part of the point of – Foucault's 'Preface to Transgression' (1977), an essay which, while fascinating in itself, is of limited use for my purposes.

2 A helpful perspective on this question is provided by Crewe (1986: 19–21).

3 An especially useful text on this point is Rossiter (1961: 274–92). See also the more recent discussion by Wiles (1987: 164–5).

4 See, e.g., Goldberg (1985: 116–17).

5 See Edward Berry (1984: 109–37, esp. 114–15).

6 See Griswold (1986: 38–54), including her table of 'Tricksters in Drama and Popular Literature' (39–40).

7 Cf. Skura (1981: 34–7).

8 Cf. Kott (1987: 49) and Carroll: 'Puck exemplifies the spirit of metamorphosis for its own sake. . . . His function in the play is principally to move and to change' (Carroll 1985: 173).

9 See also Willeford (1969: 226–35), Hassel (1980: 1–17), Blum (1983: 264–5), and Billington (1979: 44–6).

10 See also Goldsmith (1955: 15–31), who, writing before Spivack, traced the evolution of the stage fool from the Vice.

11 See, e.g., Garber (1981), Edward Berry (1984), and Boose (1982).

12 See Turner (1969; 1974: esp. 272–99; 1982: 20–60).

13 On 'nothing' in relation to the fool, see Willeford (1969: esp. 61–72 and 210–13).

14 The literally marginal status of the grotesque in the visual art of the Middle Ages is made clear by Farnham (1971: 1–146).

15 Even apart from the reservations of some materialist critics, Bakhtin has not wholly carried the day. See Harpham (1982: 71–6), who accuses him of 'underestimating the force of alienation in the grotesque' (72) – a qualification that would seem to allow more fully for the trickster's destructive aspect.

16 See, e.g., Tennenhouse (1986), Bristol (1985), and Wiles (1987: 164–81).

17 He has failed in this attempt – witness the approach of Pfister, based

on the conviction that 'it is with the problem plays . . . that the carnivalesque becomes a particularly powerful challenging and corrosive counter-force' (Pfister 1987: 39). Pfister's application of Bakhtinian subversion across the canon produces some readings that are nearly the inverse of my own.

18 Cf., however, Pfister, who argues that carnivalesque 'periods of reduced tension', even as they reinforce the established order, 'can also function as a testing-ground for alternative values and practices, some of which may be integrated, albeit infinitely modified and extenuated, into the post-festal everyday reality' (Pfister 1987: 29).

19 This is by no means to deny the development in the Renaissance of forms of self-consciousness involving a sense of the self as unstable – see Delany (1969: 11–17).

20 On this concept see also Willeford (1969: 174–91) and Ralph Berry (1979/80).

21 See, e.g., Goldberg (1985: 116–17) and McLuskie (1985).

22 Williamson asserts that 'Portia is one of the most skillful disguisers of power in dramatic literature' (Williamson 1986: 178).

23 On the boy's subversiveness, cf. Farnham (1971: 41) and Weimann (1978: 139–40).

24 Cf. Greenblatt (1980: 203–21) on Barabas as a vehicle for Marlowe's subversive playfulness.

25 Cf. Weimann (1978: 64–72).

26 Holderness (1985: 23–6) points out that Renaissance humanism and medieval providentialism had ideological 'common cause' (25).

2 CREATION ACCORDING TO KATE

1 For useful surveys of opinion, see Bean (1980: 65–6), who distinguishes 'revisionist' and 'anti-revisionist' schools in defining his own middle ground, and Woodbridge (1984: 221 n.22), who finds the play about equally brutal as its contemporary analogues (206–7).

2 See Morris (1981: 12–50) on this vexed question, to which my intertextual approach neither implies nor requires a solution.

3 However, as Leggatt documents (1973: 78–98), citizen comedies generally argue that the husband's supposedly natural 'authority must be exercised humanely, without bullying' (81). For broader studies of social attitudes, see Dusinberre (1975: 77–109) and Woodbridge, who drily observes that 'the extreme brutality of the earlier shrew-taming tradition had . . . been muted into mere psychological sadism by the 1590s' (Woodbridge 1984: 206).

4 Cf. Wayne (1985).

5 Cf. Elam (1984: 130), Fineman (1985: 154), and Tennenhouse (1986: 52). Especially in view of such resonances, I cannot share the common view that Katherina's 'playfulness and irony here are indisputable' (Newman 1986: 95). The plays on words, the linguistic give and take, create a farcical surface, not a subversive subtext, and

while her sarcastic embellishments do suggest an attempt to assert freedom (see Kahn 1981: 113), they are desperately defensive.

6 See Dusinberre (1975: 78–9), Ornstein (1986: 70), and Bryant (1986: 109).

7 The term 'chaos' is also omitted from the first formal English translation extant, *The First Day of the worldes creation* (published 1595; entered 1591). This may be coincidental (the 1595 rendering is generally looser), but Du Bartas's use of this pagan concept was controversial, because it could be construed as undermining the doctrine of creation *ex nihilo*. See the defensive explication by Goulart (*A Learned Summary*, 16), originally appended as commentary to the edition of 1582, and the almost obsessive attack by de Gamon (*La Semaine*, 4–9), who on this point virtually unwrites his progenitor, sometimes line by line, in *La Semaine ou creation du Monde. Contre celle du Sieur du Bartas* (first published 1599).

8 Although Dusinberre (1975) associates this 'theology' (wrongly, I think) with Du Bartas, and Morris describes the speech as 'patched out with allusions' to him (Morris 1981: 48), neither documents the borrowing. The first six lines of the speech are based on 1.19–24 of *La Première Sepmaine*; after the translated description of chaos, the author skips nine lines, then more loosely – to the point of garbling the original, unless some text has dropped out – follows 1.236–8 before leaving Du Bartas behind entirely.

9 Scott, in his thorough commentary on the *Asclepius* attributed to Hermes Trismegistus, relates that work's presentation of the idea to the *Timaeus*, to Plutarch's *De Iside et Osiride*, and to various heretical and orthodox Christian thinkers (3: 68–81). See also Thévenaz (1938: 68–70).

10 The *Moralia*, which includes both these essays, appeared in several Latin translations and one into French (by Jacques Amyot) in the early 1570s.

11 As often, Neoplatonism and alchemy converge. In a treatise by the medieval alchemist George Ripley, as 'set foorth' in 1591 by Ralph Rabbards with a dedication to Queen Elizabeth, an account of creation from chaos very close to that of Du Bartas is used as an analogy for the alchemist's work (*The Compound of Alchymy*, sig. B3^v). See also Titus Burckhardt (1971: 123–201) on the symbolism of the union between sulphur and quicksilver, which are identified, respectively, with male and female, form and matter. 'She' is the dissolving power who at first 'works at cross purposes with Sulphur, wresting the "substance" from the former, in order subsequently to offer "herself" to "him" as a newer, unlimited and more receptive substance' (T. Burckhardt 1971: 143). For a Renaissance illustration of the *prima materia* as fool, see Willeford (1969: 19).

3 CATALYTIC CHAOS

1 In the case of Puck, the sinister overtones are enriched by the associations of the folklore figure from whom he gets his name – see Schleiner (1985: 65–8).

2 It would seem that the application of the term to an ill-tempered woman represents a stereotype-influenced specialization not necessarily originating with the name of the animal; the sense of 'a mischievous or vexatious person' (*OED* 1), regardless of gender, persisted at least into the late sixteenth century.

3 This is not to posit an essentially female creative and restorative energy in Shakespearean drama, as does, e.g., Berggren (1980).

4 On this scene cf. Blanpied (1983: 106-7).

5 Cf. Sigurd Burckhardt (1968: 135-9).

6 See Sigurd Burckhardt (1968: 140) and Kastan (1982: 52-4), for whom the Bastard's moment of despair ('I am amaz'd') 'provides the perfect emblem of man in Shakespeare's history plays' (Kastan 1982: 57).

7 On Richard as trickster, see Mallett (1979), Blanpied (1983: 15 and 70-5), and Ralph Berry (1984: 115-16).

8 On Aaron, cf. Calderwood (1971: 42-6).

9 On *Richard III* as romance, see Kastan (1982: 132-3).

10 See the thoughtful discussion of Smith (1980: 29-48); especially well-balanced considerations of providentialism in *Richard III* are offered by Sanders (1968: 72-120) and Prior (1973: 34-58).

11 Cf. Kastan (1982: 93-5).

12 See, notably, Spivack (1958: 386-407) and Rossiter (1961: 1-22).

13 See my article (R. Hillman 1979b).

14 Kastan (1982: 132) points out the ironic allusion to destiny in Richard's word 'determined'; Weimann (1978: 160) notes the irony in his claim that he is 'not shap'd for sportive tricks' (*R3*, I. i.14).

15 Cf. Blanpied (1983: 62-3). There are prototypes earlier in the tetralogy for the subversive energy of Richard - Joan de Pucelle in Part 1, Jack Cade and his rebels in Part 2. In these cases, the subversion is external and overtly opposed to the forces of institutionalized political violence, so that it can be defused and indeed appropriated by those forces. Thus the killing of Cade transforms Alexander Iden from a figure of pastoral content, self-sufficient within his walled garden, to a bloodthirsty participant in the processes of history. It takes Richard, who incarnates the violence of the established structures themselves, to fulfil the self-destructive tendencies of the society which Iden destroys himself by embracing. On Cade as 'antic', cf. Blanpied (1983: 14-15) and Barber (1959: 13, 29, and 204); on Joan as a fool-like challenger of authority, see Ralph Berry (1979/80: 625).

16 Sylvester's version (pub. 1605), as if to avoid problematic implications, suppresses the specifically destructive features; thus God

> Did not unlike the Beare, which bringeth forth
> In th'end of thirty dayes a shapelesse birth,
> But after, licking, it in shape she drawes,
> And by degrees she fashions out the pawes,
> The head, and necke, and finally doth bring
> To a perfect beast that first deformed thing.

(1.1.447-52)

Still, it is remarkable, given the almost certain priority of Shakespeare's text, that Sylvester adjusts key epithets to create the highly Riccardian 'shapeless birth' and 'deformed thing'. Similar is his production of 'a *Chaos* most diforme' (1.1.248) by conflating 'un meslange difforme' (1.224) and '[u]n Chaos de Chaos' (1.226).

17 For a stimulating comparison of bear-baiting to the experience of the theatre, see Wiles (1987: 167).

18 On the perversion of birth-images and Richard's hatred of women, see Miner (1980). Cf. also Douglas:

> It is consistent with the ideas about form and formlessness to treat initiands coming out of seclusion [i.e., ritually reborn] as if they were themselves charged with power, hot, dangerous, requiring insulation and a time for cooling down. Dirt, obscenity and lawlessness are as relevant symbolically to the rites of seclusion as other ritual expressions of their condition. *They are not to be blamed for misconduct any more than the foetus in the womb for its [superstitiously attributed] spite and greed.*
>
> (Douglas 1966: 97; emphasis mine)

19 On the multilayered motif of devouring, cf. Miola (1983: 67–8).

20 Cf. Tourneur, *The Atheist's Tragedy*: 'Why, what is't but a rape to force a wench/To marry, since it forces her to lie/With him she would not?' (I.iv.129–31).

21 Cf. Miola (1983: 68).

22 It can be argued that Edmund's silent presence on stage during the love test and the subsequent confrontation enriches the dynamic of his villainy, since he is thereby offered ambivalent models of the successful duping of a father by falsely professing children and of a truly loving child unjustly disinherited. As far as I am aware, however, all modern editions except the new Oxford follow Capell in unnecessarily appending 'with Edmund' to the First Folio's stage direction, 'Exit Gloucester', at I.i.35.

23 The comparison is also found, in a less sustained form, in *A Shrew* (ix.46–52). The soaring hawk is made into an emblem of dangerous ambition by the falconers themselves in *2H6* (I.iv.8ff.). Cf. Chapman, *Bussy D'Ambois* (III.ii), where Bussy, the king's 'eagle', is given less freedom to 'hawk' at his great enemies than he wants – or will later take; also Marvell, 'An Horatian Ode', in which the comparison of Cromwell to a falcon is used at once to praise and to raise doubts about the state's control of his killing power:

> So when the Falcon high
> Falls heavy from the Sky,
> She, having kill'd, no more does search,
> But on the next green Bow to pearch;
> Where, when he first does lure,
> The Falckner has her sure.
>
> (91–6)

24 Cf. Homan (1986: 128) and Blanpied (1983: 70-5).

4 TRICKERY AND IMAGINATION

1 See also Kott (1987: 29-68) and Tennenhouse (1986: 43-4 and 74-5), who, as a New Historicist, supplies a context of the ultimate reaffirmation of order.

2 This view has recently been renewed in old and new forms. Hassel (1980) would restore primacy to the Pauline–Erasmian tradition, with its anagogic telos. The anthropologically oriented Edward Berry considers that the clown's 'confusion is a world through which lovers pass en route to marriage' (E. Berry 1984: 137) – a concept that accords with Garber's study of liminality and rites of initiation (1981: esp. 1-26), with Carroll's (1985) investigation of metamorphosis, and with Huston's (1981) metadramatic approach through 'play'.

3 Cf. Parker on the 'middle space of "error" and putting off' (Parker 1986: 189) as the site of the play. James Hillman (1975: 159-64) relates 'errancy' as a mechanism for self-exploration to the concept of the trickster.

4 Cf. my book (R. Hillman 1992: 106-23).

5 Cf. Garber (1981: 32).

6 On Puck as trickster, cf. Farrell (1975: 103) and Kott (1987: 49-50).

7 This is, naturally, the key element for such transformational critics as Barber ('the magic is imagination' (1959: 140)), Young (1966: 126-41 and 155-66), and Farrell (1975: 104). Dent (1964) may be considered founder of the substantial school which applies – generally at the expense of Puck and Bottom – the common Renaissance distinction between the reason-subverting and reason-controlled imaginations.

8 Cf. Huston (1981: 104-17), who treats Oberon as 'surrogate playwright figure' (113-14).

9 The apparent contradiction as to the season, then, is highly functional – neither to be rationalized away (see Bryant 1986: 75-6), nor to be simply absorbed into the idea of holiday (Barber 1959: 120). The same applies to the contradiction between the phase of the moon established in I.i and the presence of moonlight in the forest scene. The mechanicals' decision to 'disfigure, or to present, the person of Moonshine' (III.i.60-1) parallels Theseus' effective creation of May-day.

10 Those New Historicist readings that see Theseus as merely appropriating the fruits of subversion on behalf of authority (Montrose 1983; Tennenhouse 1986: 74) credit him with a more complete understanding and domination of his world than I find consistent with his portrayal here or elsewhere. Cf. Calderwood (1971: 126-7) on the gap between the change in Theseus and his understanding of it.

11 Carroll points out that the linguistic transgressions of the Prologue look forward to 'the other transformations to come' and evoke 'a

typical dream logic' (Carroll 1985: 160). Cf. Farrell (1975: 114).

12 See Barber (1959: 154n.) and Leggatt (1974: 100), who aptly compares Falstaff's rising from Shrewsbury field.

13 Carroll deals with 'the ideal of two becoming one' (Carroll 1985: 68) as part of his useful analysis of metamorphosis and identity in the play (65–80). See also Nevo (1980: 26–31), Garber (1981: 31 and 188), Kahn (1981: 197–205), and Freedman (1980: 233–43).

14 Cf. the radically divergent perceptions of Prospero's island displayed by Gonzalo, on the one hand, and Sebastian and Antonio, on the other. On the two aspects of the city, see Leggatt (1974: 7–9 and 18).

15 On this paradox, cf. Henze (1971).

16 See Parker (1979).

17 The problematics of the Proteus–Valentine relation have come in for renewed attention recently – see Adelman (1985a: 76–9), Nevo (1980: 58), and Ornstein (1986: 53–4).

18 The ways in which the clowns supply a commentary on the lovers have often been discussed, e.g., by Leggatt (1974: 22–4). See also Weimann (1978: 242–3 and 255–60).

19 See Goldberg (1986: 68–100) for a discussion of Silvia's silence as 'textually inscribed' (100).

20 On the dramatic silencing of women, cf. Belsey (1985: 149–91).

21 For a persuasive account of the play in these terms, see Ralph Berry (1972: 72–88); cf. the same author's 'Woman' (1979/80: esp. 622–3).

22 Graziani links the messenger Mercadé with the Dance of Death and sees signs in several later plays that 'Shakespeare is himself being drawn to a spirit of comedy in tune with that of the dance macabre, where laughter engages with death, tragedy, and horror' (Graziani 1986: 395).

23 Cf. Elam (1984: 126–9), for whom the Academicians' commitment to the 'phenomenal and numinal fullness of the linguistic sign' is part of their naïve Neoplatonic project. He perceives 'a like reverence towards nomination' beneath Berowne's scepticism (126).

24 On his foolishness as self-protective, cf. Farrell (1975: 85).

25 On this point, cf. Ralph Berry (1979/80: 623).

26 On the need for Berowne to become a 'jesting priest', cf. Farrell (1975: 94).

5 THE DEATH OF MERCUTIO

1 On the alchemical Mercurius as trickster, see Jung (1953–79b: 255); cf. James Hillman (1975: 163).

2 Cf. Mistress Ford's indignant image: 'What tempest, I trow, threw this whale (with so many tuns of oil in his belly) ashore at Windsor?' (II.i.64–5).

3 On the development of the later character-type, see Somerset, who argues that 'it was Shakespeare [not Robert Armin] who forged the new conception of the wise fool' (Somerset 1984: 78). For a recent restatement of the contrary view, see Wiles (1987).

4 These three theatrical manipulators are often linked. An interesting perspective is offered by Altieri (1981: 239), who is concerned with the processes of romance idealization.

5 Krieger (1979: 25-6) makes a similar point.

6 Cf. Carroll on Portia as 'a kind of domesticated Medea' retaining 'remnants of Medea's powers of transformation' (Carroll 1985: 118).

7 Ornstein notes Portia's hypocrisy and finds her more 'a product of her society' than Desdemona (1986: 102); see also Bradshaw (1987: 27-9).

8 Berger (1981: 161) extends this anticipation to Portia's clue-giving.

9 Novy effectively articulates this view: 'Shylock's main role is to speak for the aggressive and acquisitive motives that his society follows but does not admit' (Novy 1984: 66-7).

10 See, notably, Hyman (1970), Berger (1981), and Richard A. Levin (1985: 30-85).

11 Cf. Stallybrass and White (1986: 55-6) and Tennenhouse (1986: 56-7).

12 See, e.g., Bryant (1986: 94) and Richard A. Levin (1985: 81-2).

13 Cf. Carroll (1985: 126).

14 See, notably, Berger (1981: 162), Hyman (1970: 112), Hineley (1980: 229-39), and Williamson (1986: 50).

15 Cf. Fiedler (1972: 135-6) and Nuttall, who comments that Shakespeare 'finds the single point where language most powerfully asserts the interdependence of economics and humanity, in the etymological affinity between a person's *life* and a person's *living*' (Nuttall 1983: 129-30).

16 Cf. Berger (1981: 161) and Williamson (1986: 39).

17 Williamson (1986: 27) discusses the threat of cuckoldry as one of women's few sources of power and considers Portia 'nearly unique in the amount of power she contrives to retain to the end of the action' through 'fantasies of cuckoldry and forgiveness' (51). See also Neely (1985: 22 and 34-5).

18 Blanpied's concept of Falstaff as 'antic' is part of a discussion of the Henry-plays (1983: 153-249) that I find stimulating even when our readings diverge. See also Calderwood on Falstaff as the 'lie' from whose 'unseemly material' Shakespeare, through Hal as surrogate playwright, seeks to create 'an authentic order and meaning' (Calderwood 1979: 52-3).

19 Kern (1984) attempts to synthesize the readings of Barber (1959) and Battenhouse (1975) under the trickster rubric. For an application of Bakhtin, see Rhodes (1980: 89-130). Cf. Kaiser (1963: 195-275), Farnham (1971: 47-96), Wiles (1987: 116-35), Dessen (1986: 91-112), Salingar (1980), Richard L. Levin (1971: 140), Driscoll (1983: 36-43), French (1981: 107), and Aronson (1972: 55), who sees Falstaff as both trickster and 'shadow'.

20 Thus Greenblatt places on the same level Hal's setting-up and cutting-down of Francis in II.iv.28-79 (1985: 31-2).

21 Cf. Calderwood (1979: 119-33) on Falstaff-as-'lie' as integrated into the apparatus of state.

22 Erickson (1985: 54-5) persuasively discusses *Henry V* in these terms.

23 These are incorporated by Greenblatt into the pattern of authority's production of subversion (1985: 18-22).

24 Cf. Battenhouse (1975: 47): 'It is Falstaff who has been practicing the true sense of Ephesians v: redeeming time through manifest "unfruteful workes of darknes". . . . Prince Hal's purpose has been but a counterfeit redeeming, reductively political, which Falstaff *redeems* in the sense of re-estimates, re-evaluates.' Still, Battenhouse himself banishes Falstaff's darkest side.

25 On Hal as a language student, cf. Greenblatt (1985: 35-6) and Garber (1981: 92-5).

26 For a psychoanalytic view of this link, see Berger (1984: 58-78), for whom the play is a 'festered carnival' (75); on the 'tongues', see also Blanpied (1983: 180-3).

27 Cf. Garber on the transfer of power with language here (1981: 90).

28 Homan (1986: 149) discusses the shift in terms of the failure of Pistol's 'counterlanguage' in the face of Fluellen's dialect. Cf., from the perspective of genre, Altieri (1981: 237-8) and Dean (1981: 22-4).

29 On the play's uneasy romance closure, though not in terms of Henry's effective manipulation of genre, see Altieri (1981: 230) and Dean (1981: 26-7).

30 See, e.g., Bryant (1986: 114-24), Roberts (1979: 77-83), and Carroll (1985: 186-94).

31 Cf. Barton (1985: 142-6) on Windsor as a 'sound, stable, and remarkably well defined' (142) community not 'vulnerable' to Falstaff's 'particular kind of dissent' (145).

32 Jonson may also have been inspired by Simple's attempt to consult the 'wise woman of Brainford' (IV.v.26).

33 Given the reminiscence in her language of Prince Hal's scornful accounts of Falstaff in the role-playing scene (*1H4*, II.iv.446ff.) and the banishment speech ('How ill white hairs becomes a fool and jester!' (*2H4*, V.v.48)), it is tempting to catch a punning reference to the prison in Beatrice's line, 'I am sure he is in the fleet; I would he had boarded me' (II.i.142-3).

34 Richard A. Levin notes the 'language denigrating romance' and observes that 'the conventional world wants to bring them [Beatrice and Benedick] within its orbit' (R. A. Levin 1985: 99). Cf. Howard (1987: 175-9) and Neely (1985: 40).

35 Cf. Huston (1981: 136-50) on Don Pedro's metadramatics as lacking the ludic energy and spontaneity of the early comedies.

36 On the two brothers as complementary 'good' and 'evil' manipulators, cf. Robert Grams Hunter (1965: 94), Huston (1981: 144-5), and Howard (1987: 174-6). Given the superficial black-and-white contrast, it is subversively suggestive that behind Shakespeare's bastard-villain evidently lies a bastard-hero: the celebrated Don John of Austria, who in 1571 led the forces of the Holy League from Messina to defeat the Turks at Lepanto – an occasion for rejoicing in England as elsewhere in Christendom. *His* Spanish half-brother, Philip II, was hardly a positive figure for Elizabethans.

37 Howard is one of the few critics to argue that 'Dogberry and Verges

perform a sentimental, utopian function', in contrast with Shake-speare's 'more rebellious, clever, and even dangerous lower-class figures' (Howard 1987: 177).

38 Bryant (1986: 130) also finds this significant.

39 See, notably, Barber (1959: 222-60).

40 On this point, cf. Leggatt (1974: 226).

41 On the resolution as 'an impersonal organic process' and Viola's passivity in comparison to Rosalind, see Leggatt (1974: 248-9). Carroll notes that the element of water, symbolic of transformation, imagistically 'engulfs most of the characters' (Carroll 1985: 81).

42 In Lodge's *Rosalynde*, Alinda's spirited defence of her friend, which includes a declared willingness to share the sentence of exile, provokes her furious father into banishing both together (177-8).

43 For a provocative discussion of this performance as 'a model for royal power', see Goldberg (1983: 153).

44 The quality of Lodge's verse throughout is surely glanced at by Orlando's poetry and Touchstone's commentary on it.

6 LOVE'S TYRANNY

1 On the association of the two characters, cf. French (1981: 191), Skura (1981: 255-6), and Goldberg (1983: 236-9).

2 It is the ultimate ironic tribute to Vincentio's success that he is often more-or-less loosely referred to as a trickster, especially in confirming his status as embodiment of righteous power in the play's own terms – see, e.g., Tennenhouse (1986: 155) and Williamson (1986: 105).

3 This point is also made by McGuire (1985: 69-70), who examines the multiple final silences in detail (63-96), with an emphasis on the implications for production.

4 Cf. Wheeler's (1981) relation of the 'problem comedies' to their author's sexual repression; also Stockholder (1987: 66-83 and 223-4).

5 On links between the Duke and Angelo, see Van Laan (1978: 95-6) and, in terms of a response by the Duke to an inner conflict over sexuality, Wheeler (1981: 135-9), Stockholder (1987: 81 and 224), Leggatt (1988: 345-6), and Richard A. Levin (1982).

6 The concept of the Duke as internal dramatist has held the status of critical commonplace since Barton (1962: 178-80), who terms Lucio an 'unruly extempore actor' interrupting the Duke's script; cf. Van Laan (1978: 94-101). This perspective lends itself to New Historicist readings in terms of the theatrics of power – too readily, according to Dawson, who argues persuasively that the metatheatrical ending undermines the 'linkage between sex and knowledge, between verbal power, sexual domination, and legal authority' (1988: 337). Cf. Leggatt, who finds the Duke inept as a playwright and therefore considers this aspect of his role primarily ironic (1988: 358-9). However, the audience's distance and insight do not, I think, diminish the Duke's final achievement of moral, political, psychological, and sexual hegemony *within* the play-world, thanks to

what Swann, who stresses the false harmony of the 'shape' imposed by the Duke, aptly terms the 'mystified acceptance' of his 'power' (1987: 68) by other characters (Lucio being a subversive exception).

7 See also Goldberg (1983: 231-9) and Tennenhouse (1986: 156-9).

8 A favourite critical phrase – see Skura (1981: 254), Nuttall (1983: 130), and Leggatt (1988: 346).

9 See, e.g., Garber (1981: 221), who specifically credits the Duke's withholding of the truth about Claudio.

10 See, e.g., Arthur Kirsch (1981: 115-16).

11 See Dessen (1986: 113-33) on Parolles as Vice, although he comes close to accepting the eventual scapegoating as efficacious.

12 On the place of virginity in a male-determined system of symbolic commodity-exchange, see Irigaray (1985: 186), much of whose discussion of sexuality as a manifestation of power-relations (170-97) suits the three Problem Plays. On the sexual politics of this exchange, cf. French (1981: 174-6) and Neely (1985: 58-104).

13 A doubtful line, it should be noted, followed by an apparent gap in sense.

14 See, e.g., G. K. Hunter (1959: xxxvi) and Robert Grams Hunter (1965: 103).

15 The persuasive argument of Richard A. Levin that Parolles is 'society's scapegoat' hardly warrants his fabrication of an elaborate conspiracy of which Helena is 'the secret mastermind' (1980: 139-42).

16 Cf. Bayley (1975: 64) on Thersites as uniquely, among Shakespeare's 'cynics and railers', in conformity with his milieu.

17 On Pandarus as motiveless go-between, cf. Fly (1976: 38).

18 I am substantially in agreement with French's (1981) analysis of the first scene and, in particular, of Troilus' self-absorption.

19 Cf. Ornstein (1960: 245) and Bryant (1986: 199).

20 See Bayley (1975), Lyons (1971: 69-99), and Yoder (1972: 15-16).

21 There is an intriguing resemblance between Troilus' sexual initiation, with the help of a 'wise' older male, and the structure of various primitive rituals that effect the transition to manhood and warrior-status, often by way of a symbolic repudiation of the mother and a symbolic death to childhood. See Eliade (1965: *passim*).

22 Woodbridge notes that the 'most prominent stage misogynists are or have been soldiers' (Woodbridge 1984: 279), including Troilus and Claudio in *Much Ado*.

23 Cf. Yoder (1972: 22-3), Bryant (1986: 197-200), and Girard (1985).

24 See Bayley (1975: 67-71), Greene (1980: 143-5), Yoder (1972: 22), Burns (1980: 122-7), Voth and Evans (1975: 236), Roy (1973: 112-13), Novy (1984: 119), Dollimore (1984: 47-9), and Asp (1977: 413-14), who emphasizes Cressida's self-image as a psychological influence throughout.

25 While the bedroom exchange earlier in the scene parodically recalls the parting of Romeo and Juliet in III.v – 'Wilt thou be gone? it is not yet near day' (1ff.) – this is close to Juliet's desperate response to Friar Lawrence: 'Go get thee hence, for I will not away' (V.iii.160).

26 On Troilus' conduct here, cf. Yoder (1972: 20-1), Burns (1980: 121-2), and Girard (1985: 194).

7 TRAGIC HEROISM

1 For a recent example, see Stockholder (1987: 65-6 and 72).
2 On Hamlet as revenger, cf. Wheeler's psychoanalytic approach in terms of 'true' and 'false' selves (1981: 194-5).
3 On the Gravedigger as Death, cf. Farnham (1971: 116-17 and 128-9).
4 Farrell (1975: 184-6) reads the encounter similarly. Treatments of the carnivalesque element are also offered by Bristol (1985: 188-93), Pfister (1987: 37-8), Weimann (1978: 239-42), and Willeford (1969: 199-200).
5 Cf. Sorge (1987) and Bristol (1987).
6 Campbell's (1961) classic study is representative of the traditional approach in terms of Elizabethan faculty psychology.
7 For roughly parallel views of the worlds of the late tragedies as psychic projections, see Coursen (1986) and Wheeler (1981: 215). Cf. Stockholder's remark that Hamlet's 'self-considering mind . . . will pass into the fools and tricksters who hover around the edges' (Stockholder 1987: 64) of the later tragedies.
8 Cf. Long on Cassio's 'inability to hold his drink' as indicating Venetian society's denial of 'the entire Falstaff-element in man' (Long 1976: 44) – the key to the tragedy, as he argues.
9 See, e.g., Cavell (1979), Greenblatt (1980: 222-54), and Newman (1987).
10 Cf. Long on nature, in Othello's formulations, as a sort of 'devil-beast . . . mollified by romance' (Long 1976: 47). That the monstrous could be viewed in the Renaissance as part of a harmonious universe is made clear by Céard (1980).
11 Aronson (1972: 99-102) identifies them, as well as Banquo's ghost, with Macbeth's 'shadow'. On the ghost, see also Coursen (1986: 167-71).
12 On the issue of interpretation, cf. Goldberg (1987: 260).
13 Cf. Tennenhouse (1986: 128-9).
14 Cf. Bristol (1985: 184-5) and Weimann (1978: 244-5).
15 Cf., in political terms, Goldberg (1983: 186-93).
16 See, e.g., Adelman (1980), Kahn (1981: 155-72), and Sprengnether (1986).
17 On his self-destructiveness in terms of gender-related anxieties, cf. Sprengnether (1986: 104).
18 See also Adelman (1980: 141-3), Kahn (1981: 70), Sprengnether (1986: 105), and Goldberg (1983: 189).
19 The importance of Timon's threshold is noted by Fly (1976: 127).
20 On Timon's playing of Christ, cf. Fly (1976: 130) and Frye (1967: 110-11).
21 Cf. Fly (1976: 129-31), Kahn (1981: 193), and French (1981: 277-9).
22 On the ending as subversive, cf. Dollimore (1984: 203).

23 A similar view is offered by Coursen (1986: 124-7 and 148-50) in terms of Jungian 'inflation'. See also Wheeler (1981: 216).

24 Cf. Willeford (1969: 222-3) and Driscoll (1983: 131-2). There are striking parallels with the death ritual of the Nyakyusa ('a voluntary embrace of the symbols of death is a kind of prophylactic against effects of death') and with Dinka ritual murder: 'By [the old man's] free, deliberate decision he robs death of the uncertainty of its time and place of coming' (Douglas 1966: 77-8).

25 Quinones (1972: 412) comments similarly on Edmund's line.

26 See, e.g., Novy (1984: 196-7), Erickson (1985: 172), and French (1981: 251-65).

27 See also Proser (1965: 171-235) and Van Laan (1978: 221-2).

28 Goldman documents a pattern of vertical movement connecting the lovers' excessiveness with the overflowing tides that produce fertility – a process 'described at length by Antony for Caesar's benefit during their Bacchic feast' (Goldman 1985: 130), which exposes Caesar's fear of a loss of self-control in terms of carnival: 'the wild disguise hath almost/Antick'd us all' (II.vii.124-5).

29 Cf. the analysis of their exchange by Proser (1965: 178-82).

30 For a discussion of Renaissance 'polytheism' from a psychological perspective, see James Hillman (1975: 193ff.). Jung posits a concept of possession whereby 'some content, an idea or a part of the personality, obtains mastery of the individual' and illustrates it with this mythological analogy: 'The garment of Deianeira has grown fast to his skin, and a desperate decision like that of Heracles is needed if he is to tear this Nessus shirt from his body and step into the consuming flame of immortality, in order to transform himself into what he really is' (Jung 1953-79a: 122-3).

31 Thus Waith (1962: 119): 'Rage is the characteristic response of the Herculean hero to an attack on his honour.'

32 On Mardian here, see Bono (1984: 185-7) and Waddington (1966: 210-27).

33 See Panovsky (1930) and Simon (1955).

34 See Coates (1978: 50), Waddington (1966: 221-4), and Adelman (1973: 81-101).

35 Cf. Adelman (1973: 92-6), Wind (1967: 91ff.), Waddington (1966: 223-4), and, with reference to Isis, Bono (1984: 212-13).

36 On the doctrine presented in the masque, see Wind (1967: 206). A reading in terms of the politics of masquing is offered by Goldberg (1983: 62-5, 67, 83-4, and 126-7), who, however, in arguing for Hercules' transformation into a representation of James, finds 'in the figure of Hercules reconciliation, not opposition to pleasure' (63). Rather, the point, uniting Neoplatonic doctrine and flattery, is that Hesperus (i.e., James) corrects the limited Hercules, who is *merely* 'Virtue [without Pleasure] looking on' (192).

8 THE TRICKSTER MADE SPIRIT

1 In keeping with most recent criticism, my approach to *Pericles* assumes its status as a textual whole, whatever the precise nature of Shakespeare's contribution.

2 See Farrell (1975: 216-20) for a suggestive reading of the bear, Antigonus, and the folly of the Clown.

3 See my article (R. Hillman 1979a).

4 It is by no means clear how Henry V might hope to deliver, in a non-romance universe, on his promise: 'For he to-day that sheds his blood with me/Shall be my brother; be he ne'er so vile,/This day shall gentle his condition' (*H5*, IV.iii.61-3).

5 Commentators have made much of his name, which is that of Mercury's son, and have tended to offer more-or-less qualified celebrations of him as 'life-force' – see, e.g., Traversi (1965: 138-9), McFarland (1972: 131-2), Felperin (1972: 217-18), and Hartwig (1972: 117-20).

6 See my book (R. Hillman 1992: 120-3).

7 So does the Orphic parody detected by Hartwig (1972: 79-80).

8 In light of the precedent of Antony, cf. Novy, for whom Cloten is a parodic figure of masculine violence, one of the instruments by which, in the romances, 'the values of Mars and Hercules are superseded by the values of fertility and peace' (Novy 1984: 168). On Cloten's parodic relation to Posthumus, see also Robert Grams Hunter (1965: 157-8), Schwartz (1970: 226-31), and Arthur Kirsch (1981: 153-9).

9 On this resemblance, cf. Arthur Kirsch (1981: 147-8).

10 The recalcitrance of Antonio and Sebastian serves as a meeting ground for various critics whose readings have provided helpful background for my own – see, e.g., Leech (1950: 155), Felperin (1972: 279), Marsh (1962: 187-8), Hartwig (1972: 161), and Berger (1969: 275).

11 On Prospero's role-playing here, cf. Berger (1969: 274-6).

12 It is a common observation that the action of the play, as Hartwig puts it, 'begins at the point of dénouement which occurs in the last act of the other three plays' (Hartwig 1972: 138).

13 Cf. Berger (1969: 258).

14 On these lines as defining Gonzalo's romance response, cf. Patrick (1983: 174).

15 See, e.g., Kermode (1966: xlix) and Frye (1965: 153).

16 On Prospero as chess-player, cf. Loughrey and Taylor (1982: 116); on the courtly love symbolism, see Hartwig, who perceives 'a symbolic concord of reason and passion in romantic love' (Hartwig 1972: 159).

17 I have more fully developed the reading that follows in my book (R. Hillman 1992: 117-20).

18 Kott, for one, accepts this labelling when he relates Ariel to Mercury in Neoplatonic and alchemical terms (Kott 1987: 112-13). Cf. Stockholder (1987: 205 and 263 n.10) on Ariel as trickster and phallus.

19 The doctrine of the King's Two Bodies offers a precedent for

conceiving of a figurative form of immortality in terms of a 'soul' – see Kantorowicz (1966: 13).

20 The belief, Stoic in origin, that the soul is a fiery substance that dissolves in air was much discussed in the Renaissance – see, e.g., Burton (*Anatomy of Melancholy*, 1: 185–7).

REFERENCES

PRIMARY SOURCES

Note: STC numbers refer to *A Short-Title Catalogue of Books Printed in England, Scotland, and Ireland and of English Books Printed Abroad 1475–1640*, first compiled by A. W. Pollard and G. R. Redgrave, 2nd edn, revised and enlarged, begun by W. A. Jackson and F. S. Ferguson, completed by Katharine F. Pantzer, 2 vols, London: The Bibliographical Society, 1986.

Ariosto, Lodovico, *Orlando Furioso*, trans. Sir John Harington, ed. Graham Hough, London: Centaur, 1962.

Bodin, Jean, *Method for the Easy Comprehension of History*, trans. Beatrice Reynolds (Records of Civilization - Sources and Studies 37, 1945) New York: Octagon, 1966.

Bullough, Geoffrey (ed.), *Narrative and Dramatic Sources of Shakespeare*, 8 vols, London: Routledge; New York: Columbia University Press, 1957–75.

Burton, Robert, *The Anatomy of Melancholy*, ed. A. R. Shilleto, 2 vols, 1893, London: Bell, 1920.

Cawley, A. C. (ed.), *Mactatio Abel, The Wakefield Pageants in the Towneley Cycle*, Manchester: Manchester University Press, 1958, 1–13.

Chapman, George, *Bussy D'Ambois*, ed. Nicholas Brooke (The Revels Plays), London: Methuen, 1964.

Chaucer, Geoffrey, *Troilus and Criseyde, The Riverside Chaucer*, gen. ed. Larry D. Benson, 3rd edn, based on *The Works of Geoffrey Chaucer*, ed. F.N. Robinson, Boston, MA: Houghton Mifflin, 1987, 473–585.

Du Bartas, Guillaume de Salluste, Sieur, *The Divine Weeks and Works of Guillaume de Saluste Sieur du Bartas*, trans. Joshua Sylvester, ed. Susan Snyder, 2 vols, Oxford: Clarendon Press, 1979.

—— *The First Day of the worldes creation: or of the first week of W. Salustius Lord of Bartas*, trans. anon., London: I. Iackson for G. Seaton, 1595; STC 21658.

—— *La Première Sepmaine. The Works of Guillaume de Salluste Sieur du Bartas: A Critical Edition with Introduction, Commentary, and*

Variants, 3 vols, ed. Urban Tigner Holmes, Jr, John Coriden Lyons, and Robert White Linker, Chapel Hill: University of North Carolina Press, 1935–40; vol. 2, 1938.

Fletcher, John, 'To the Reader', *The Faithful Shepherdess*, in Cyrus Hoy (ed.), *The Dramatic Works in the Beaumont and Fletcher Canon*, gen. ed. Fredson Bowers, vol. 3, Cambridge: Cambridge University Press, 1966.

Gamon, Christofle de, Sieur de Chomenas, *La Semaine, ou creation du Monde. Contre celle du Sieur du Bartas*, n.p.: Gedem Petit, 1609.

Goulart, Simon, *A Learned Summary upon the Famous Poeme of William of Saluste Lord of Bartas*, trans. T.L.D.M.P. [Thomas Lodge], London, 1621; STC 21666.

Jonson, Ben, *Virtue Reconciled to Pleasure, Ben Jonson: The Complete Masques*, ed. Stephen Orgel (The Yale Ben Jonson), New Haven, CT: Yale University Press, 1969.

Kyd, Thomas, *The Spanish Tragedy*, ed. Philip Edwards (The Revels Plays), London: Methuen, 1959.

Lodge, Thomas, *Rosalynde: Euphues Golden Legacie* (1590 edn), in Geoffrey Bullough (ed.), *Narrative and Dramatic Sources of Shakespeare*, 8 vols, London: Routledge; New York: Columbia University Press, 1957–75, vol. 2, 158–256.

Marvell, Andrew, 'An Horatian Ode upon Cromwel's Return from Ireland', *The Poems and Letters of Andrew Marvell*, ed. H. M. Margoliouth, 2 vols, 3rd edn, rev. Pierre Legouis with the collaboration of E.E. Duncan Jones, Oxford: Clarendon Press, 1971, vol. 1.

Mucedorus, Elizabethan and Stuart Plays, ed. Charles Read Baskervill, Virgil B. Heltzel, and Arthur H. Nethercot, 1934, New York: Holt, Rinehart, & Winston, 1962, 525–52.

Paracelsus (Theophrastus Bombast von Hohenheim), *Selected Writings*, ed. Jolande Jacobi, trans. Norbert Guterman (Bollingen Series 28), 2nd edn, New York: Pantheon for Bollingen Foundation, 1958.

Plutarch, 'A Commentarie of the Creation of the Soule, Which Plato Describeth in his Book Timaeus', *The Philosophie, Commonly Called, The Morals*, trans. Philemon Holland, London: [Arnold Hatfield], 1603, 1030–47.

—— 'Of Isis and Osiris', *The Philosophie, Commonly Called, The Morals*, trans. Philemon Holland, London: [Arnold Hatfield], 1603, 1286–1319.

Ripley, George, *The Compound of Alchymy*, 'set foorth' by Ralph Rabbards, London, 1591; STC 21057 (rpt. *The English Experience* 887, Amsterdam: Theatrum Orbis Terraram; Norwood, NJ: Walter J. Johnson, 1977).

Scott, Walter (ed. and trans.), *Hermetica: The Ancient Greek and Latin Writings Which Contain Religious or Philosophic Teachings Ascribed to Hermes Trismegistus*, 4 vols, Oxford: Clarendon, 1924–36.

Shakespeare, William, *The Riverside Shakespeare*, textual ed. G. Blakemore Evans, Boston, MA: Houghton Mifflin, 1974.

Sidney, Sir Philip, *The Defence of Poesie, The Prose Works of Sir Philip*

Sidney, ed. Albert Feuillerat, 4 vols, 1912, Cambridge: Cambridge University Press, 1963, vol. 3, 1-46.

The Taming of a Shrew, in Geoffrey Bullough (ed.), *Narrative and Dramatic Sources of Shakespeare*, 8 vols, London: Routledge; New York, Columbia University Press, 1957-75, vol. 1, 69-108.

Tourneur, Cyril, *The Atheist's Tragedy, or, The Honest Man's Revenge*, ed. Irving Ribner (The Revels Plays), London: Methuen, 1964.

SECONDARY SOURCES

Adelman, Janet (1973) *The Common Liar: An Essay on* Antony and Cleopatra, New Haven, CT: Yale University Press.

—— (1980) ' "Anger's My Meat": Feeding, Dependency, and Aggression in *Coriolanus*', in Murray M. Schwartz and Coppélia Kahn (eds), *Representing Shakespeare: New Psychoanalytic Essays*, Baltimore, MD: Johns Hopkins University Press, 129-49.

—— (1985a) 'Male Bonding in Shakespeare's Comedies', in Peter Erickson and Coppélia Kahn (eds), *Shakespeare's Rough Magic: Renaissance Essays in Honor of C. L. Barber*, Newark: University of Delaware Press; London: Associated University Presses, 73-103.

—— (1985b) ' "This Is and Is Not Cressid": The Characterization of Cressida', in Shirley Nelson Garner, Claire Kahane, and Madelon Sprengnether (eds), *The (M)other Tongue: Essays in Feminist Psychoanalytic Interpretation*, Ithaca, NY: Cornell University Press, 119-41.

Altieri, Joanne (1981) 'Romance in *Henry V*', *Studies in English Literature* 21: 223-40.

Aronson, Alex (1972) *Psyche and Symbol in Shakespeare*, Bloomington: Indiana University Press.

Asp, Carolyn (1977) 'In Defense of Cressida', *Studies in Philology* 74: 406-17.

Bakhtin, Mikhail (1968) *Rabelais and His World*, trans. Helene Iswolsky, Cambridge, MA: MIT Press.

Bamber, Linda (1982) *Comic Women, Tragic Men: A Study of Gender and Genre in Shakespeare*, Stanford, CA: Stanford University Press, 1982.

Barber, C. L. (1959) *Shakespeare's Festive Comedy: A Study of Dramatic Form and Its Relation to Social Custom*, Princeton, NJ: Princeton University Press.

Barton, Anne (1962) *Shakespeare and the Idea of the Play*, pub. under name of Anne Righter, London: Chatto.

—— (1985) 'Falstaff and the Comic Community', in Peter Erickson and Coppélia Kahn (eds), *Shakespeare's Rough Magic: Renaissance Essays in Honor of C. L. Barber*, Newark: University of Delaware Press; London: Associated University Presses, 131-48.

SECONDARY SOURCES

Battenhouse, Roy (1975) 'Falstaff as Parodist and Perhaps Holy Fool', *PMLA* 90: 32-52.

Bayley, John (1975) 'Time and the Trojans', *Essays in Criticism* 25: 55-73.

Bean, John C. (1980) 'Comic Structure and the Humanizing of Kate in *The Taming of the Shrew*', in Carolyn Ruth Swift Lenz, Gayle Greene, and Carol Thomas Neely (eds), *The Woman's Part: Feminist Criticism of Shakespeare*, Urbana: University of Illinois Press, 65-78.

Belsey, Catherine (1985) *The Subject of Tragedy: Identity and Difference in Renaissance Drama*, London: Methuen.

Berger, Harry, Jr (1969) ' "Miraculous Harp": A Reading of Shakespeare's *Tempest*', *Shakespeare Studies* 5: 253-83.

—— (1981) 'Marriage and Mercifixion in *The Merchant of Venice*: The Casket Scene Revisited', *Shakespeare Quarterly* 32: 155-62.

—— (1984) 'Sneak's Noise or Rumor and Detextualization in *2 Henry IV*', *The Kenyon Review*, n.s. 6.4: 58-78.

Berggren, Paula S. (1980) 'The Woman's Part: Female Sexuality as Power in Shakespeare's Plays', in Carolyn Ruth Swift Lenz, Gayle Greene, and Carol Thomas Neely (eds), *The Woman's Part: Feminist Criticism of Shakespeare*, Urbana: University of Illinois Press, 17-34.

Berry, Edward (1975) *Patterns of Decay: Shakespeare's Early Histories*, Charlottesville: University Press of Virginia.

—— (1984) *Shakespeare's Comic Rites*, Cambridge: Cambridge University Press.

Berry, Ralph (1972) *Shakespeare's Comedies: Explorations in Form*, Princeton, NJ: Princeton University Press.

—— (1979/80) 'Woman as Fool: Dramatic Mechanism in Shakespeare', *The Dalhousie Review*, 59: 621-32.

—— (1984) '*Richard III* - Bonding the Audience', in J. C. Gray (ed.), *Mirror up to Shakespeare: Essays in Honour of G. R. Hibbard*, Toronto: University of Toronto Press, 114-27.

Billington, Sandra (1979) ' "Suffer Fools Gladly": The Fool in Medieval England and the Play *Mankind*', in Paul V. A. Williams (ed.), *The Fool and the Trickster: Studies in Honour of Enid Welsford*, Cambridge: Brewer, 36-54.

Blanpied, John W. (1983) *Time and the Artist in Shakespeare's English Histories*, Newark: University of Delaware Press.

Blum, Claude (1983) 'La Folie et la mort dans l'imaginaire collectif du Moyen Age et du début de la Renaissance (xiie-xvie siècles): positions du problème', in Herman Braet and Werner Verbeke (eds), *Death in the Middle Ages (Mediaevalia Lovaniensia*, Ser. 1, Studia 9), Louvain: Louvain University Press, 258-85.

Bono, Barbara J. (1984) *Literary Transvaluation: From Vergilian Epic to Shakespearean Tragicomedy*, Berkeley: University of California Press.

Boose, Linda E. (1982) 'The Father and the Bride in Shakespeare', *PMLA* 97: 325-47.

Bradshaw, Graham (1987) *Shakespeare's Scepticism*, Brighton, Sussex: Harvester.

Bristol, Michael D. (1985) *Carnival and Theatre: Plebeian Culture and the Structure of Authority in Renaissance England*, New York and London: Methuen.

—— (1987) 'Lenten Butchery: Legitimation Crisis in *Coriolanus*', in Jean E. Howard and Marion F. O'Connor (eds), *Shakespeare Reproduced: The Text in History and Ideology*, New York: Methuen, 207-24.

Brooke, Nicholas (1968) *Shakespeare's Early Tragedies*, London: Methuen.

Bryant, J. A., Jr (1986) *Shakespeare and the Uses of Comedy*, Lexington: University of Kentucky Press.

Burckhardt, Sigurd (1968) *Shakespearean Meanings*, Princeton, NJ: Princeton University Press.

Burckhardt, Titus (1971) *Alchemy: Science of the Cosmos, Science of the Soul*, trans. William Stoddart, 1967, Baltimore, MD: Penguin.

Burns, M. M. (1980) '*Troilus and Cressida*: The Worst of Both Worlds', *Shakespeare Studies* 13: 105-30.

Calderwood, James L. (1971) *Shakespearean Metadrama: The Argument of the Play in* Titus Andronicus, Love's Labour's Lost, Romeo and Juliet, A Midsummer Night's Dream, *and* Richard II, Minneapolis: University of Minnesota Press.

—— (1979) *Metadrama in Shakespeare's Henriad:* Richard II *to* Henry V, Berkeley: University of California Press.

—— (1987) *Shakespeare and the Denial of Death*, Amherst: University of Massachusetts Press.

Campbell, Lily Bess (1961) *Shakespeare's Tragic Heroes: Slaves of Passion*, rpt of 1930, London: Methuen.

Carroll, William C. (1985) *The Metamorphoses of Shakespearean Comedy*, Princeton, NJ: Princeton University Press.

Cavell, Stanley (1979) 'On *Othello*', *The Claim of Reason: Wittgenstein, Skepticism, Morality, and Tragedy*, Oxford: Clarendon, 481-96.

Céard, Jean (1980) 'Tératologie et tératomancie au xvie siècle', in M. T. Jones-Davies (ed.), *Monstres et prodigues au temps de la Renaissance*, Paris: Université de Paris-Sorbonne, Insitut de Recherches sur les Civilisations de L'Occident Moderne, Centre de Recherches sur la Renaissance, 5-16.

Coates, John (1978) ' "The Choice of Hercules" in *Antony and Cleopatra*', *Shakespeare Survey* 31: 45-52.

Coursen, H. R. (1986) *The Compensatory Psyche: A Jungian Approach to Shakespeare*, Lanham, MD: University Press of America.

Crewe, Jonathan (1986) 'The Politics of Theater (I)', *Hidden Designs: the Critical Profession and Renaissance Literature*, New York: Methuen, 19-34.

Dawson, Anthony B. (1978) *Indirections: Shakespeare and the Art of Illusion*, Toronto: University of Toronto Press.

—— (1988) '*Measure for Measure*, New Historicism, and Theatrical Power', *Shakespeare Quarterly* 39: 328-41.

Dean, Paul (1981) 'Chronical and Romance Modes in *Henry V*',

Shakespeare Quarterly 32: 18–27.

Delany, Paul (1969) *British Autobiography in the Seventeenth Century*, London: Routledge.

Dent, R. W. (1964) 'Imagination in *A Midsummer Night's Dream*', *Shakespeare Quarterly* 15: 115–29; rpt. in James G. McManaway (ed.), *Shakespeare 400: Essays by American Scholars on the Anniversary of the Poet's Death*, New York: Holt, Rinehart, & Winston, 115–29.

Dessen, Alan C. (1986) *Shakespeare and the Late Moral Plays*, Lincoln: University of Nebraska Press.

Dollimore, Jonathan (1984) *Radical Tragedy: Religion, Ideology, and Power in the Drama of Shakespeare and His Contemporaries*, Chicago: University of Chicago Press; Brighton, Sussex: Harvester.

—— (1985) 'Transgression and Surveillance in *Measure for Measure*', in Jonathan Dollimore and Alan Sinfield (eds), *Political Shakespeare: New Essays in Cultural Materialism*, Manchester: Manchester University Press, 72–87.

—— (1986a) 'The Dominant and the Deviant: A Violent Dialectic', *Critical Quarterly* 28: 179–92.

—— (1986b) 'Subjectivity, Sexuality, and Transgression: The Jacobean Connection', *Renaissance Drama* n.s. 17: 53–79.

Douglas, Mary (1966) *Purity and Danger: An Analysis of Concepts of Pollution and Taboo*, London: Routledge.

Dreher, Diane Elizabeth (1986) *Domination and Defiance: Fathers and Daughters in Shakespeare*, Lexington: The University Press of Kentucky.

Driscoll, James P. (1983) *Identity in Shakespearean Drama*, Lewisburg, PA: Bucknell University Press; London: Associated University Presses.

Dusinberre, Juliet (1975) *Shakespeare and the Nature of Women*, Basingstoke, Hampshire: Macmillan.

Eco, Umberto (1984) 'The Frames of Comic "Freedom" ', in Thomas A. Sebeok (ed.), assisted by Marcia E. Erickson, *Carnival!*, Berlin: Mouton, 1–9.

Elam, Keir (1984) *Shakespeare's Universe of Discourse: Language-Games in the Comedies*, Cambridge: Cambridge University Press.

Eliade, Mircea (1958) *Patterns in Comparative Religion*, trans. Rosemary Sheed, orig. title *Traité d'histoire des religions*, London: Sheed & Ward.

—— (1965) *Rites and Symbols of Initiation: The Mysteries of Birth and Rebirth*, trans. Willard R. Trask, orig. pub. 1958 as *Birth and Rebirth*, New York: Harper Torchbooks.

Erickson, Peter (1985) *Patriarchal Structures in Shakespeare's Drama*, Berkeley: University of California Press.

Evans, Bertrand (1979) *Shakespeare's Tragic Practice*, Oxford: Clarendon.

Evans, Malcolm (1985) 'Deconstructing Shakespeare's Comedies', in John Drakakis (ed.), *Alternative Shakespeares*, London: Methuen, 67–94.

—— (1986) *Signifying Nothing: Truth's True Contents in Shakespeare's Text*, Athens, GA: University of Georgia Press.

Farnham, Willard (1971) *The Shakespearean Grotesque: Its Genesis and Transformation*, Oxford: Clarendon.

Farrell, Kirby (1975) *Shakespeare's Creation: The Language of Magic and Play*, Amherst: University of Massachusetts Press.

Felperin, Howard (1967) 'Shakespeare's Miracle Play', *Shakespeare Quarterly* 18: 363–74.

—— (1972) *Shakespearean Romance*, Princeton, NJ: Princeton University Press.

Fiedler, Leslie A. (1972) *The Stranger in Shakespeare*, New York: Stein & Day; London: Croom Helm.

Fineman, Joel (1985) 'The Turn of the Shrew', in Patricia Parker and Geoffrey Hartman (eds), *Shakespeare and the Question of Theory*, London: Methuen, 138–59.

Fly, Richard (1976) *Shakespeare's Mediated World*, Amherst: University of Massachusetts Press.

Foucault, Michel (1977) 'A Preface to Transgression', *Language, Counter-Memory, Practice: Selected Essays and Interviews*, ed. with an introduction by Donald F. Bouchard, trans. Donald F. Bouchard and Sherry Simon, Ithaca, NY: Cornell University Press, 29–52.

Freedman, Barbara (1980) 'Errors in Comedy: A Psychoanalytic Theory of Farce', in Maurice Charney (ed.), *Shakespearean Comedy*, New York: New York Literary Forum, 233–43.

French, Marilyn (1981) *Shakespeare's Division of Experience*, New York: Summit.

Frye, Northrop (1965) *A Natural Perspective: The Development of Shakespearean Comedy and Romance*, New York: Columbia University Press.

—— (1967) *Fools of Time: Studies in Shakespearean Tragedy*, Toronto: University of Toronto Press.

Garber, Marjorie (1981) *Coming of Age in Shakespeare*, London: Methuen.

Gilmore, Myron P. (1956) 'Freedom and Determinism in Renaissance Historians', *Studies in the Renaissance* 3: 49–60.

Girard, René (1985) 'The Politics of Desire in *Troilus and Cressida*', in Patricia Parker and Geoffrey Hartman (eds), *Shakespeare and the Question of Theory*, London: Methuen, 188–209.

Goldberg, Jonathan (1983) *James I and the Politics of Literature: Jonson, Shakespeare, Donne, and Their Contemporaries*, Baltimore, MD: Johns Hopkins University Press.

—— (1985) 'Shakespearean Inscriptions: The Voicing of Power', in Patricia Parker and Geoffrey Hartman (eds), *Shakespeare and the Question of Theory*, London: Methuen, 116–37.

—— (1986) *Voice Terminal Echo: Postmodernism and English Renaissance Texts*, London: Methuen.

—— (1987) 'Speculations: *Macbeth* and Source', in Jean E. Howard and Marion F. O'Connor (eds), *Shakespeare Reproduced: The Text in History and Ideology*, New York: Methuen, 242–64.

Goldman, Michael (1985) *Acting and Action in Shakespearean Tragedy*, Princeton, NJ: Princeton University Press.

Goldsmith, Robert Hillis (1955) *Wise Fools in Shakespeare*, with an Introduction by Oscar James Campbell, East Lancing: Michigan State University Press.

Graziani, René (1986) 'M. Mercadé and the Dance of Death: *Love's Labour's Lost, V.ii.705–11*', *Review of English Studies*, 37: 392–9.

Greenblatt, Stephen (1980) *Renaissance Self-Fashioning: From More to Shakespeare*, Chicago: University of Chicago Press.

—— (1985) 'Invisible Bullets: Renaissance Authority and Its Subversion, *Henry IV* and *Henry V*', in Jonathan Dollimore and Alan Sinfield (eds), *Political Shakespeare: New Essays in Cultural Materialism*, Manchester: Manchester University Press, 18–47.

Greene, Gayle (1980) 'Shakespeare's Cressida: "A Kind of Self" ', in Carolyn Ruth Swift Lenz, Gayle Greene, and Carol Thomas Neely (eds), *The Woman's Part: Feminist Criticism of Shakespeare*, Urbana: University of Illinois Press, 133–49.

Griswold, Wendy (1986) *Renaissance Revivals: City Comedy and Revenge Tragedy in the London Theatre 1576–1980*, Chicago: University of Chicago Press.

Harpham, Geoffrey Galt (1982) *On the Grotesque: Strategies of Contradiction in Art and Literature*, Princeton, NJ: Princeton University Press.

Hartwig, Joan (1972) *Shakespeare's Tragicomic Vision*, Baton Rouge: Louisiana State University Press.

Hassel, R. Chris, Jr (1980) *Faith and Folly in Shakespeare's Romantic Comedies*, Athens, GA: University of Georgia Press.

Hawkes, Terence (1980) 'Comedy, Orality, and Duplicity: *A Midsummer Night's Dream* and *Twelfth Night*', in Maurice Charney (ed.), *Shakespearean Comedy*, New York: New York Literary Forum, 155–63.

Hawkins, Sherman (1967) 'The Two Worlds of Shakespearean Comedy', *Shakespeare Studies* 3: 62–80.

Henze, Richard (1971) '*The Comedy of Errors*: A Freely Binding Chain', *Shakespeare Quarterly* 22: 35–41.

Hillman, James (1975) *Re-Visioning Psychology*, New York: Harper & Row.

Hillman, Richard (1979a) 'The "Gillyvors" Exchange in *The Winter's Tale*', *English Studies in Canada* 5: 16–23.

—— (1979b) 'Meaning and Mortality in Some Renaissance Revenge Plays', *University of Toronto Quarterly* 49: 1–17.

—— (1992) *Intertextuality and Romance in Renaissance Drama: The Staging of Nostalgia*, Basingstoke, Hampshire: Macmillan.

Hineley, Jan Lawson (1980) 'Bond Priorities in *The Merchant of Venice*', *Studies in English Literature 1500–1900* 20: 217–39.

Holderness, Graham (1985) *Shakespeare's History*, Dublin: Gill & Macmillan; New York: St Martin's.

Homan, Sidney (1986) *Shakespeare's Theater of Presence: Language, Spectacle, and the Audience*, Lewisburg, PA: Bucknell University Press; London: Associated University Presses.

Howard, Jean E. (1987) 'Renaissance Antitheatricality and the Politics of Gender and Rank in *Much Ado About Nothing*', in Jean E. Howard and Marion F. O'Connor (eds), *Shakespeare Reproduced: The Text in History and Ideology*, New York: Methuen, 163–87.

Hunter, G. K. (1959) Introduction, *All's Well That Ends Well*, by William Shakespeare (The Arden Shakespeare), London: Methuen, xi–lix.

Hunter, Robert Grams (1965) *Shakespeare and the Comedy of Forgiveness*, New York: Columbia University Press.

Huston, J. Dennis (1981) *Shakespeare's Comedies of Play*, London: Macmillan.

Hyman, Lawrence W. (1970) 'The Rival Lovers in *The Merchant of Venice*', *Shakespeare Quarterly* 21: 109–16.

Irigaray, Luce (1985) *This Sex Which Is Not One*, trans. Catherine Porter with Carolyn Burke, Ithaca, NY: Cornell University Press.

Jung, C. G. (1953–79a) 'Concerning Rebirth', *The Archetypes and the Collective Unconscious*, trans. R. F. C. Hull, 2nd edn, *The Collected Works of C. G. Jung*, ed. Herbert Read, Michael Fordham, and Gerhard Adler, 20 vols in 21 (Bollingen Series 20), Princeton, NJ: Princeton University Press, vol. 9 (part 1), 111–47.

—— (1953–79b) 'On the Psychology of the Trickster-Figure', *The Archetypes and the Collective Unconscious*, trans. R. F. C. Hull, 2nd edn, *The Collected Works of C. G. Jung*, ed. Herbert Read, Michael Fordham, and Gerhard Adler, 20 vols in 21 (Bollingen Series 20), Princeton, NJ: Princeton University Press, vol. 9 (part 1), 255–72.

Kahn, Coppélia (1981) *Man's Estate: Masculine Identity in Shakespeare*, Berkeley: University of California Press.

Kaiser, Walter (1963) *Praisers of Folly: Erasmus, Rabelais, Shakespeare* (Harvard Studies in Comparative Literature 25), Cambridge, MA: Harvard University Press.

Kantorowicz, Ernst H. (1966) *The King's Two Bodies: A Study in Mediaeval Political Theology*, rpt of 1957, Princeton, NJ: Princeton University Press.

Kastan, David Scott (1982) *Shakespeare and the Shapes of Time*, Hanover, NH: University Press of New England.

Keller, Luzius (1974) *Palingène, Ronsard, Du Bartas: Trois études sur la poésie cosmologique de la Renaissance*, Berne: Francke.

Kermode, Frank (1966) Introduction, *The Tempest*, by William Shakespeare, ed. Frank Kermode (The Arden Shakespeare), 6th edn, rpt of 1958, London: Methuen, xi–xciii.

Kern, Edith (1984) 'Falstaff – A Trickster Figure', *The Upstart Crow* 5: 135–42.

Kirsch, Arthur (1981) *Shakespeare and the Experience of Love*, Cambridge: Cambridge University Press.

Kirsch, James (1966) *Shakespeare's Royal Self*, Foreword by Gerhard Adler, New York: Putnam's for the C. G. Jung Foundation for Analytical Psychology.

Knight, G. Wilson (1969) *The Crown of Life: Essays in Interpretation of Shakespeare's Final Plays*, rpt of 1947, London: Methuen.

Kott, Jan (1987) *The Bottom Translation: Marlowe and Shakespeare and the Carnival Tradition*, trans. Daniela Miedzyrzecka and Lillian Vallee, Evanston, IL: Northwestern University Press.

Krieger, Elliot (1979) *A Marxist Study of Shakespeare's Comedies*, London: Macmillan.

Leech, Clifford (1950) *Shakespeare's Tragedies and Other Studies*, London: Chatto.

Leggatt, Alexander (1973) *Citizen Comedy in the Age of Shakespeare*, Toronto: University of Toronto Press.

—— (1974) *Shakespeare's Comedy of Love*, London: Methuen.

—— (1988) 'Substitution in *Measure for Measure*', *Shakespeare Quarterly* 39: 342–59.

Levin, Richard A. (1980) '*All's Well That Ends Well*, and "All Seems Well" ', *Shakespeare Studies* 13: 131–44.

—— (1982) 'Duke Vincentio and Angelo: Would "A Feather Turn the Scale"?', *Studies in English Literature 1500–1900* 22: 257–70.

—— (1985) *Love and Society in Shakespearean Comedy: A Study of Dramatic Form and Content*, Newark: University of Delaware Press.

Levin, Richard L. (1971) *The Multiple Plot in English Renaissance Drama*, Chicago: University of Chicago Press.

Lloyd, Michael (1959) 'Cleopatra as Isis', *Shakespeare Survey* 12: 88–94.

Long, Michael (1976) *The Unnatural Scene: A Study in Shakespearean Tragedy*, London: Methuen.

Loughrey, Bryan, and Neil Taylor (1982) 'Ferdinand and Miranda at Chess', *Shakespeare Survey* 35: 113–18.

Lyons, Charles R. (1971) *Shakespeare and the Ambiguity of Love's Triumph*, The Hague: Mouton.

McAlindon, T. (1986) *English Renaissance Tragedy*, Vancouver: University of British Columbia Press.

McFarland, Thomas (1972) *Shakespeare's Pastoral Comedy*, Chapel Hill: University of North Carolina Press.

McGuire, Philip C. (1985) *Speechless Dialect: Shakespeare's Open Silences*, Berkeley: University of California Press.

McLuskie, Kathleen (1985) 'The Patriarchal Bard: Feminist Criticism and Shakespeare: *King Lear* and *Measure for Measure*', in Jonathan Dollimore and Alan Sinfield (eds), *Political Shakespeare: New Essays in Cultural Materialism*, Manchester: Manchester University Press, 88–108.

Mallett, Phillip (1979) 'Shakespeare's Trickster-Kings: Richard III and Henry V', in Paul V. A. Williams (ed.), *The Fool and the Trickster: Studies in Honour of Enid Welsford*, Cambridge: Brewer, 64–82.

Marsh, D. R. C. (1962) *The Recurring Miracle: A Study of* Cymbeline *and the Last Plays*, Pietermaritzburg: University of Natal Press.

Miner, Madonne M. (1980) ' "Neither Mother, Wife, nor England's Queen": The Roles of Women in *Richard III*', in Carolyn Ruth Swift Lenz, Gayle Greene, and Carol Thomas Neely (eds), *The Woman's Part: Feminist Criticism of Shakespeare*, Urbana: University of Illinois Press, 35–55.

Miola, Robert S. (1983) *Shakespeare's Rome*, Cambridge: Cambridge University Press.

Montrose, Louis Adrian (1983) ' "Shaping Fantasies": Figurations of Gender and Power in Elizabethan Culture', *Representations* 2: 61-94.

Morris, Brian (1981) Introduction, *The Taming of the Shrew*, by William Shakespeare, ed. Brian Morris (The Arden Shakespeare), London: Methuen, 1-149.

Neely, Carol Thomas (1985) *Broken Nuptials in Shakespeare's Plays*, New Haven, CT: Yale University Press.

Nevo, Ruth (1980) *Comic Transformations in Shakespeare*, London: Methuen.

Newman, Karen (1986) 'Renaissance Family Politics and Shakespeare's *The Taming of the Shrew*', *English Literary Renaissance* 16: 86-100.

—— (1987) ' "And wash the Ethiop white": Femininity and the Monstrous in *Othello*', in Jean E. Howard and Marion F. O'Connor (eds), *Shakespeare Reproduced: The Text in History and Ideology*, New York: Methuen, 143-62.

Nietzsche, Friedrich (1964) *The Birth of Tragedy or Hellenism and Pessimism*, trans. W. A. Haussmann, *The Complete Works of Friedrich Nietzsche*, ed. Oscar Levy, New York: Russell, vol. 1.

Novy, Marianne (1984) *Love's Argument: Gender Relations in Shakespeare*, Chapel Hill: University of North Carolina Press.

Nuttall, A. D. (1983) *A New Mimesis: Shakespeare and the Representation of Reality*, London: Methuen.

Ornstein, Robert (1960) *The Moral Vision of Jacobean Tragedy*, Madison: University of Wisconsin Press.

—— (1986) *Shakespeare's Comedies: From Roman Farce to Romantic Mystery*, Newark: University of Delaware Press; London: Associated University Presses.

Panovsky, Erwin (1930) *Hercules am Scheidewege und Andere Antike Bildstoffe in der Neueren Kunst*, Leipzig: Teubner.

Parker, Patricia (1979) *Inescapable Romance: Studies in the Poetics of a Mode*, Princeton, NJ: Princeton University Press.

—— (1986) 'Deferral, Dilation, Différance: Shakespeare, Cervantes, Jonson', in Patricia Parker and David Quint (eds), *Literary Theory/ Renaissance Texts*, Baltimore, MD: Johns Hopkins University Press, 182-209.

Patrick, Julian (1983) '*The Tempest* as Supplement', in Eleanor Cook, Chaviva Hošek, Jay Macpherson, Patricia Parker, and Julian Patrick (eds), *Centre and Labyrinth: Essays in Honour of Northrop Frye*, Toronto: University of Toronto Press, 162-80.

Pelton, Robert D. (1980) *The Trickster in West Africa: A Study of Mythic Irony and Sacred Delight*, Berkeley: University of California Press.

Pfister, Manfred (1987) 'Comic Subversion: A Bakhtinian View of the Comic in Shakespeare', in Werner Habicht, Jörg Hasler, and Kurt Tetzeli von Rosador (eds), *Deutsche Shakespeare-Gesellschaft West: Jahrbuch 1987*, Bochum: Kamp, 27-43.

Prior, Moody E. (1973) *The Drama of Power: Studies in Shakespeare's History Plays*, Evanston, IL: Northwestern University Press.

Proser, Matthew N. (1965) *The Heroic Image in Five Shakespearean Tragedies*, Princeton, NJ: Princeton University Press.

Quinones, Ricardo J. (1972) *The Renaissance Discovery of Time* (Harvard Studies in Comparative Literature 31), Cambridge, MA: Harvard University Press.

Rackin, Phyllis (1987) 'Androgyny, Mimesis, and the Marriage of the Boy Heroine on the English Renaissance Stage', *PMLA* 102: 29–41.

Rhodes, Neil (1980) *Elizabethan Grotesque*, London: Routledge.

Roberts, Jeanne Addison (1979) *Shakespeare's English Comedy: The Merry Wives of Windsor in Context*, Lincoln: University of Nebraska Press.

Rossiter, A. P. (1961) *Angel with Horns and Other Shakespeare Lectures*, ed. Graham Storey, London: Longmans.

Roy, Emil (1973) 'War and Manliness in Shakespeare's *Troilus and Cressida*', *Comparative Drama* 7: 107–20.

Salingar, Leo (1974) *Shakespeare and the Traditions of Comedy*, Cambridge: Cambridge University Press.

—— (1980) 'Falstaff and the Life of Shadows', in Maurice Charney (ed.), *Shakespearean Comedy*, New York: New York Literary Forum, 185–205.

Sanders, Wilbur (1968) *The Dramatist and the Received Idea: Studies in the Plays of Marlowe and Shakespeare*, Cambridge: Cambridge University Press.

Schleiner, Winfried (1985) 'Imaginative Sources for Shakespeare's Puck', *Shakespeare Quarterly* 36: 65–8.

Schwartz, Murray M. (1970) 'Between Fantasy and Imagination: A Psychological Exploration of *Cymbeline*', in Frederick Crews (ed.), *Psychoanalysis and Literary Process*, Cambridge, MA: Winthrop, 219–83.

Simon, Marcel (1955) *Hercule et le Christianisme*, Paris: La Faculté des Lettres de l'Université de Strasbourg.

Skura, Meredith Anne (1981) *The Literary Use of the Psychoanalytic Process*, New Haven, CT: Yale University Press.

Smith, Gordon Ross (1980) 'A Rabble of Princes: Considerations Touching Shakespeare's Political Orthodoxy in the Second Tetralogy', *Journal of the History of Ideas* 41: 29–48.

Snyder, Susan (1979) *The Comic Matrix of Shakespeare's Tragedies: Romeo and Juliet, Hamlet, Othello, and King Lear*, Princeton, NJ: Princeton University Press.

Somerset, J. A. B. (1984) 'Shakespeare's Great Stage of Fools 1599–1607', in J. C. Gray (ed.), *Mirror up to Shakespeare: Essays in Honour of G. R. Hibbard*, Toronto: University of Toronto Press, 68–81.

Sorge, Thomas (1987) 'The Failure of Orthodoxy in *Coriolanus*', in Jean E. Howard and Marion F. O'Connor (eds), *Shakespeare Reproduced: The Text in History and Ideology*, New York: Methuen, 225–41.

Spivack, Bernard (1958) *Shakespeare and the Allegory of Evil: The*

History of a Metaphor in Relation to His Major Villains, New York: Columbia University Press.

Sprengnether, Madelon (1986) 'Annihilating Intimacy in *Coriolanus*', in Mary Beth Rose (ed.), *Women in the Middle Ages and the Renaissance: Literary and Historical Perspectives*, Syracuse, NY: Syracuse University Press, 89–111.

Stallybrass, Peter, and Allon White (1986) *The Politics and Poetics of Transgression*, London: Methuen.

Stilling, Roger (1976) *Love and Death in Renaissance Tragedy*, Baton Rouge: Louisiana State University Press.

Stockholder, Kay (1987) *Dream Works: Lovers and Families in Shakespeare's Plays*, Toronto: University of Toronto Press.

Street, Brian V. (1972) 'The Trickster Theme: Winnebago and Azande', in André Singer and Brian V. Street (eds), *Zandae Themes: Essays Presented to Sir Edward Evans-Pritchard*, Totowa, NJ: Rowman, 82–104.

Swann, Charles (1987) 'Lucio: Benefactor or Malefactor?', *Critical Quarterly* 29: 55–70.

Tennenhouse, Leonard (1986) *Power on Display: The Politics of Shakespeare's Genres*, New York: Methuen.

Thévenaz, Pierre (1938) *L'Ame du monde: le devenir et la matière chez Plutarch* (Collection d'Etudes Anciennes publiée sous le patronage de l'Association Guillaume Budé), Paris: Les Belles Lettres.

Tillich, Paul (1952) *The Courage to Be*, New Haven, CT: Yale University Press.

Traversi, Derek (1965) *Shakespeare: The Last Phase*, rpt of 1955, Stanford, CA: Stanford University Press.

Turner, Victor (1969) *The Ritual Process: Structure and Anti-Structure*, Chicago: Aldine.

—— (1974) *Dramas, Fields, and Metaphors: Symbolic Action in Human Society*, Ithaca, NY: Cornell University Press.

—— (1977) 'Variations on a Theme of Liminality', in Sally F. Moore and Barbara G. Myerhoff (eds), *Secular Ritual*, Assen: Van Gorcum, 36–52.

—— (1982) *From Ritual to Theatre: The Human Seriousness of Play*, New York: Performing Arts Journal Publications.

Van Gennep, Arnold (1960) *The Rites of Passage*, trans. Monika B. Vizedom and Gabrielle L. Caffee, Chicago: University of Chicago Press.

Van Laan, Thomas F. (1978) *Role-Playing in Shakespeare*, Toronto: University of Toronto Press.

Voth, Grant L., and Oliver H. Evans (1975) 'Cressida and the World of the Play', *Shakespeare Studies* 8: 231–9.

Waddington, Raymond B. (1966) '*Antony and Cleopatra*: "What Venus did with Mars" ', *Shakespeare Studies* 2: 210–27.

Waith, Eugene M. (1962) *The Herculean Hero in Marlowe, Chapman, Shakespeare and Dryden*, London: Chatto & Windus.

Watson, Robert N. (1984) *Shakespeare and the Hazards of Ambition*, Cambridge, MA: Harvard University Press.

Wayne, Valerie (1985) 'Refashioning the Shrew', *Shakespeare Studies* 17: 159–87.

Weimann, Robert (1978) *Shakespeare and the Popular Tradition in the Theatre: Studies in the Social Dimension of Dramatic Form and Function*, ed. Robert Schwartz, Baltimore, MD: Johns Hopkins University Press; orig. title *Tradition des Volkstheaters* (1967).

Welsford, Enid (1935) *The Fool: His Literary and Social History*, London: Faber.

Wheeler, Richard (1981) *Shakespeare's Development and the Problem Comedies: Turn and Counterturn*, Berkeley: University of California Press.

Wiles, David (1987) *Shakespeare's Clown: Actor and Text in the Elizabethan Playhouse*, Cambridge: Cambridge University Press.

Willeford, William (1969) *The Fool and His Sceptre: A Study in Clowns and Jesters and Their Audience*, [Evanston, IL]: Northwestern University Press.

Williamson, Marilyn L. (1986) *The Patriarchy of Shakespeare's Comedies*, Detroit: Wayne State University Press.

Wind, Edgar (1967) *Pagan Mysteries in the Renaissance*, enlarged and revised edn, Harmondsworth, Middlesex: Penguin.

Woodbridge, Linda (1984) *Women and the English Renaissance: Literature and the Nature of Womankind, 1540–1620*, Urbana: University of Illinois Press.

Yoder, R. A. (1972) ' "Sons and Daughters of the Game": An Essay on Shakespeare's *Troilus and Cressida*', *Shakespeare Survey* 25: 11–25.

Young, David P. (1966) *Something of Great Constancy: The Art of* A Midsummer Night's Dream (Yale Studies in English 164), New Haven, CT: Yale University Press.

INDEX

280